Down Goes Marianne

Monson, Delcassé, and the Anglo-French Dispute over Fashoda

Craig E. Saucier

First Southern Girl Press Edition, 2013

ISBN-10: 0615710522

ISBN-13: 978-0615710525

DEDICATION

The book is dedicated with love to Triche, the woman most responsible for any of this material ever seeing the light of day—my best friend, my wife, my cupcake.

CONTENTS

Acknowledgments v

Introduction 1

Monson 7

The Egyptian Question 33

Salisbury and the Nile Campaign 59

"Such Claims are More Worthy of Opéra-Boufee" 95

"An Uneasy Conviction . . Justice Has Not Been Done" 107

Delcassé 119

"Emissary of Civilization" or "Scum of the Desert"? 133

"As Impossible as It is Absurd" 147

Golden Bridges Falling Down 165

Reports of Revolution are "Grossly Exaggerated" 181

"I Think Sir E. Monson has been Frightened" 193

Down Goes Brisson 209

French Heartaches Continue 227

War Scare, 1898-1899 235

"The Queen Wants to Enjoy Cimiez" 257

Conclusion 263

Bibliography 275

ACKNOWLEDGMENTS

This project is a reworking of my Master's Thesis. I am deeply indebted to Professor Karl A. Roider, Jr. for his assistance, suggestions, and encouragement. His reading and rereading of the manuscript assisted me in producing a meaningful body of work. Over the years, Dr. Roider has been my friend and mentor. I am grateful to he and his wife Sue for their friendship, and for allowing me to feel like part of their family.

Professor Thomas C. Owen significantly contributed to the quality of my writing. His careful reading of the text and many stylistic suggestions enhanced and invigorated my language. I am grateful to Professor Meredith Veldman, whose several invaluable organizational suggestions that assisted me to more precisely focus and define the larger issues.

I am grateful to the incredible staff at the National Archives of the United Kingdom, formerly the Public Records Office, at Kew, London.

In the LSU Department of History, where I served as a graduate assistant and coordinator, I owe an unpayable gratitude to the boss of the department, the late Peggy Seale. I also wish to acknowledge the encouragement and influence of the various professors with whom I had the pleasure to work as a grading assistant: Dr. Randy Rogers; Dr. James D. Hardy, Jr.; Dr. Ann Holmes; Dr. Paul Hoffman; and the late Frederic A. Youngs, Jr. I wish also to extend a special and lifelong thanks to Marshall Schott and Ronald Barr, friends and scholars, two gentlemen of wit and wisdom, who helped keep me loose, focused, and well lubricated.

Finally, I wish to extend my gratitude and love to the people who define who I am and have become. My late father Chuck and my mother Renie—they made the sacrifices and provided me the opportunities. They showed me the world, figuratively and literally, taught me dignity, courtesy, respect, and responsibility, and gave me unquestioning love and support through all of my endeavors. My sister Carrie and my brother Scott, with whom I played, argued, and shared the magic and excitement of growing up over and across the globe. My daughters, Gabrielle, Sydney, and Amy, whose love and energy enriched and challenged my powers of concentration on an almost daily basis.

And, the woman who changed my life with a wave of her hand, my beautiful wife, Triche. Her love—total and unconditional—her generosity, selflessness, and absolute commitment to our lives together have refined and renewed my life. She makes me want to be a better man. She is my best friend, my soul mate, and I thank God every day for her.

Down Goes Marianne

INTRODUCTION

This work examines the role and performance of Sir Edmund John Monson, British ambassador to France, during the Fashoda crisis of 1898. The "crisis," representative of the period of empire-building by the European Powers in Africa, the Near East, and the Far East during the second half of the nineteenth century, was a diplomatic confrontation between Britain and France over imperial control of the Upper Nile valley. On the surface, the contested prize appeared to be a deserted and crumbling fortress on the Nile river, built by the Egyptians in 1870 to combat the slave trade. Some four hundred miles south of Khartoum, where nothing existed but swamps, hippopotami, and a few neighboring tribes, the fort had little intrinsic significance. In fact, the problem involved a range of larger and interrelated issues: quarrels over imperial preponderance in Africa and the Nile valley, concerns over the stability of the Ottoman Empire, and polemics over national honor.

The crisis followed the meeting at Fashoda in mid-September 1898 between Captain Jean-Baptiste Marchand, a French marine and head of small expedition, and Colonel Herbert Kitchener, head of the

Anglo-Egyptian army, both under orders to claim the region on behalf of their governments. For four months, from mid-September 1898 to mid-January 1899, the dispute brought France and Britain close to the threshold of war. The outcome at the site, however, was never in doubt. The question was never if Marchand would withdraw from Fashoda; as British gunboats, field guns, and battle-tested soldiers faced down the tiny French expedition, which had no reliable means of communication with its government, such a withdrawal was a foregone conclusion. The question rather was when and under what conditions Marchand would retire.

At the heart of the negotiations to resolve the Fashoda crisis stood the British prime minister Lord Salisbury and Théophile Delcassé, the French foreign minister. Salisbury initially proved willing to consider limited commercial concessions in return for French recognition of Britain's preponderance in the Upper Nile valley. The opposition of his cabinet colleagues, however, as well as a violent anti-French chauvinism sweeping over the British public compelled him to maintain a firm and uncompromising position. At the same time, Delcassé understood that France, weakened internally by the Dreyfus affair and externally by its diplomatic isolation and military inferiority, would be overwhelmed by British power. Although he sought only to procure some territorial compensation in the Upper Nile as a sop for French pride, however inconsequential, Britain's naval preparations and refusal to compromise forced Delcassé to order Marchand's withdrawal from Fashoda in early November 1898. Despite the French capitulation, however, the threat of war continued to strain Anglo-French relations, as London maintained its naval and military preparations well into the spring. In late January 1899, Salisbury and Paul Cambon, the new French ambassador to Britain, began negotiations in

London to resolve the Upper Nile question. The discussions culminated in an agreement, signed on 21 March 1899, which established British and French spheres of influence.

Little disagreement exists in the historical literature about the significance of the Fashoda crisis. Virtually all the major studies emphasize its importance as a turning point in the diplomatic relations between Britain and France. Historians generally agree that the crisis, which represented the high water mark of the Anglo-French colonial rivalry, advanced if not altogether forced the resolution of the Egyptian and Upper Nile questions and ultimately served as the catalyst to the rapprochement between Britain and France in the period prior to the outbreak of the First World War. The Entente Cordiale of 1904 indeed proved to be the instrument that effectively ended centuries of mutual Anglo-French antagonism and contributed effectively to the formation of the Triple Entente with Russia.

In general, most of the relevant historical literature considers the Fashoda crisis almost exclusively within the context of British and French imperial rivalries in Africa. Much of this scholarship, moreover, tends to concentrate on the diplomatic policies and practices of Salisbury and Delcassé. Thus, because the resolution of the crisis ultimately occurred between the respective foreign ministries of Britain and France, most of these works provide a limited assessment of Ambassador Monson's role and conduct during the negotiations.

Furthermore, most of these works ignore crucial domestic considerations – most significant, the Dreyfus affair and its impact upon French diplomatic policy. The confrontation in the Upper Nile occurred at precisely the moment the French government found itself suddenly engulfed by the dramatic reemergence of the Dreyfus affair. In the most critical respect, the "Affair" altered the setting in which the Fashoda negotiations were to be conducted. Throughout the discussions, the French temper, both public and private, grew more explosive and more unpredictable. As a result, the Dreyfus affair exerted a profound impression upon Monson. The ambassador initially argued that, so long as domestic pressures did not force Delcassé's hand, the French would resolve the Fashoda dispute with "calmness." As the French government, however, failed to maintain control over the domestic agitation over revision and the accompanying turmoil, Monson increasingly feared that French leaders might attempt to divert public attention away from the affair with a military confrontation with London. Consequently, the importance of the Dreyfus affair, its impact upon French diplomacy, and its influence upon Monson is central to this work.

Monson's role as the principal envoy between Salisbury and Delcassé during the Fashoda crisis followed two phases. From September to October 1898, he provided an active voice for Salisbury and as such engaged Delcassé in often heated and animated discussions. From October to November, however, growing dissatisfaction with Monson's performance diminished his influence. In Paris, Delcassé grew frustrated with his inability to persuade the ambassador to moderate Britain's hard-line position. At the same time, in London, Salisbury increasingly doubted the soundness and reliability of Monson's reporting. On the one hand, he believed Monson far too eager to placate French concerns. On the other hand, he suspected that some of Monson's dispatches betrayed rather excessive excitement and nervousness. As a result, the negotiations that resolved the Fashoda crisis shifted to London and Monson was thereafter ignored.

Consequently, the concentration on the role of the British ambassador during the Fashoda crisis presents

the reader with an interesting, if not obvious, question --
namely, why bother? Clearly, Monson played a minimal
role in the ultimate resolution of the crisis. After actively
facilitating and participating in the early negotiations, he
found himself almost completely ignored after early
October. An extended examination of his performance,
therefore, might seem curious. Given the institutional
limitations placed upon Monson -- notably, Delcassé's
efforts to avoid him and Salisbury's preference to
conduct diplomatic business in London with the French
ambassador, both of which further limited the scope of
Monson's activities to providing information, answering
questions, and responding to orders -- the reader might
question whether Monson could have played anything
but a peripheral function. Therefore, the consideration of
Monson's role during the Fashoda crisis helps to provide
a more thorough appreciation of the changing nature of
British diplomatic representation in the late nineteenth
century.

Craig E. Saucier

Chapter One

MONSON

In the ultimate resolution of the Fashoda crisis, Lord Salisbury and Théophile Delcassé bypassed the British ambassador to France, Sir Edmund Monson, initially the principal envoy between London and Paris. The primary explanations for consigning Monson to the periphery of the negotiations involved certain long-term institutional considerations and short-term evaluations of the ambassador's effectiveness as well as competence. An overall assessment of Monson's role and performance, therefore, requires an initial examination of the British diplomatic service, his career, and a general overview of the diplomatic setting.

By 1898 Monson's tenure in the British diplomatic service had extended over forty years. His career, like those of other turn of the century British diplomats, reflected the transformation of the diplomatic service by two interdependent developments in the middle of the nineteenth century: an expansion of the governmental and foreign policy bureaucracy and a revolution in communications technology. Both developments resulted in what Raymond A. Jones called the "New

Diplomatic Service."[1]

This "new" Diplomatic Service involved the institutional expansion of the Foreign Office and the corresponding decline of the British Diplomatic Service. The unreformed service of the eighteenth century had very few professional characteristics. It possessed only a rudimentary organization, little specialization of function, few regulations, irregular salaries, and virtually no promotion by merit or seniority. More often than not, embassies and missions provided an outlet for political patronage or as a "gigantic system of outdoor relief for the aristocracy." Senior posts proved almost equivalent to minor cabinet positions, junior positions offered opportunities for the sons of well-connected families, and sharp ideological differences between Whigs and Tories ensured continuing replacement of ambassadors upon the changing of the home government. In the 1850s and 1860s, however, Parliament began to apply civil service reforms to the Diplomatic Service. The Foreign Office introduced qualifying entrance examinations and established a clearly-defined hierarchy of ranks, duties, and salaries; it took over junior appointments, created new positions, and reduced the dependence of junior diplomats upon their ambassadors. In the years after 1860, therefore, senior appointments began to depend less on political patronage and more on career criteria. The percentage of aristocrats in the Diplomatic Service declined to below 40 percent while the percentage of commoners in the service rose to over 60 percent. As a result, the Diplomatic Service became a regular career profession in which advancement resulted from performance and ability rather than simply by influence and patronage.

---

[1]Raymond A. Jones, *The British Diplomatic Service, 1815-1914* (Waterloo, Ontario, Canada: Wilfrid Laurier University Press, 1983).

One unfortunate result of these reforms was a notable glut of personnel in the lower ranks of the Service, caused by an excessively large number of appointments made in the 1850s. The 1861 Milnes Committee stabilized the situation by creating third and second secretaries out of the ranks of former attachés, thus providing an extra rung of promotions. This overabundance of personnel led to much frustration and a more or less regular block in promotions in the late 1860s, which in turn prompted large numbers of resignations among the lower ranks of the Service.[2] This contributed to a very slow passage to promotion within the senior levels as well, at least until the years after 1876, when ambassadorial level representation expanded from five embassies to nine.[3] Still, promotion remained slow and based principally on seniority, although the possibility was always left open for promotion by exceptional merit. As foreign secretary Lord Stanley wrote to the Queen in September 1867: "The diplomatic service has of late years become a profession [in which] promotion by seniority . . . is expected. It is a badly paid service in which promotion lags slower every year. Good men are only kept in it from the ambition of distinguishing themselves in its higher ranks."[4]

One other result of these reforms, however, was an expansion of control by the Foreign Office, not only over British foreign policy but over the Diplomatic Service as well. By the turn of the nineteenth century,

---

[2]Ibid, 48, 94-109; 144-150; 152-153; 159-163; 215-217; Zara S. Steiner, *The Foreign Office and Foreign Policy, 1898-1914* (Cambridge: Cambridge University Press, 1969), 172-174.

[3]Until 1876, Britain maintained embassies in five states: France, the Ottoman Empire, Austria-Hungary, Russia, and Prussia/Germany. In the years after 1876, ambassador-level representation was established in Italy [1876], Spain [1887], the USA [1893], and Japan [1905].

[4]Jones, 153, 176; Steiner, 70.

the Foreign Office carried out three essential activities. First, the Foreign Office served as a permanent bureaucracy, life-time servants of the state. It remained in tenure, unbroken except by death, retirement, promotion, or transfer to a foreign post. In this way, the staff preserved the institutional memory of the Foreign Office. Second, it engaged in fact-finding and thus became a necessary and reliable source of information of current importance. Third, in addition to the daily voluminous flow of telegrams and official dispatches, the Foreign Office staff carried out private letter writing and correspondence with British representatives abroad. While the foreign secretary kept up the correspondence with ambassadors and ministers, the undersecretaries and private secretaries also kept up a correspondence, which could guide or check an ambassador. It was not only a way to handle British representatives abroad, it also proved useful in a regular ordinary way to convey the pace and temper of a desired relationship and the general context in which it was to be understood.[5]

The extent of this growing Foreign Office control over the Diplomatic Service created some antagonism between the two services. The Foreign Office staff, for example, thought that "only clerks trained in the office could handle the work properly" and therefore considered diplomats as "amateurs" who were "unaccustomed to work or to regular hours."[6]

Furthermore, there were increasing concerns about the quality of British ambassadors. Some maintained that the Service failed to produce enough men qualified to occupy the top positions. In 1888, for example, in explaining his choice of Lord Lytton as his choice for

---

[5]Agatha Ramm, "Lord Salisbury and the Foreign Office," in *The Foreign Office, 1782-1982*, ed. Roger Bullen (Frederick, Maryland: University Publications of America, Inc., 1984), 55-59.

[6]Steiner, 22.

the embassy in France, Lord Salisbury wrote the Queen that Sir Robert Morier was not possible, Sir Augustus Paget was disqualified by having a German wife, Sir John Lumley was retiring, Sir William White was too useful at Constantinople, Lionel West was not clever, Sir Clare Ford was not sufficiently polished, Lord Vivian was wanted in Russia, and Monson had "not enough ability." Consequently, Lord Rosebery lamented in April 1893 that there was a "deficiency of proper candidates for important embassies." Not only did British diplomats continue to be recruited from a rather narrow social base, the Diplomatic Service did not always attract the ambitious or the energetic, given the slow pace of promotion and the little variety of social life at most foreign posts. In fact, the practice began under Salisbury of appointing high ranking officials within the Foreign Office bureaucracy to posts overseas.[7]

The revolution in communications technology, however, proved to be a far more crucial development. The speeding up of communications in the middle of the nineteenth century, fundamentally altered the character of diplomatic representation. British ambassadors in the eighteenth century tended to exercise great independence due in large part to the slowness of contemporary means of communication: the European postal service and the King's Messengers. Typically, an ambassador arrived at his post with formal instructions, drawn up with the intention of acquainting him with the broad objectives of government policy. Although he was not to deviate from his instructions, the distance from London often presented opportunities for independent initiative. After 1860, however, the widespread introduction of telegraph cables between Britain and foreign capitals began to transform ambassadors into mere bureaucrats, described by

---

[7]Jones, 175-176, 185-188; Steiner, 183.

historian Raymond Jones as "self-effacing, subordinate, and anonymous - fit persons to execute the policy of the foreign secretary at the behest of the electric telegraph."[8] The impact, even the necessity, of the telegraph proved to be a matter of debate. While some argued that the telegraph reduced the responsibility of the ambassador, others argued that faulty information and premature instructions in fact required additional responsibility.[9]

Whether a result of the institutional expansion of the Foreign Office or the revolution in communications technology, the power, influence, and initiative of British ambassadors during the second half of the nineteenth century decreased. Foreign Secretaries rarely permitted diplomats any role in the shaping of policy. This too represented a notable change from the eighteenth century practice, called the "English Plan," in which the established and preferred methods for conducting negotiations was to employ British representatives in foreign capitals instead of foreign diplomats accredited to London. By the last quarter of the century, however, the Foreign Office relied upon its diplomats principally for information and for the execution of its policy, while decisions about policy were made almost entirely in London. Diplomats were expected simply to report intelligently, represent British interests, and conduct any negotiations the foreign secretary might deem necessary. Differences of opinion existed, of course, but few diplomats acted with complete independence or in direct contradiction to their instructions. It was generally only British representatives in remote places such as Constantinople or St. Petersburg, or those who were engaged in complex local

[8]Jones, 116.

[9]Daniel R. Headrick, *The Invisible Weapon. Telecommunications and International Politics, 1851-1945* (New York and Oxford: Oxford University Press, 1991), 73-75; Jones, 116-126, 137-138, 218-219.

negotiations, who were given real freedom. As London was the most significant post for most foreign nations, most British diplomatic business was conducted at home. For that reason, few disagreed with Sir Francis Bertie's snide observation that at Downing Street, "one can at least pull the wires whereas an Ambassador is only a damned marionette."[10]

By the turn of the twentieth century, the age of the great independent British ambassador was over. This, therefore, was the professional diplomatic context in which Edmund Monson was appointed British ambassador to France in the late summer of 1896.[11]

Sir Edmund John Monson was born on 6 October 1834 at Chart Lodge, Seal, near Sevenoaks in Kent. He was the third son of William John Monson, sixth Baron Monson, and his wife Eliza. His background can be traced to the earliest Normans who settled in Lincolnshire in the twelfth century. One famous ancestor, Sir William Monson, fought against the Spanish Armada and was knighted by the Earl of Essex. He was educated first at a private school in the Isle of Wight. He proceeded to Eton, then to Balliol College, Oxford, where he graduated B.A. in 1855 with a first class degree in law and modern history. Monson was elected a fellow of All Souls College in 1858 and proceeded to the M.A in the same year. In 1868 he was

---

[10]Jones, 117, 216-219; Steiner, 173, 176, 183. Bertie served as ambassador to Italy [1903-1905] and became Monson's successor at Paris in 1905. He served in Paris until 1918.

[11]For Monson's background, see: Leonard Clair Wood, "Sir Edmund Monson, Ambassador to France" (Ph.D diss., University of Pennsylvania, 1960), 1-12; Sir Sidney Lee, ed., *Dictionary of National Biography. Supplement, January 1901-December 1911* (Oxford: Oxford University Press, 1912), s.v. "Sir Edmund John Monson" by Thomas Henry Sanderson, 687-688; Godfrey E.P. Hertslet, ed., *The Foreign Office List and Diplomatic and Consular Yearbook For 1910* (London: Harrison and Sons, 1910), 417-418.

chosen to act as an examiner of modern languages for the Taylorian scholarship. Monson married Eleanor Catherine Mary Munro in 1881. Over the course of their marriage, which produced three sons, Lord and Lady Monson were enormously popular in society and admired for their "grace and tact."

Monson entered the Diplomatic Service in July 1856 and following his qualifying examination was appointed as a paid attaché to the British embassy in Paris. In April 1858 he was sent to Florence, briefly returned to Paris, and thereafter to Washington DC. For nearly five years Monson acted as the private secretary to Lord Lyons, the British Minister to the United States, during which time the minister was occupied with the critical questions that resulted from the outbreak of the American Civil War. By the time of his appointment to Washington, Monson had already established a reputation for sound judgment, loyalty, and unimpeachable integrity.[12] Little of that, however, proved sufficient in the stifling heat of Washington DC. In the early months of the Civil War, Lyons requested additional assistants from the Foreign Office: "I conjure you to send me out two or at least one good working attaché as soon as possible. Brooke is completely out of health; Warre is always prostrated by the abominable heat of this place; Monson can do a great deal, but his constitution is not of iron."[13] In 1863 following his second foreign service examination, Monson was transferred to Hanover as attaché but soon promoted to third secretary and within months dispatched to Brussels as Third Secretary of Legation. In March 1865 apparently dissatisfied with the slowness of promotion or wearied by monotonous routine, he

---

[12]*Dictionary of National Biography*, 637; Wood, 2-6.

[13]Lord Newton, *Lord Lyons: A Record of British Diplomacy, 1890-1902*, vol. 1 (London: Edward Arnold, 1913), 87.

resigned from the Service and sought election to Parliament. Monson contested the seat for Reigate in the Liberal interest but was defeated. Although a Liberal, Monson strongly supported Tory diplomacy. While posted to Hungary, he wrote numerous letters to his brother, William John Monson, Viscount Oxenbridge and ultimately Seventh Baron Monson, in which he expressed reservations about Gladstone's foreign policy. "My great issue with the Liberal Government," he wrote on 5 February 1876, referring to Gladstone's intention to attack the purchase of the Suez Canal, "is the line they take abroad." He thought [21 March 1876] the proposal to make Queen Victoria "Empress" of India to be "foolish." On 20 September 1876 he wrote that Gladstone "is, as always in foreign politics, as impractical and visionary as ever." A month later, he described Gladstone's policy in the Balkans as "insane."[14]

He remained unemployed until May 1869, when he reentered the Diplomatic Service as a consul in the Azores, an appointment intended as a stepping stone to renewed diplomatic employment.[15] In December 1871, when the independent position conceded to Hungary by the Ausgleich of 1867 necessitated the presence of a British agent, Monson assumed the newly created post of consul-general at Budapest, where he remained until March 1874 when he transferred to the British embassy at Vienna as second secretary. His letters, however, continued to betray deep frustration about the dullness of routine and the slowness of promotion. On 9 August 1875, he complained that, in response to his recent inquiry

---

[14]The Papers of Sir Edmund John Monson, Modern Papers Reading Room, New Bodleian Library, Oxford University (hereafter cited as Monson MSS): c.590, 5 February 1876, Monson to Monson; 21 March 1876, Monson to Monson; 20 September 1876, Monson to Monson; 19 October 1876, Monson to Monson; Wood, 7-8.

[15]Monson MSS, c.589, 21 May 1869, Lord Lyons to Monson.

about a possible transfer into a recent vacancy, the Foreign Office replied, "You may rely upon your name coming before Lord Derby with those of other candidates for promotion and transfer." Monson rationalized to his brother that this was "the regular stereotypical answer, which means and promises nothing at all. . . . I fear that I doomed to continue here." Similarly, on 21 March 1876: "All my personal friends seem to have luck, and I hope that something may eventually turn up for me." In early June, following the news that Charles Mansfield would succeed Lord Hussey Vivian as the Consul-General to Wallachia and Moldavia, he grumbled, "I am somewhat disgusted for he is a horrid earl, and has done nothing to deserve his promotion except intrigue tooth and nail to get it. Moreover, as he hates me, it is a triumph for him over me . . . Truly, it is a very thankless lot, ours. . . . However, come what may, I will never kow-tow to the powers that be – and must resign myself to my fate of being passed over *ad infinitum*."[16] Nevertheless, he began to enjoy an uninterrupted although relentlessly slow advancement. From September 1876 to May 1877, he represented the British government on a special mission to the Montenegrin capital of Cetinje when it became evident that Serbia and Montenegro were going to enter into active hostilities against Turkey. For his efforts, Monson was promoted to Minister Resident and appointed CB.[17] After assignments as Minister Resident and Consul-

---

[16]Monson MSS., c.590: Monson to Monson, 9 August 1875; Monson to Monson, 21 March 1876; Monson to Monson, 2 June 1876

[17]The Most Honourable Order of the Bath is a British order of chivalry founded by George I in 1725. The name derives from the elaborate medieval ceremony for creating a knight, which involved bathing (as a symbol of purification) as one of its elements. The knights so created were known as "Knights of the Bath." The Order consists of three classes of members: (1) Knight Grand Cross (GCB); (2) Knight Commander (KCB); and (3) Companion (CB).

General to the Republic of Uruguay (June 1879-January 1884), the Argentine Republic and Paraguay (January-December 1884), during which he was promoted to Envoy Extraordinary and Minister Plenipotentiary, Monson was transferred to Denmark, where he served from December 1884 to February 1888. While in Copenhagen, the Danish and American governments selected Monson to serve as arbitrator on the claims of the American firm of Butterfield and Company against the Danish government. The American complaint was based on alleged ill-treatment of two vessels, which had been detained by Danish authorities in the island of St. Thomas in 1854 and 1855, on the grounds that they had been freighted with contraband of war for Venezuela. The case had been the subject of contention for over thirty years. Ultimately Monson settled the case in favor of Denmark (although the award was not delivered until January 1900). For his efforts, Monson was knighted KCMG.[18] In February 1888 he was transferred to Athens, where he enjoyed an enviable position as friend and even adviser of King George of Greece. Although his influence may have been due to the good relations between London and Athens, it probably depended more on Monson's earlier days at the Danish court and the friendships he formed with George and his father, the King of Denmark Christian IX.[19]

Indeed, throughout his career, Monson sought to conduct diplomatic business on a personal level and to establish working relationships based on friendship and mutual confidence. He believed that collegial relations

---

[18]Knight Commander of the Most Distinguished Order of Saint Michael and Saint George, an order of chivalry founded in 1818 by George, Prince Regent, later George IV. It is awarded to those who render extraordinary or important non-military service in a foreign country. It can also be conferred for important or loyal service in relation to foreign and Commonwealth affairs.

[19]*Dictionary of National Biography*, 637; Hertslet, 417-418; Wood, 8-9, 290.

with foreign counterparts would enable him to maintain more effective and cordial formal relations between the governments. Among his superiors in London, however, Monson sometimes appeared overly sympathetic to the governments to which he was accredited and projected their point of view too enthusiastically. Moreover, whenever he failed to establish confidential diplomatic relationships with the resident foreign minister, as would be the case in Paris, his efforts often proved ineffective.

At the end of June 1892, Monson was promoted to GCMG[20] and replaced Lord Vivian as British minister to Brussels. This was a potentially significant career appointment; among other things, Monson's contacts with King Leopold II of Belgium brought him to the attention of Queen Victoria, whose interest in the promotion of aspiring diplomats was an important consideration in the appointment of ambassadors.[21] More important, British relations with Leopold at that moment were strained by disputes over territorial rights in central Africa. Under the MacKinnon Treaty of May 1890, the British East Africa Company (BEAC) agreed to give Leopold sovereign rights between the Congo Free State and Lado, a small outpost on the Nile. Leopold, believing that the treaty left him free to extend his dominions toward the Upper Nile, sent Captain Guillame van Kerckhoven to Lado with a considerable force in September 1890. Lord Salisbury protested that because the BEAC was not acting on behalf of the British government, London was not legally bound by the treaty. He worried as well about the possibility that the French would attempt to challenge the British position there and in Egypt. Salisbury therefore warned Leopold

---

[20]Grand Cross of the Most Distinguished Order of Saint Michael and Saint George.

[21]Jones, 189.

in early 1892 through Vivian that the British government would not tolerate his ambition to extend Belgian control into the Upper Nile.

This is the point at which Salisbury appointed Monson to Brussels. His instructions were to uphold the position, as outlined by Salisbury, and to press for a recall of Van Kerckhoven's expedition. Monson's initial efforts, however, had little success, as Leopold treated his repeated requests for information with indifference and protests of ignorance.[22]

Monson first became concerned about the possibility of a French drive into the Upper Nile while stationed in Brussels. Leopold, who attempted to hustle Monson into supporting a favorable arrangement in the Nile-Congo divide, plied the Minister with reports that a Franco-Congolese arrangement was imminent. At a carefully arranged interview in early July 1892, Leopold warned Monson that current territorial disputes would allow France to secure a road to the Nile "with a view to future designs on Egypt." Moreover, Monson learned through the Belgian foreign minister, Baron Auguste Lambermont, that Leopold intended to sign an agreement with the French affording them access to the Nile valley. Lambermont, with whom Monson successfully established himself on good terms, maintained reservations about the potential impact of Leopold's African intrigues on Anglo-Belgian relations. As each took the other into his confidence, Lambermont confirmed in early 1893 that the king was conducting simultaneous discussions with London and Paris and that, contrary to the reports of Lord Dufferin the British ambassador in Paris, Leopold and the French were close to an agreement. Based on this information, Monson

---

[22]William L. Langer, *The Diplomacy of Imperialism, 1890-1902*, 2d ed., (New York: Alfred A. Knopf, 1965), 124-125; Wood, 14-22.

warned London -- nearly a year and a half before the Franco-Congolese Treaty of August 1894 -- that Leopold and the French foreign minister Gabriel Hanotaux would sign an agreement by which France could push into the Nile valley and secure an outlet for French posts.[23] Leopold was sufficiently offended by Monson's reports to London of Belgian deceptions and duplicity that he summoned the Minister and subjected him to a stern lecture on the sanctity of treaties and "the moral rights of the weak against the strong." He also complained to Queen Victoria in March 1893 that Monson "had been lacking in deference" and pressed for his dismissal. In response to the Queen's inquiries, Lord Rosebery, the new Liberal foreign minister under William Gladstone, wrote that he was sorry "to learn that Your Majesty's new Ambassador has not been found conciliatory by the King of the Belgians. It is only fair to remember that we have grave cause to complain of the King in his capacity as Sovereign of the Congo." Indeed, in May 1893, the Belgian foreign ministry confirmed that Van Kerckhoven had firmly established a position and Belgian authority at Lado.[24]

In August 1893 Rosebery appointed Monson ambassador to Austria-Hungary. Although he would repeatedly give assurances of his confidence through numerous and engaging letters,[25] Rosebery found himself compelled by political considerations to bypass Monson in the conduct of British diplomacy with

---

[23]G. N. Sanderson, *England, Europe and the Upper Nile, 1882-1899* (Edinburgh: Edinburgh University Press, 1965), 98-99, 104-105; Wood, 23-38.

[24]George Earle Buckle, ed., *The Letters of Queen Victoria. A Selection From Her Majesty's Correspondence and Journals Between the Years 1886-1901* (London: John Murray, 1932), third series, vol. 3, *1896-1901* (hereafter cited as LQV), 244-245; Langer, *The Diplomacy of Imperialism*, 124-125;Wood, 29-31.

[25]Monson MSS, c.593, 2 January 1894, Rosebery to Monson; 15 January 1894, Rosebery to Monson; 13 February 1894, Rosebery to Monson.

Austria. Although both nations were attempting to assess the impending détente between France and Russia, Rosebery gave Monson neither instructions nor direction regarding conversations with Count Gustav Kálnoky, the Austro-Hungarian foreign minister. By contrast the correspondence between Vienna and its ambassador in London, Count Franz Deym, were explicit and detailed. Rosebery considered an official silence to Monson as absolutely imperative simply because he agreed with Salisbury's policy for friendship with Austria-Hungary. Gladstone, however, did not. Consequently, while Franco-Russian relations warmed and British relations with both continued to strain, Rosebery sought to reassure Austria-Hungary and Italy of British friendship through confidential and personal discussions with Count Deym. Had he conducted conversations through Monson, other cabinet members, who were hostile to Salisbury's diplomacy and constitutionally entitled to read the official correspondence of an ambassador, would have been immediately alerted. In order to maintain his policy, therefore, Rosebery was content to leave Monson in the dark.[26]

Monson nevertheless attempted to assess the unsettled conditions in the Balkans but initially could get little information from Kálnoky. At the same time, although unknown to Monson, Count Deym pressed Rosebery for British support against the threat of a Franco-Russian combination. By December 1893 Kálnoky, suspecting that Monson was aware of Deym's representations in London, dropped the pretense and spoke candidly of his concerns that Russia would use the French combination to improve her position at Constantinople. Austria's fleet, he feared, was insignificant, the Germans indifferent, and the Italians

---

[26] Jones, 186-189; Wood, 46-50.

useless and ineffectual. Struck by the abrupt change in the foreign minister's tone, Monson began drafting urgent dispatches in December 1893 and January 1894 to Rosebery, who systematically ignored them.

London continued to disregard Monson throughout the spring of 1894. In February he was not invited to participate in discussions between Kálnoky and the newly appointed British ambassador to Turkey, Sir Philip Currie. Deym informed Kálnoky that Currie, who was en route to Constantinople, enjoyed Rosebery's complete confidence and possessed accurate knowledge of his intentions. With respect to Monson, however, Rosebery had no reason to fear that he might commit any indiscretion but "would be pleased if [Kálnoky] were somewhat reserved with reference to his statements; the more so as he had as yet committed nothing to writing concerning our conversations, and had not yet informed the ambassador about them."

The secretive manner with which Rosebery conducted his diplomacy annoyed Monson, although he was aware in any event of the political realities in London. Nevertheless, for the next three years, he continued to report his observations and opinions about Austria's needs and difficulties and spent much of his time, meeting and socializing with numerous dignitaries, aristocrats, politicians, and other ambassadors. He believed that a critical part of an ambassador's ability to collect information and thus an essential diplomatic responsibility depended upon dinner parties, balls, and soirées. Monson thus adhered to the advice of Sir George Hamilton Seymour, British Minister to Portugal, who commented in 1850 that "I have no idea of man being a good diplomatist who does not give good dinners." For that reason, there remained considerable relevance in Sir Francis Bertie's observation that at Downing Street, "one can at least pull the wires whereas an Ambassador is only a damned marionette."[27] His relationship with Kálnoky was particularly warm, due not only to the improved relations between London and Vienna but to Monson's genuine interest in Austrian affairs. The two men were similar in views and temperaments and thus established great confidence in the views of the other. At least one observer, however, discounted the ties between Monson and Kálnoky. William Lavino, the Vienna correspondent for the *Times*, wrote in February 1895 that London could not rely on Kálnoky, whose policy had in fact become more hostile to London. The foreign minister had never been as friendly to Great Britain "as our Foreign Office has been led to believe," he wrote. "The longer Monson is here the more Austrian he gets, and I think he would look upon any suspicion of Kálnoky as next door to a crime. It is not admiration; it is the infatuation of a man of unsound judgment."[28] Monson betrayed his sensitivity to his hosts more outwardly in August 1895. Following the return of the Conservatives to office, Lord Salisbury considered Monson the leading candidate to replace Sir Edward Malet in Berlin. Monson wavered, maintaining that an appointment to Germany would be considered a serious slight to the Austrian government. Accordingly, when rumors began to circulate in the summer of 1896 that he would be appointed to Paris, London newspapers reported disappointment throughout Vienna. The *Standard* [19 August 1896] noted that Monson's personal qualities and great diplomatic experience contributed to maintaining cordial relations, while the *Times* [22 August 1896] reported regret in Vienna, where "H.E. and Lady Monson, who enjoy special favor at Court, have become two of the most welcome and

---

[27]Jones, 98; Steiner, 183.

[28]Wood, 50-69, 78-80.

popular figures in the society of the Austrian capital."[29]

In August 1896, a few months after having been made GCB,[30] Salisbury appointed Monson to replace Lord Dufferin as the British ambassador to the French Republic. While the embassy at Paris remained a brilliant and prestigious position in the foreign service, its significance by the 1890s was regarded increasingly in social rather than diplomatic terms. Salisbury once wrote the Queen that Paris was so close, British policy toward France was "absolutely in the hands of the Foreign Office."[31] Philip Currie, British ambassador to the Ottoman Empire, observed that "at Constantinople, there is real work to do, whereas at Paris, official responsibility is reduced to a minimum."[32]

When Monson arrived in December 1896, Europe was struggling to resolve problems arising within the Ottoman Empire, the so-called "Eastern Question." From London's point of view, the Eastern Question involved efforts to reform and defend the Ottoman Empire. Salisbury believed that unless reformed, the Ottoman Empire would disintegrate and that Russia would take advantage of the chaos to assert its influence over the Straits of Constantinople.[33] Moreover, Anglo-French relations were languishing from bitter, acrimonious, and

---

[29]Newspaper quotes in Monson MSS., c. 1290; Jones, 190; Wood, 11.

[30]Knight Grand Cross of the Bath.

[31]Jones, 185-186.

[32]Monson MSS., c. 1290. Currie's quote in the *Leeds Mercury*, 19 August 1896. See also: Marguerite Steinheil, *My Memoirs* (New York: Sturgis and Walton Company, 1912), 70.

[33]Foreign Office, Public Records Office, London (hereafter cited as FO). See reports in FO 27/3267, FO 27/3268, FO 27/3314, FO 27/3315, FO 27/3316, FO 27/3317, FO 27/3318, FO 27/3319, FO 27/3320, FO 27/3394, and FO 27/3400; J.A.S. Grenville, *Lord Salisbury and Foreign Policy: The Close of the Nineteenth Century* (London: University of London and the Athlone Press, 1964), 26-31, 46-52, 74-77; Wood, 83-114.

seemingly endless disputes arising out of colonial claims and competing spheres of influence throughout the world: China, Siam, Indo-China, Newfoundland -- but especially throughout Africa: Tunis, Madagascar, Morocco, the Niger valley, and Egypt.

Monson arrived, however, without clear instructions to engage the French in discussions over any of the issues that had embittered relations. Because neither side seemed particularly eager or willing to make concessions, Monson worked not to resolve issues but to defend and explain British policy to the French. For his superiors in London, he served essentially as an observer, reporter, and analyst. Given the ambiguous nature of his instructions, Monson endeavored to leave nothing to question in his dispatches. He wished to call attention to every fact, consideration, and imponderable of any given situation. In a letter to Permanent Undersecretary of State Sir Thomas Sanderson in December 1896, Monson noted that an ambassador should "furnish the Secretary of State with as much official information as he can properly managed to send; and to supplement it by a private summary, and his own comments and views." As a result, his dispatches were masterpieces of numbing overkill; they were of inordinate length, often ten to twelve pages.[34] One representative example was a nine page letter to Salisbury in which Monson related a conversation with a French financier about the arrears of the Belgian contribution due the Ottoman government, complete with chronology and conjecture.[35] Such ambitions, while generally appreciated in London, provoked considerable exasperation among the embassy staff. Maurice Baring, one of Monson's attachés in Paris, wrote that "there never seemed to be any

---

[34]Wood, 217-218.

[35]FO 27/3314, D.14, 10 January 1897, Monson to Salisbury.

reason why Sir Edmund's dispatches should ever end . . . one had the sensation of coasting pleasantly downhill on a bicycle that had no brake, and save for an accident was not likely to stop."[36] In a letter to Monson, dated 8 November 1897, Bryan Clark-Thornhill, also of the British embassy, wrote "I don't want to complain, but I do want to justify our position . . . [U]ntil 6 November, over 1,439 more documents were handled in the Chancery than during the whole of last year . . . You write rather more than Lord Dufferin."[37]

During his tenure in France, Monson dealt with two foreign ministers, Gabriel Hanotaux and Théophile Delcassé. Given the passive character of his position, however, he found relations with both men exasperating. In the absence of substantive instructions, Monson's tactics were largely defensive. He refrained from initiating any discussions on African questions; when they were raised, he either evaded them, elaborated on Salisbury's answers to the French ambassador in London, Baron Alphonse de Courcel, or deferred the matter to the Foreign Office. Furthermore, he did not get along personally with either minister. Monson developed a profound distrust if not outright contempt for Hanotaux, whom he regarded as a liar and disgustingly infatuated with Russia; he could never decide "how far it is ever possible to place reliance upon his Excellency's word." Moreover, he became convinced that the French foreign ministry inspired much of the anti-British sentiment in certain Parisian newspapers and in the Chamber of Deputies.[38] Monson believed that

---

[36]Wood, 217-218.

[37]Monson MSS., c.358, 24 December 1896, Monson to Sanderson; c.594, 8 November 1897,Thornhill to Monson.

[38]FO 27/3267, D.383, 10 December 1896, Monson to Salisbury. See also: FO 27/3267, D.384, 10 December 1896, Monson to Salisbury; FO 27/3267, D.388, 11 December 1896, Monson to Salisbury.

Hanotaux's request for British concessions, whether in Tunis or Madagascar, in exchange for French good will was generally a political ploy by the foreign minister to assuage French sentiment and to secure a diplomatic victory, but more to the point to enhance his own prestige.[39] His relationship with Delcassé, although more cordial than with Hanotaux, similarly was never one of confidence or satisfaction. While they managed to work amicably together, Delcassé's extreme reserve and constant unwillingness to be drawn out on important questions annoyed and disconcerted Monson. Throughout his tenure in France, Monson repeatedly complained about his inability to establish even the most elementary relations of confidence with Delcassé; he repeatedly complained about the foreign minister's hesitation to enter into any precise detail. Consequently, as in Vienna, Monson relied heavily on local informants, friends in government circles, and newspaper reports for much of his own information.[40]

During his first two years in Paris, Monson had little to do aside from taking note of virulent anti-British attacks in Parisian newspapers and observing the more or less annual rise and fall of successive French ministries. He devoted much time to society, endeavoring as always to facilitate cordial relations through personal contacts. At the annual banquet of the British Chamber of Commerce in Paris on 3 May 1897, he expressed his "fervent hope that the old 'entente cordiale' between England and France may be again established; and to add my conviction that if the two countries could only know and understand each other better such a consummation might be achieved."[41] While

---

[39]Wood, 118-121.

[40]FO 27/3396, D.413, 18 August 1898, Monson to Salisbury.

[41]FO 27/3316, D.314, 7 May 1897, Monson to Salisbury; FO 27/3316, D.329, 11 May 1897, Monson to Salisbury.

he tended to attribute the strong anti-British sentiment in France to certain politicians "who are both ignorant and malicious," he maintained consistently that the principal culprit in France was the Parisian press. "Active hostility against us is felt, I believe, but by comparatively few Frenchmen; but it is because those who are so inspired are loud and demonstrative in expressing their feelings, that such hostility is supposed to be general."[42] At times, his zealousness contributed to sloppiness in language, which undercut his own efforts. In June 1897, for example, he verbally communicated to Hanotaux Salisbury's acceptance of six proposals regarding the Eastern Question. He reported that the foreign minister:

> [d]id not quite like the words 'conspicuously vague' but I explained that Your Lordship's meaning was undoubtedly complimentary to the adroitness with which His Excellency had drawn up the proposals, and that the expression should be taken in conjunction with the context, which implied that as much ground as possible should be covered without committing the Powers to inconvenient or to unpalatable obligations.

He noted that Hanotaux accepted this view. In a diplomatic minute, however, Arthur Balfour, First Lord of the Treasury wrote that "'Conspicuously' vague was intended for Sir E. Monson's consumption, not for formal communication to the French Minister." Salisbury noted: "I agree – but it does not matter."[43]

At other times, Monson demonstrated an unfortunate

---

[42]FO 27/3316, D.329, 11 May 1897, Monson to Salisbury. See also: FO 27/3316, D.369, 28 May 1897, Monson to Salisbury; FO 27/3318, D.524, 6 August 1897, Monson to Salisbury.

[43]FO 27/3317, D.398, 11 June 1897, Monson to Salisbury; minutes by Balfour and Salisbury [12 June 1897].

carelessness or confusion, which could not have inspired much confidence in either London or Paris. In December 1896 he reported that Hanotaux supported the use of coercion against the Ottoman government in an effort to bring anti-European violence in Constantinople under control. Salisbury responded forcefully by informing French ambassador Courcel "that under no circumstances would he agree to the employment of coercive measures against the Sultan." Courcel assured Salisbury that Monson must have misunderstood Hanotaux's language. Furthermore, Hanotaux himself complained to the ambassador that Monson had "certainly misrepresented him." Monson's defense was the vagueness of Hanotaux's language. The foreign minister, he noted, had spoken of the dangers in the Ottoman Empire "in a vague and sketchy manner which renders it difficult to make a clear and intelligible report of his conversation. This may have been his deliberate purpose, for before I left him he observed that as I had not yet been received in audience by the President our interview could not be considered official."[44]

Through the summer Monson devoted much attention to the Franco-Russian alliance and its implications for Britain. He believed that the Russian connection encouraged France to avoid resolving the Eastern Question. He noted, for example, that following the visit of Hanotaux and President Félix Faure to St. Petersburg in August 1897, Hanotaux expressed strong opposition to Salisbury's proposal of a united guarantee by Britain, France, and Russia to assist Greece in paying its war indemnity.[45] The foreign minister's "very frank

---

[44]FO 27/3267, Tel.43, 3 December 1896, Monson to Salisbury. See also: FO 27/3267, D.379, 4 December 1896, Monson to Salisbury; FO 27/3267, D.394, 17 December 1896, Monson to Salisbury.

[45]In April 1897, war broke out between Greece and Turkey. The Powers intervened to save Greece from the worst consequences.

declaration of his absolute indifference to the results of the war as regards the territorial position of Greece" proved to be quite a surprise to Monson, given Hanotaux's previous professions of Philhellenism and given how strongly the French, during Monson's stay in Athens, "put forward their claim to be the especial, if not the sole, patrons of Greece." At the same time, however, Monson was not too terribly surprised, considering current French infatuation with Russia:

> I cannot believe that M. Hanotaux, in spite of the fatal facility with which he changes his opinions and discards on the morrow the theories of yesterday, would have made so reckless an assertion were it not an echo of language which he has heard from Count Muraviev. . . . M. Hanotaux clinched this cynical avowal of a change of views . . . by asserting his conviction that there is no one in France who would now lift up his finger to aid Greece. . . . In the actual fervour for Russia which pervades this country, it is certain that the policy which the former dictates will be implicitly accepted by the latter.[46]

France's groveling and the "delirious exhibition of satisfaction at Russian protection" disgusted Monson.[47] Amidst the initial hysteria in France concerning the impending visit of French President Faure to Russia, which had completely dominated the media and public attention, Monson was prompted to write that "No more striking illustration would, I think, be given of the aptness of Prince Bismark's [sic] assertion that there is something feminine in the French temperament. I can well understand," he continued, " the susceptibility which, as he told me himself, drove the late Prince

---

[46]FO 27/3319, D.575, 2 September 1897, Monson to Salisbury.

[47]FO 27/3319, D.572, 31 August 1897, Monson to Salisbury.

Lobanoof [*sic*] away from Paris at the time of the Toulon visit and caused him, to use his expression, 'a sensation of nausea.'"[48]

While Monson believed that most Frenchmen were not so naive as to believe the Russian alliance would bring about a war to regain the lost provinces of Alsace and Lorraine, he saw it as justification for a militant colonial policy that could be aimed only at Britain; in any event, Monson speculated, French action in Africa would become bolder.[49]

---

[48]FO 27/3318, D.550, 22 August 1897, Monson to Salisbury.

[49]Wood, 130-135, 296-297.

Craig E. Saucier

Chapter Two

THE EGYPTIAN QUESTION

The conflict over Fashoda, to all appearances a race for control of an abandoned fortress, grew directly out of the Anglo-French struggle for imperial preponderance in Egypt. This struggle involved competing visions of Africa: a British vision of empire through eastern Africa stretching south from the Mediterranean Sea to the Cape of Good Hope, which conflicted with a French vision of empire across north-central Africa from the Atlantic Ocean to the Red Sea. More to the point, the confrontation over Fashoda, which began in earnest following the British occupation of Egypt in 1882, developed almost entirely out of consideration for British imperial strategy in the Near East. Between 1882 and 1898, three primary goals drove British policy: protection of Egypt and the Suez Canal, maintenance of the British position in the Mediterranean Sea, and protection of the Upper Nile valley.

Egypt initially represented a bridge between the Mediterranean and Red Seas, affording a shorter overland route to India. British imperial policy since the eighteenth century sought to protect the route to India, which remained London's base of commercial and military power in the East. British institutions in India secured and promoted trade and investment throughout central and southeast Asia, the Far East, Australia, and New Zealand. Consequently, the opening of the Suez Canal in 1869 magnified the importance of Egypt by revolutionizing communication and commerce between Europe and the East. In strategic terms, the canal became the "indispensable link" between the Mediterranean Fleet and the Indian Army, the two pillars of British power that supported London's diplomacy both east and west of Egypt. In economic terms, the canal proved critical to British commerce, as over eighty percent of its ship traffic was of British registry.[50]

Inherent in its policy of protecting the Near Eastern route to India, London understood the necessity for control of the Mediterranean Sea; thus, the Royal Navy maintained bases at Malta and Gibraltar, prepared to act if London's diplomacy failed. From the middle of the nineteenth century, however, the existing instability and threat of dissolution in the Ottoman Empire endangered the British position in the Mediterranean. Moreover, and far more important, because Egypt remained formally a province of the Ottoman Empire, instability throughout the Sultan's domains heightened British interest. The primary threat came from Russian designs on the Straits of Constantinople and the Balkans. Salisbury believed the collapse of the Ottoman Empire inevitable and thus worked to safeguard British interests if Russia chose to seize the Straits. This problem became particularly critical in the 1890s, following the Franco-Russian alliance, when it became clear that it would be

---

[50]Ronald Robinson, John Gallagher, and Alice Denny, *Africa and the Victorians: The Climax of Imperialism in the Dark Continent* (New York: St. Martin's Press, 1961), 11-13; J.A.S. Grenville, *Lord Salisbury and Foreign Policy: The Close of the Nineteenth Century* (London: University of London and the Athlone Press, 1964), 291, 296.

impossible henceforth to seal the Straits against Russia.[51] In October 1896 Salisbury invited the Powers to meet in conference at Constantinople, to work out a program of reform that would assure the stability of the Ottoman Empire. In spite of an agreement reached by early February 1897, war broke out between Greece and Turkey in April before the sultan could be made to accept the reforms. As a result, the conference failed. By 1897, therefore, the focus of London's efforts to maintain the British position in the Mediterranean shifted from the Straits to the Nile. Salisbury wrote to ambassador Currie in Constantinople:

> I have regarded the Eastern question as having little serious interest for England . . . On the other hand, our interest in Egypt is growing stronger . . . The only policy which it seems to me is left to us . . . is to strengthen our position on the Nile . . . and to withdraw as much as possible from all responsibilities at Constantinople.[52]

For London indeed protection of Egypt required control of the Upper Nile valley. The Nile River, the longest river in the world at approximately 4,130 miles, is the primary water resource and life artery for Egypt. The Nile has two major tributaries, the White Nile and Blue Nile. The White Nile is longer and rises in the Great Lakes region of central Africa. It flows north through Tanzania, Lake Victoria, Uganda and South Sudan. The Blue Nile is the source of most of the water

---

[51]Michael Barthorp, *War on the Nile: Britain, Egypt and the Sudan, 1882-1898* (Poole, New York and Sydney: Blandford Press, 1984), 16-18; Grenville, 46-52, 97; Sanderson, 100, 402.

[52]Grenville, 83-94; Robert Taylor, *Lord Salisbury*, ed. Chris Cook (New York: St. Martin's Press, 1975), 171.

and fertile soil. It begins at Lake Tana in Ethiopia and flows into Sudan from the southeast. The two rivers meet near the Sudanese capital of Khartoum. The northern section of the Nile flows toward the Mediterranean Sea almost entirely through desert, from Sudan into Egypt. The *Upper* Nile is in southeastern Sudan, bordered by Ethiopia to the east, the Sudanese territory of Bahr el Ghazal to the west, and the region of Equatoria to the south. In reality, the Upper Nile was largely barren and inhospitable territory. The Egyptian economy, however, depended on the flow of the Nile for its summer water, which was essential to sustain the £10 million cotton crop. Moreover, because of an abnormally low river flood and an almost chronic inadequacy of the summer water supply during the late 1880s, there was increased interest in building dams, reservoirs, or barrages at the outlets of Lakes Victoria and Albert. Because any interference with the White Nile could have impoverished Egypt, however, the very discussion provoked fears that such technology would be used for malevolent purposes.

The British government believed that some enemy or power hostile to Egypt could deliberately employ modern technology to interfere with the flow of the Nile and thereby disrupt the Egyptian economy. Sir Samuel Baker, the British explorer who discovered Lake Albert, wrote in 1884 that the abandonment of the Sudan exposed Egypt to a terrible danger:

> Should a civilized, or even a semi-civilized, enemy be in possession of [Khartoum], the waters of the Rahad, Dinder, Blue Nile, and the Atbara Rivers could be diverted from their course and dispersed throughout the deserts, to the utter ruin and complete destruction of Egypt proper. . . . the plan is feasible, and that, should any European be in command at the rebellious centre of the Sudan, his first strategical

operation would be to deprive Egypt of the water that
is necessary for her existence.[53]

Therefore, the waters of the Upper Nile linked the
protection of the Sudan to the protection of Egypt and
thus to the security of the British position in Egypt. For
that reason, London regarded the protection of the Upper
Nile from European interference as a fundamental
objective of its imperial diplomacy.

The Anglo-French dispute over Fashoda was born
out of the Egyptian Question. Over the middle decades
of the nineteenth century Anglo-French relations had
been warm or at least cooperative, particularly in the
Near East. Britain and France were allies during the
Crimean War and thereafter worked together to shore up
the Ottoman Empire against the territorial encroachment
of Russia. In the mid-1870s London and Paris
established a partnership over the Egyptian treasury to
alleviate the financial difficulties of Ismail Pasha, the
Khedive of Egypt and nominally the viceroy of the
sultan. Ismail, who wished to rule as a modern pharaoh
over the richest empire in Africa, borrowed and spent
vast sums of money for construction and modernization
of his lands. He soon found himself, however, in severe
financial difficulties. In 1875 when Ismail put his shares
of the Suez Canal Company up for sale, British Prime
Minister Benjamin Disraeli procured a loan from the
Rothschilds and purchased the shares -- 40 percent of
total Suez Canal shares -- for £4 million. Although the
purchase did not represent a controlling share of canal
stock, it made Britain the chief stockholder and gave it in
practice a determining voice in the decisions of the

---

[53]Langer, *Diplomacy of Imperialism*, 103-107, 559, 574; Sanderson, 10-11, 402-
403; Patricia Wright, *Conflict on the Nile: The Fashoda Incident of 1898*
(London: William Heinemann Ltd., 1972), 44-45.

company. By 1876 Ismail's bankruptcy forced him to accept foreign intervention in the form of an international commission of debt control, the *Caisse de la Dette Publique*. Britain and France, the states most immediately concerned, subsequently established a dual directorship of Egyptian finances, which quickly extended into Egyptian governmental affairs by 1878. As their scrutiny and control over Egyptian affairs became more rigorous, however, discontent increased among the middle ranks of the Egyptian officer corps. Conscious of his loss of power and prestige, Ismail began to intrigue and rally support among these increasingly radicalized officers for throwing off European intervention. In 1879, London and Paris prevailed upon the Turkish sultan Abdul Hamed to overthrow and replace Ismail with the Khedive's son, Mohammed Tewfik, who was inevitably regarded as a puppet for the Europeans. By 1881, therefore, growing Egyptian nationalism and a deepening resentment of European influence threatened the Anglo-French dual control.[54]

The subsequent tension that emerged between Britain and France -- and ultimately the extreme French petulance -- over the British occupation of Egypt is mystifying, considering that it was in fact Paris which initially pushed for an aggressive and forward policy, while London hesitated. Throughout late 1881 militancy spread and public order began to break down in Egypt, prompting concerns in London and Paris not only for the safety of the 90,000 Europeans living there but more significantly for the stability of their dual financial control. The French first broached the possibility of a joint expedition for the purpose of preserving stability in

---

[54]Barthorp, 20-30; William L. Langer, *European Alliances and Alignments, 1871-1890*, 2d ed., (New York: Alfred A. Knopf, 1950), 258-268; Jones, 255; Thomas Pakenham, *The Scramble For Africa, 1876-1912* (New York: Random House, 1991), 78, 125-128.

Egypt. The British cabinet of William Gladstone, far away more concerned with electoral reform and Irish home rule, preferred that the Turks should undertake any expedition should one become necessary. That solution, however, was unacceptable to Paris, which worried that the Turks would inspire a pan-Islamic movement across northern Africa, at the very moment the French were consolidating control in Tunis and Algeria. In late December 1881 the French Prime Minister Léon Gambetta pushed for an aggressive joint policy and persuaded a very reluctant Gladstone to consent to the issuing of a Joint Note on 8 January 1882, which stressed their mutual determination to maintain the Khedive on the throne and to preserve law and order. Gladstone, who had won the election of 1880 in part by attacking the imperial foreign policy of Disraeli, had reservations about committing British force, preferring once again to leave intervention to a Turkish expedition under a mandate from the European powers. In late January, however, Gambetta's ministry collapsed and was replaced by the more pacific and accommodating Charles de Freycinet. The result was a decided change in French policy; Paris now repudiated the idea of using force and maintained that there was no immediate need to act in Egypt. Freycinet agreed that the proper course in Egypt was at the very least to secure a European mandate for British and French intervention.

In the meantime, the impact of the 8 January Note proved catastrophic: it alarmed Tewfik, angered the Egyptian army, drove Egyptian moderates to side with the militants, and directed the growing nationalist movement more and more against all European influence. In May 1882, therefore, the British and French dispatched a joint naval squadron to Alexandria to safeguard law and order. The arrival of the warships, however, triggered even more religious hysteria and prompted outrages against Christian European communities in Cairo and Alexandria. On 11 June riots broke out in Alexandria, which left fifty Europeans dead and many more injured. The failure of the naval demonstration and the outbreak of rioting made a deep impression in London and ultimately compelled a change in British policy; in particular, the Gladstone government began to consider possible military intervention. They invited the French to join in formally requesting a Turkish intervention with "a mandate from the Concert of Europe," which would thereby avoid the necessity for a British landing. Again, however, the French government refused to support a Turkish advance. In the meantime, at Alexandria, anti-western elements in the Egyptian army continued work on defensive batteries and earthworks abreast allied warships. British admiral Sir Beauchamp Seymour, sufficiently alarmed by the ongoing preparations and concerned for the safety of his ships and crews -- and on his own authority -- issued an ultimatum on 10 July; unless the forts were surrendered within 24 hours, he would open fire. Seymour invited the French to cooperate. In Paris, however, Freycinet declined. He declared that his ministry could not agree to participate in an act of war without the consent of the Chamber of Deputies. The next morning at 0700, having received no reply to the ultimatum, the British began bombarding the forts; French ships withdrew to Port Said. Following three days of riots and chaos, Seymour landed troops on 14 July to restore order. On 20 July, in the absence of any indication that the sultan would take any action to restore stability within Egypt and after hearing reports that Egyptian radicals intended to blow up the Suez Canal as a reprisal for the attack on Alexandria, Gladstone reluctantly agreed to undertake a large military expedition to strengthen the Khedive and maintain the security of the Canal. A week later on 27 July, the House of Commons, by an overwhelming majority, voted the credit of £2,300,00 to pay for the expedition. In Paris, the Freycinet ministry announced that they were willing to join the British and accordingly asked the Chamber of Deputies for the vote of credit for the operation. On 29 July, however, the Freycinet ministry was overwhelmingly defeated by a huge majority on the grounds that the Suez Canal was not a French interest. The new ministry, under Charles Duclerc, had to withdraw from the joint plan to protect the Canal and announced that Paris would do nothing further in Egypt. In the meantime, between mid-August and mid-September 1882, the British army under General Sir Garnet Wolseley, commander-in-chief of the British Army, defeated the Egyptian forces and proceeded to occupy the country.[55]

The catalyst for the British occupation of Egypt, therefore, was the strategic necessity to secure the stability of Egypt, the Suez Canal, and ultimately, the lifeline to India. Historians Ronald Robinson and John Gallagher argue that over the long run the British occupation of Egypt altered the European balance of power. France was humiliated and began to search for compensation by attacking British interests in West Africa. At the same time, the Germans began moving into East and Southwest Africa although primarily in an effort to extort British support in Europe. Thus, by altering the European balance of power, the British occupation inflated the importance of trivial disputes in tropical Africa and set off a "scramble" for control of the Dark Continent.[56] For the British government, however,

---

[55]Barthorp, 30-37, 49-73; Langer, *European Alliances*, 266-277; Pakenham, 130-135; Robinson and Gallagher, 94-120.

[56]Robinson and Gallagher, 17, 162.

the occupation created two new long-term problems: the evacuation of Egypt -- specifically, how and when -- and the hostility and resentment of France.

Gladstone quickly announced that Britain wanted to withdraw from Egypt as soon as possible. Already in September 1882, the cabinet was making out a timetable from which to retire British forces. For the time being, however, the cabinet decided that its forces would remain in Egypt until they had secured the complete restoration of tranquility, stability, security, and the authority of the Khedive. They further believed that these goals would be achieved only by a complete overhaul of all Egyptian institutions under British auspices, guided and assisted by British advisors, inspired with and adhering to British standards. In the meantime, French influence would be ousted, the Dual Control over Egyptian finances abolished, and a greater share of the management of the Suez Canal assumed by London. Until a new Egyptian army could be raised and trained to safeguard the country effectively, a British garrison would have to remain.[57] Therefore, the official word was that occupation would be temporary. How long "temporary" meant remained unclear; the cabinet, for example, could not agree on how to proceed and how to determine the point at which the Khedive's authority was in fact reestablished.

The schedule for evacuation became problematical due to growing instability in the Sudan, which had been conquered by Egypt in the early nineteenth century. In the early 1880s the Sudan became engulfed in an uprising of Islamic fanaticism known as "Mahdism." In Islamic eschatology, the *Mahdi* is believed to be the messianic successor of the Prophet who will rule for

---

[57]Barthorp, 74; Pakenham, 180-181; Robinson and Gallagher, 122-124; Sanderson 13-14; Wright, 13-20, 23-29.

seven, nine, or nineteen years before the Day of Judgment and will rid the world of evil. In late June 1881, Muhammad Ahmad proclaimed himself the Mahdi. He declared Jihad against the Turkish and Egyptian oppressors and incited local Sudanese tribes to rise in support. This led the British government to dispatch in 1884 the ill-fated mission of General Charles "Chinese" Gordon to Khartoum to secure the evacuation of loyal Egyptian soldiers and British civilians. Besieged by the Mahdi's forces, Gordon organized a city-wide defense that lasted almost a year. Although his heroic defense of the city won him the admiration of the British public, the government had not supported his expedition and had not planned to relieve him. Only when public pressure to rescue Gordon's besieged mission had become too great did the government reluctantly dispatch a relief force. It arrived two days after the city had fallen and Gordon had been killed; accounts of his heroism and horrific death at the hands of the Mahdi's forces elevated the general nearly into British sainthood, a martyr sacrificed by an ingrate government.

By 1885, therefore, the entire region of the Upper Nile to the Egyptian frontier was under the undisputed control of the Mahdi and his successor, the Khalifa. Because the Mahdists had neither the resources nor the expertise to interfere with the flow of the Nile or to threaten the borders of Egypt, the British government was content for the time being that they stay. So long as the Mahdists were in control of the vast and unproductive area, there was no need to go to the trouble or expense to subdue them. In London and Cairo, however, there remained some apprehension that efforts would be made to interfere with the head waters of the Upper Nile, Egypt's all-important water supply. More to the point, the British feared that one of its European rivals might try to move into the Upper Nile.

The occupation of Egypt created a second serious problem for London: the enmity of France. Following the collapse of the Freycinet ministry in July 1882, Paris formally adopted a policy of noninterference in Egypt; although the French would not participate in any military operations, they would not obstruct the British. Relations between London and Paris nevertheless grew tense as it became clear that the British withdrawal would not be immediately forthcoming. In addition to the economic and strategic implications for France's position in the Near East, the British occupation represented a loss of national prestige. The French long believed that it was their destiny to modernize and enlighten Egypt. France indeed had been the dominant European influence in Egypt since Napoleon's Egyptian expedition in 1798. In spite of the expulsion of Napoleon's army three years later, French scholars, scientists, and technical experts continued to dominate European culture and influence in Egypt. They built a fleet and a large army, with which Mohammed Ali had conquered the Sudan in 1820; they helped Egypt embark upon an ambitious modernization program; and a French engineer, Ferdinand de Lesseps, constructed the Suez Canal. The British, by contrast, had not played any meaningful role in Egypt until Disraeli's purchase of the Suez Canal shares in 1875.[58]

The British occupation of Egypt stirred debate on the proper orientation of French foreign policy. The debate

---

[58]Christopher Andrew, *Théophile Delcassé and the Making of the Entente Cordiale: A Reappraisal of French Foreign Policy, 1898-1905* (London: Macmillan and Company, 1968), 21-22; Barthorp, 14, 17-18, 77-132; Darrell Bates, *The Fashoda Incident of 1898: Encounter on the Nile* (Oxford: Oxford University Press, 1984), 12; Morrison Beall Giffen, *Fashoda: The Incident and its Diplomatic Setting* (Chicago: University of Chicago Press, 1930), 27-28; Langer, *Diplomacy of Imperialism*, 102-103, 108, 110; Langer, *European Alliances*, 281-282; Pakenham, 74-75, 467-468, 505-506; Robinson and Gallagher, 125-127; Sanderson, 114-115; Wright, 6, 31-40.

centered around two fundamental positions. On one hand, the *continentalists* argued that France's most serious problems were its diplomatic isolation and the constant threat of Germany. They were wary of colonial expansion, which not only diverted resources from the containment of the German threat, but also courted the serious possibility of confrontation with Britain. The continentalists generally favored rapprochement with Britain, along with Russia, in order to counter German power. French resources, therefore, should be devoted to meeting the German challenge on the continent. On the other hand, the *colonialists* argued that France was not only a European power but a world power. Because its influence in world politics was a function of the size of its empire, expansion would decidedly strengthen France's European position. Because overseas French expansion often encountered British opposition, many among the colonialists favored an understanding with Germany as a means of strengthening French global power. Not surprisingly, tension emerged between these two currents of opinion. According to Roger Glenn Brown, this tension found its institutional expression in interdepartmental rivalry for control of French foreign and colonial policy; specifically, between the Ministry of Foreign Affairs (which became the focus of continentalist opinion) and the agency charged with colonial affairs. Throughout much of the nineteenth century, that agency had been the Ministry of Marine. The Third Republic, however, created an Undersecretariat of State for Colonies, which was raised to full ministerial status in 1894.[59]

The Duclerc ministry bitterly resented being ousted

---

[59]Roger Glenn Brown, *Fashoda Reconsidered: The Impact of Domestic Politics on French Policy in Africa, 1893-1898* (Baltimore and London: The Johns Hopkins Press, 1970), 17-19; Richard Ned Lebow, *Between Peace and War: The Nature of International Crisis* (Baltimore and London: The Johns Hopkins Press, 1981), 72.

from the dual financial control in Cairo. Numerous statesmen regarded the occupation as France's worst humiliation since 1871 and demanded compensation. In the mid-1880s, French colonialists began to agitate for colonial expansion in Tunis, Algeria, Senegal, the Ivory Coast, and north of the Congo. They cooperated with Germany in opposing British ambitions in the Congo and southwest Africa, and pressed their own claims in the New Hebrides, Madagascar, Morocco, Indochina, China, and Newfoundland. The main source of acrimony, however, always remained Egypt.[60]

British leaders continued to pledge publicly to evacuate Egypt but only when it was strategically acceptable. Lord Salisbury's primary concern during his second ministry (1886-1892)[61] involved the balance of power in the Mediterranean. In protecting Britain's routes to the East, the preconditions of which included the security of Egypt and the stability of the Ottoman Empire, Salisbury understood that the longer Britain remained in Egypt, French resentment and the Russian threat to the Straits increased the danger in the Mediterranean. At the same time, however, if London withdrew from Egypt prematurely and the Ottoman Empire continued to disintegrate, the Suez Canal might fall into the hands of another power.

By the late 1880s Salisbury began to shift away from the idea of evacuation altogether. The catalyst for this consequential shift in British policy was the failure

---

[60]Langer, *European Alliances*, 285-287, 297-306, 371-397; Graham H. Stuart, *French Foreign Policy: From Fashoda to Serajevo (1898-1914)* (New York: The Century Company, 1921), 12-16.

[61]In June 1885, Salisbury's first cabinet replaced the second Gladstone ministry (June 1880-June 1885), which had been beset with economic depression. Although Salisbury's first cabinet was short-lived (June 1885 to February 1886), Gladstone's third ministry quickly fell apart in July 1886 over the issue of Irish home rule.

of the Drummond-Wolff mission. Sir Henry Drummond-Wolff, minister at Teheran, went to Constantinople in January 1887 to negotiate the British withdrawal from Egypt; Salisbury, however, insisted on the right of reoccupation if Egypt slipped back into anarchy. Although Drummond-Wolff secured an agreement by late May, the sultan refused to ratify the convention under pressure from France and Russia. Salisbury realized, therefore, that the Ottoman Empire was even weaker than he originally believed and began to doubt that the route to India could ever be defended as effectively at the Straits as at the Suez Canal. Moreover, France was becoming an active menace, not merely a disgruntled rival. It was not that the terms of the Drummond-Wolff Convention were unacceptable to Paris; it was their greater resentment over London's attempt to resolve the Egyptian question without French participation.[62] Tensions between London and Paris in 1887 prompted Salisbury's sarcastic quip that, "in view of the irritation resulting from this and other questions, it is very difficult to prevent oneself from wishing for another Franco-German War to put a stop to this incessant vexation."[63] Furthermore, events in the Upper Nile -- the lowest flood on record and a series of internal crises that weakened the Mahdist state, rendering it perhaps too weak to resist a European offensive -- exposed the vulnerability of the Egyptian borders and the necessity for stability in the area. Finally, the possibility of German penetration from East Africa into Equatoria, one of the southernmost of Egypt's former Sudanese

---

[62]Pakenham, 338-340; Langer, *European Alliances*, 397-404, 429-430 ; Dame Lillian M. Penson, *Foreign Affairs Under the Third Marquis of Salisbury* (London: University of London and Athlone Press, 1962), 17; Robinson and Gallagher, 254, 264-268; Sanderson, 41, 115-116.

[63]Newton, 386.

provinces,[64] and the possibility of Italian penetration toward Khartoum from Somaliland[65] further threatened the waters of the Upper Nile.

By 1890, therefore, Salisbury concluded that Britain must remain in Egypt in order to secure the headwaters of the Nile and to secure the Suez Canal. At the same time, he understood that the Sudan would eventually have to be reconquered and restored to Egyptian control. Until that point diplomacy would have to suffice to safeguard British interests and to keep European rivals out of the Upper Nile. The British government negotiated treaties with Germany in July 1890[66] and Italy in April 1891.[67] London concluded its more significant arrangement with Leopold II of Belgium in April 1894, the Anglo-Congolese Agreement, by which the king effectively recognized the basin of the White Nile to be a British sphere of influence. In return, London granted to Leopold a perpetual lease over the Bahr al-Ghazal, one of Egypt's former and southernmost Sudanese provinces, thereby effectively denying that region to France.[68] The

---

[64]The easiest approach to Equatoria and the headwaters of the Nile was from the east coast, where German agents were active.

[65]In May 1889, Italy and the King of Ethiopia concluded the Treaty of Uccialli, which allowed Italy to edge towards Khartoum, at the confluence of the White Nile and the Blue Nile.

[66]In return for the island of Heligoland in the North Sea the British established a protectorate over Zanzibar, security in Kenya, and access to Uganda (which meant access to the headwaters of the Nile), thereby protecting London's concern for a Mombasa-to-Lake Victoria railroad.

[67]Italy abandoned all claims to any political foothold within the Upper Nile basin in return for the right to occupy Kassala (in eastern Sudan).

[68]In return for the perpetual lease over Equatoria and Bahr al-Ghazal, Leopold leased to Britain a corridor running along the eastern border of the Congo state and the western border of German East Africa and thereby preserving the possibility of a continuous line of British communications from Cairo to the Cape of Good Hope.

cumulative effect of these diplomatic arrangements was to eliminate three potential threats to the British position in the Upper Nile. In exchange for concessions, the German, Italian, and Belgian governments effectively agreed to recognize the entire basin of the White Nile -- the stretch of the Nile River from Lake Victoria to Khartoum -- as a British sphere of influence.[69]

The French, meanwhile, remained persistent in their opposition to British policy. They argued that the entire region of the Upper Nile had become *res nullius*; in other words, all foreign authority had disappeared with the evacuation of the British in 1885 following the fall of Khartoum. They continued to hope that London might be persuaded to end its occupation of Egypt through negotiation; yet discussions were never productive. As many French leaders tended to blame Salisbury for the stalemate, they pinned their hopes on Gladstone's return to power in 1892. This optimism, however, faded in the face of Gladstone's preoccupation with Irish affairs.[70]

French belligerency intensified with the appointment in May 1894 of Théophile Delcassé as the new minister for the colonies. Delcassé, a former journalist who specialized in foreign and colonial affairs, was a rabid and committed imperialist. He believed that colonies were vital not merely to secure necessary markets but also as a symbol of national prestige. He thus considered the extension of the French Empire first and foremost as a means of restoring France to its former rank

---

[69]For a complete discussion of the diplomatic arrangements in London's efforts to protect its position in the Upper Nile, see: Bates, 13-15; Langer, *Diplomacy of Imperialism*, 6-7, 108-124; Langer, *European Alliances*, 492-495; David L. Lewis, *The Race to Fashoda: European Colonialism and African Resistance in the Scramble For Africa* (New York: Weidenfeld and Nicolson, 1987), 9, 38, 111-112; Pakenham, 355-357, 449-450, 468, 472-473; Robinson and Gallagher, 284, 290-295, 330-331; Sanderson, 41-46, 67-80, 162-170, 203.

[70]Andrew, 24-25.

in Europe. In 1892 Delcassé helped to establish the *parti colonial*, an interparty union of approximately 90 members of the Chamber of Deputies who advocated greater French colonial expansion in Africa. The *parti colonial* effectively became the principal front through which small but influential pro-colonialist groups exerted significant influence over the Chamber of Deputies. One of the most significant included the *Comité de l'Afrique Française*, which sought to ensure that France obtained its share in the spoils of Africa. From its inception in 1890, it promoted and subsidized expeditions and ventures designed to expand French influence and markets in West Africa and the region of Lake Chad; beginning in 1892, it shifted its main interests to the east, to the Bahr al-Ghazal and to the Nile basin. A second pro-colonialist group, the *Union Coloniale Française*, represented an association of French firms with colonial interests in French colonies. Following his appointment as the undersecretary for the colonies in early 1893 and his elevation to minister for the colonies the following year, Delcassé maintained a close relationship with leading members of the *parti colonial*, whose ultimate objective was a continuous belt of French territory across Africa from Senegal to the Red Sea. Moreover, their immediate commercial aim was to secure a port on the Nile that would serve existing French possessions in Equatoria and prevent the British goal of dominating eastern Africa.[71]

In February 1893, as the undersecretary for the colonies in the ministries of Alexandre Ribot (December

---

[71]Andrew, 3-32; Brown, 19-22, 24-25; Susan Peterson, *Crisis Bargaining and the State: The Domestic Politics of International Conflict* (Ann Arbor: The University of Michigan Press, 1996), 106-107; Charles W. Porter, *The Career of Théophile Delcassé* (Philadelphia: University of Pennsylvania Press, 1936), 8-9, 11-15, 29-34; P.J.V. Rolo, *Entente Cordiale: The Origins and Negotiation of the Anglo-French Agreements of 8 April 1904* (London: Macmillan & Company, 1969), 75-83; Sanderson, 119-120.

1892-April 1893) and Charles Dupuy (April-December 1893). Delcassé proposed the dispatch of an expedition under the command of Major Parfait-Louis Monteil to the Bahr al-Ghazal and ultimately into the Nile valley. Monteil was a French colonial military officer and explorer who had already made an epic journey in West Africa between 1890 and 1892, traveling east from Senegal to Lake Chad. The goal of the mission was to provide France with a commercial outlet on the Nile. Delcassé believed that, by striking into the Bahr al-Ghazal, the French could threaten the headwaters of the Nile and thus force the British to address French interests in Egypt. Delcassé proved highly influenced by the views of Victor Prompt, a hydraulic engineer, who in January 1893 argued that the waters of the Nile could be regulated with the building of dams at strategic points on the river. What caught Delcassé's attention was the prospect of reopening the Egyptian question by the implied threat of interference.[72] Recognizing that the expedition would need to be reinforced, Delcassé sought the cooperation and support of Menelik the King of Ethiopia. Menelik, already disposed to friendly relations with the French, agreed to send a mission to occupy regions around the White Nile.[73] He also understood that the Quai d'Orsay[74] would never approve of anything that was likely to disturb good relations with both Britain and Belgium. In May, therefore, Delcassé persuaded the

---

[72]Langer, *Diplomacy of Imperialism*, 127-129; Lewis, *Race to Fashoda*, 47-50; Pakenham, 456-457. Sanderson, 141-143.

[73]As early as 1888 the French government considered good relations with Ethiopia as a way of applying pressure on the British position in Egypt. They helped Menelik, who came to power in 1889, procure arms and munitions. In return, Menelik formally denounced the Treaty of Uccialli in February 1893. Bates, 44-45; Sanderson, 152-158.

[74]A metonym for the French Ministry of Foreign Affairs, which is located on the Quai d'Orsay in the seventh arrondissement of Paris.

president of the Republic, Sadi Carnot, to approve the expedition; the Ministry of Foreign Affairs was not even consulted. Carnot is said to have told Monteil: "*Il faut occupier Fachoda.*"[75] Preparations moved forward but Monteil procrastinated. A series of delays and diversions followed, coupled with bureaucratic inertia so that the necessary stores for the expedition did not leave until June 1894. Monteil himself did not depart for Africa until mid-July 1894 and was ultimately ordered to the Ivory Coast. In the meantime, the Dupuy ministry collapsed and was replaced by Jean Casimir-Perier, who dismissed Delcassé and never gave the Monteil operation any more than lukewarm support. The mission into the Bahr al-Ghazal never got seriously underway.[76]

Until the spring of 1894, in spite of the preparations made to send Monteil into the Upper Nile, official French policy and public opinion considered the Egyptian question a matter of remote territorial importance. African questions were irrelevant compared to the more critical continental questions such as Alsace and Lorraine. It was, however, the Anglo-Congolese Agreement of April 1894 between King Leopold II and Lord Rosebery, who became the British prime minister when Gladstone resigned in March, that exacerbated and transformed the Upper Nile question into a major issue of Great Power diplomacy and began to stir feelings of national prestige and public excitement. This agreement, in part a result of concerns raised by rumors and reports of the Monteil expedition, deliberately sought to keep France out of the Upper Nile.

Furthermore, it made an antagonist of the new French foreign minister, Gabriel Hanotaux, who

---

[75]"It is necessary to occupy Fashoda."

[76]Andrew, 41-42; Bates, 6-8; Brown, 27; Langer, *Diplomacy of Imperialism*, 131-134, 139; Lebow, 73; Lewis, *Race to Fashoda*, 47-50, 52-53; Sanderson, 144-151, 188-189, 192-211; Wright, 113-114.

assumed office with the return in late May 1894 of Charles Dupuy. Hanotaux originally opposed the Monteil expedition to the Upper Nile. Not only was it contrary to traditional French policy, which long recognized the integrity of the Ottoman Empire, but it would hinder his efforts to improve relations with Britain. The Anglo-Congolese Agreement dealt his policy a heavy blow and triggered in France a renewal of Anglophobia. Hanotaux immediately attacked it and announced his intention to order Monteil back to duty. He soon discovered, however, that France lacked significant international support. More serious were the immoderate threats of the British ambassador, Lord Dufferin. Having seen reports in the newspapers of a French mission to the Upper Nile, "to confront us with a *'fait accompli*,'" the ambassador appeared at the Quai d'Orsay and demanded to know what Monteil was up to. When Hanotaux tried to explain that Monteil had not even set sail and that there was plenty of time for London and Paris to resolve their differences, the impulsive Dufferin interrupted "that it would simply mean war between the two countries; and that it would be a terrible thing if we were to revive in Africa the miserable combats which had deluged India with French and British blood in the middle of the last century." Dufferin's intemperate remarks upset Lord Rosebery almost as much as they did Hanotaux but the French did not know this at the time. Uncertain whether Britain would seriously go to war, Hanotaux agreed to scale down Monteil's instructions, confining the expedition to the Upper Ubangi and promising that "not a single man was to be placed on the White Nile."[77]

---

[77]Andrew, 41-43; Brown, 27-29; Langer, *Diplomacy of Imperialism*, 131-134; Lewis, *Race to Fashoda*, 47-50, 52-55, 55; Pakenham, 451, 457; Robinson and Gallagher, 333; Sanderson, 144-151, 161, 188-189, 192-211; Wright, 113-114.

In moderating the French tone, Hanotaux was playing a double game; he hoped not only to appease London but also to facilitate his own secret discussions with Leopold. In the meantime, while both the British and French hoped to use Leopold in the Congo to block the expansion of the other, Leopold endeavored to take advantage of the Anglo-French rivalry, play both powers against each other, and subsequently double his African real estate. Accordingly, four months after he concluded the Anglo-Congolese Agreement with London, Leopold concluded with Hanotaux the Franco-Congolese Agreement of August 1894, in which he essentially surrendered to France all the leases obtained from Britain in the area of the White Nile. It was a clear breach of the Anglo-Congolese Agreement but Rosebery, hindered by cabinet hostility toward Salisbury's imperial objectives, was unwilling to object. Therefore, by August 1894, the Upper Nile once again lay exposed to the possibility of a French advance.[78]

Delcassé understood that Hanotaux's new instructions to Monteil rendered the mission virtually inconsequential. Seeking to exert the independence of the Colonial Ministry and still believing that such a venture would force London to reopen the Egyptian question, he proposed another expedition. Victor Liotard, already extending French influence into central Africa near the Nile watershed, would be ordered to take over as civilian governor of a province whose eastern boundaries were left purposefully undefined. The timing, Delcassé reasoned, was opportune. By November 1894, discussions with London to resolve colonial differences were at an impasse. In addition, Paris began to hear rumors of a British expedition into the Upper Nile under

[78] Bates, 16-17; Langer, *Diplomacy of Imperialism*, 134; Lewis, *Race to Fashoda*, 9, 38; Pakenham, 450-451; Sanderson, 168-184.

Colonel Henry Colville. Delcassé's concerns about Colville were largely exaggerated. The Gladstone cabinet dispatched Colville to Uganda in 1893 for commercial and philanthropic ventures. His actual activities in Uganda proved to be quite brief and he departed in early 1895. In addition, Hanotaux opposed a new mission as unnecessarily provocative and likely to upset his efforts to improve relations with London. The foreign minister, however, found himself at a political disadvantage in the ensuing showdown because earlier that month, he had been the only member of the ministry to oppose taking action against a certain Captain Alfred Dreyfus, recently accused of selling military secrets to the Germans. Delcassé therefore convinced the ministry to authorize this new expedition to the Nile; he instructed Liotard to occupy as much of the Nile basin as he could before Colville could arrive from Uganda.[79]

London and Paris pursued diplomatic efforts to resolve colonial differences and disputes into 1895, but without result. Although they sought to limit the scope of the expeditions currently in the field, London remained determined to prevent France from entering the Upper Nile, while Paris remained as determined to exercise its right to do so. On both sides of the Channel, political rhetoric enflamed the issue. In France, nationalists and colonialists urged the government to occupy the Upper Nile before the arrival of the British. On 28 February, François Deloncle, one of France's leading colonialists stood up in the Chamber of Deputies and declared that London must be compelled to settle the paramount Egyptian question. If Britain persisted in refusing to keep its promise to evacuate Egypt once internal order was restored, then France would "take

---

[79]Andrew, 43-44; Bates, 18-21, 39-41; Brown, 28-32; Langer, *Diplomacy of Imperialism*, 261-263; Lebow, 73-74.

Britain in the rear" by marching across Africa from the Atlantic into the Upper Nile, thereby forcing its rival to the conference table. In London, the Liberal government under Lord Rosebery came under pressure from Conservative members of Parliament to clarify its position about the various French expeditions said to be encroaching upon British spheres of influence in west and central Africa. When asked specifically on 28 March about French advances on the Nile and Niger rivers, Sir Edward Grey the undersecretary of state for foreign affairs announced in the House of Commons that the advance of a French expedition "under secret instructions right from the other side of Africa into a territory over which our claims have been known for so long, would not be merely an inconsistent and unexpected act, but it must be perfectly well known by the French government that it would be an unfriendly act and would be so viewed in England." The effect of Grey's comments, which he had not cleared with Rosebery, was explosive. At home the objections came not from the Conservatives, who in fact welcomed the clarification but from Grey's fellow Liberals. Henry Labouchère, for example, condemned the remarks as "a quasi-declaration of war against France." The storm caused by Grey's *"fameuse manifestation"* was particularly more intense in Paris, where it appeared that London was threatening war over its claim to the entire Nile valley. This was far more an unfriendly act, ambassador Courcel complained to the British foreign secretary Lord Kimbereley, than to send a "wandering column of explorers" into the Upper Nile.

Hanotaux, however, was more anxious than ever to reach a rapprochement with London. He was becoming ever more disenchanted with the Russians, while the Germans simply appeared eager to exploit French frustrations. Outside the Nile and the Niger questions, he believed that the interests of Britain and France could be easily reconciled. Hanotaux gratefully saw a fortuitous opportunity to renew his conciliatory efforts when, in the British parliamentary election of June 1895, the Liberals lost their majority in the House of Commons. The fall of Lord Rosebery's government resulted in the triumphant return to office of the Conservatives under Robert Gascoyne-Cecil, the Third Marquess of Salisbury, for a third term as prime minister.[80]

---

[80]Bates, 21-24; Brown, 33-35; Giffen, 264-267; Lewis, *Race to Fashoda*, 5-6; Pakenham, 466.

Craig E. Saucier

Chapter Three

SALISBURY AND THE NILE CAMPAIGN

In 1895 Lord Salisbury, who served as his own foreign minister, was at the height of his influence. He was first elected to the House of Commons in 1854 and served as secretary of state for India in Lord Derby's Conservative government from 1866 until 1867. In 1868 upon the death of his father, Lord Robert Cecil was elevated to the House of Lords. He returned to government as secretary of state for India in 1874 under Benjamin Disraeli and in 1878 was appointed Foreign Secretary, playing a leading role at the Congress of Berlin. After the Conservatives lost the 1880 general election and following the death of Disraeli the year after, Salisbury emerged as Conservative leader in the House of Lords. He became prime minister for the first time in June 1885 following Gladstone's resignation; he held the office until the return of the Liberals in early 1886. When Gladstone became converted to a position in favor of Home Rule for Ireland, Salisbury formed an alliance with the breakaway Liberal Unionists and won the subsequent general election in August 1886. He remained prime minister until the 1892 general election. Although the Unionists won the largest number of votes and seats, Gladstone formed a government with the support of the Irish Nationalist Party.

A representative of the landed aristocracy, hostile to democracy, Salisbury adhered to the reactionary credo, "Whatever happens will be for the worse, and therefore it is in our interest that as little should happen as possible." He concerned himself above all with the maintenance of stability within in the cabinet and in foreign policy. He consulted his ministers on important foreign policy decisions and took special pains to keep them fully informed, particularly those in an inner circle concerned with diplomatic affairs: Arthur Balfour, First Lord of the Treasury; Michael Hicks Beach, Chancellor of the Exchequer; Joseph Chamberlain, Colonial Secretary; Lord Lansdowne, Secretary of War; Lord George Hamilton, Secretary of State for India; the Duke of Devonshire, head of the Defense Committee; and Queen Victoria. He generally had little trouble maintaining control of his cabinets as he often allowed his colleagues a free hand and rarely intervened in their departmental concerns. In theory, any member of the cabinet could veto a decision. Although it was usually left for the prime minister to decide, he deferred to their wishes in the few instances when they ran counter to his own. Cabinet decisions, therefore, were often decided by consensus. Political maneuvering, however, increasingly threatened the stability of his government. The coalition of 1895 was a fragile one, a delicate combination of Conservatives and "unionist" Liberals; disputes were not uncommon. In particular, the hardline Colonial Secretary Chamberlain proved a major opponent of Salisbury's more moderate positions on foreign and colonial policy. Moreover, Salisbury's increasingly frail health and failing strength began to alarm his colleagues. His eyes bothered him, he got fatter, he suffered from bronchitis, his patience decreased, his sharp wit began to fade, and his trips to Whitehall became less and less frequent.

Increasingly, important issues were discussed insufficiently, much time was wasted on trivialities and irrelevant questions, and cabinet decisions were not always clear. The concern became more acute as the prime minister was compelled to take increasing physical breaks to relieve his health. Salisbury took leave between March and May 1897 as the crisis between Greece and Turkey became serious. He fell ill in February 1898 and retired to the continent just before the cabinet was to decide whether to risk war with Russia. In August 1898 he departed as Chamberlain was making one final effort to conclude an alliance with Germany, as London was negotiating over the Portuguese colonies, and as the Spanish, bitter over London's indifference during the Spanish-American War, began to erect fortifications commanding Gibraltar Bay. Consequently, the prime minister's colleagues began to wonder whether he should continue in office, especially in light of continuing international crises.[81]

In his conduct of diplomacy, Salisbury adhered to several broad principles, none more important than his desire to avoid war. Driven by a deep religious faith and broad ethical principles, he believed that human suffering was an evil. At the same time, he was equally driven by more pragmatic concerns. As Britain's wealth, power, and position throughout the world were uniquely vulnerable to wars or even rumors of war, the potential cost of protecting its global system of trade and finance from rivals grew to exceed its available resources. Provided that national interests were not adversely affected, the peaceful settlement of disputes was much more to Britain's advantage than recourse to war. As a matter of course, he opposed those who regarded war as

---

[81]Grenville, 8-11, 92-93, 142-150, 173-176, 190-194; Peterson, 102-103; Steiner, 25-26.

an extension of foreign policy. Moreover, he never sought diplomatic victories for their own sake. He believed that a spectacular diplomatic victory was almost as bad as war; to humiliate a rival complicated the task of conciliation later on. Thus, he developed a reputation for resolving disputes with face-saving gestures and "graceful concessions." The victories of diplomacy, Salisbury believed, were won by a "series of microscopic advantages; a judicious suggestion here, an opportune civility there, a wise concession at one moment and a farsighted persistence at another." Salisbury also refused to deploy "bluff" as a diplomatic tactic. He was convinced that any "Bismarckian" policy based on false foundations would lead to disaster. He therefore insisted upon knowing precisely whether Britain's military strength was equal to supporting whatever policy happened to be under cabinet discussion.[82]

Although the foreign policy principle with which historians most associate Salisbury was "splendid isolation," the most authoritative historian of Salisbury's foreign policy, J.A.S. Grenville, argues that he was not an isolationist. Faced with an increasingly volatile and complex international environment, no foreign minister could adopt a completely isolationist position. Salisbury was simply not prepared or willing to promise material assistance by concluding alliances, arguing that international cooperation could only be based on "mutual

---

[82]Barbara W. Tuchman, *The Proud Tower: A Portrait of the World Before the War, 1890-1914* (New York: The Macmillan Company, 1966), 31. See also: Grenville, 6, 16-18, 22; Lillian M. Penson, "The New Course in British Foreign Policy, 1892-1902," in *Transactions of the Royal Historical Society*, 4th series, vol. 25 (London: Offices of the Royal Historical Society, 1943), 129; Penson, *Foreign Affairs Under the Third Marquis of Salisbury*, 12, 167-17; A. N. Porter, "Lord Salisbury, Foreign Policy and Domestic Finance, 1860-1900," in *Salisbury: The Man and His Policies*, ed. Lord Blake and Hugh Cecil (New York: St. Martin's Press, 1987), 151; Ramm, 20-21.

interests and not on sentimental or even 'racial' affinities." In a changing world, circumstances might alter, thus leaving a nation in conflict with its written engagements and commitments.[83] He expressed his views very clearly in a memorandum of May 1901 when the question of alliance with Germany once again came under discussion:

> The fatal circumstances is that neither we nor the Germans are competent to make the suggested promises. The British Government cannot undertake to declare war, for any purpose, unless it is a purpose of which the electors of this country would approve. If the Government promised to declare war for an object which did not commend itself to public opinion, the promise would be repudiated and the Government would be turned out. . . . The course of the English Government in such a crisis must depend on the view taken by public opinion in this country, and public opinion would be largely, if not exclusively, governed by the nature of the *casus belli*.[84]

His ultimate objective, however, and the ultimate principle driving his foreign policy was the defense of the British Empire. In one respect, he was reluctant to assume direct governmental responsibility for the large tracts of African lands that the chartered companies were attempting to control. He indeed referred to himself as a "reluctant imperialist." He was often critical of the rush to carve up the globe and bemoaned the tendency of imperialists to trigger "constant wars at distant points which bring us large bills and such little credit and which it is afterwards their onerous task to justify." He remained conscious that Britain ruled over many

---

[83]Grenville, 16-17.

[84]Penson, 20-21.

different races, faiths, and traditions; he thus feared that the attempt to establish and impose an alien British pattern everywhere would surely undermine the British Empire as racial and religious animosities were certainly undermining the sultan's dominions. Nevertheless, Salisbury's cabinmets not only oversaw the addition of vast new territories to the British Empire, he personally defended Britain's imperial interests and pursued a policy that endeavored to forestall rival Powers.[85]

In the actual practice of carrying out his foreign policy, Salisbury supplied the coherent, overall principle of the policy to be pursued or the settlement to be concluded; anything else was delegated. Consequently, while he kept the larger political issues and questions in his own hands "as his own independent exercise" Salisbury reduced consultation with the Foreign Office chiefs to an minimum and delegated responsibility for certain matters to the principal and assistant undersecretaries, with varying degrees of independence: minor negotiations, interviews with the representatives of the less exalted powers, control over junior personnel, and selections for promotion to all but the higher appointments. He preferred to have cognizance of what was going forward in these matters but that was all.[86]

Upon his return to office in the summer of 1895 Salisbury sought to resolve several long-standing disputes with France. Although he previously had tried to maintain friendly relations with the Triple Alliance, he came to the conclusion that Germany could never be relied upon to help protect British interests. More to the point, he realized that an eventual British push up the Nile would provoke the French to even greater irritation. Consequently, in the tense aftermath of Sir Edward

---

[85]Grenville, 19-21; Peterson, 103; Taylor, 13, 67.

[86]Ramm, 48-54, 59.

Grey's provocative declaration, the cabinet appeared receptive to Hanotaux's overtures to find common ground. Salisbury made a determined effort to placate the French in other parts of the world. Negotiations over Siam began in August 1895. By 1896 London agreed to abandon its presence in the Upper Mekong valley. Salisbury further promised to negotiate a new convention over Tunis and intimated a softening of its opposition to French aspirations in the Congo and Morocco. In June 1896, believing the collapse of the Ottoman Empire as inevitable, he suggested that France might be interested in acquiring Syria. Similarly, in August, he proposed that France might acquire Crete.[87]

More important, in October, he promised a new commission to consider French and British claims in West Africa. Anglo-French rivalry in West Africa had begun in the early 1890s. Colonial Minister Delcassé, who sought to unify France's scattered conquests into a single bloc stretching from the Congo to the Mediterranean, sent out military expeditions to link French coastal colonies to the African interior before the expansion of other powers along the Niger River, mainly Britain, robbed them of the hinterlands. In 1893-1894 the French made Dahomey a protectorate, pushed into the Kingdom of Borgu, and made a treaty with Liberia. These actions, which threatened the British colonies of Sierra Leone and the Gold Coast, led to bickering with London and a sharpening of polemic over West Africa. Despite efforts in late 1893 to resolve rival claims, new disputes erupted through 1894 and 1895 as both made treaties and disputed those of the other.

Salisbury considered West Africa to be nothing more than worthless swamps, jungles, and "malarious

---

[87]Grenville, 132-133; Langer, *Diplomacy of Imperialism*, 45, 251; Pakenham, 467-468; R. Taylor, 173; Sanderson, 235.

deserts" of value to nobody, and, by comparison to Egypt, a place of secondary importance. He was quite willing to grant concessions to Paris and give up British claims there in return for French recognition of British rights in the Nile valley. With respect specifically to more explosive issue of Egypt, however, his position had grown more firm. Salisbury had long considered Egypt a "disastrous inheritance" and desired initially to restore stability to the region, thereby allowing British forces to withdraw as soon as possible. By 1895, however, he understood that in light of London's vital need to secure the headwaters of the Nile and thus the Suez Canal, British forces would remain in Egypt indefinitely, at least until the Sudan was restored to Egyptian control. Nevertheless, he went so far as to privately assure Courcel that Britain's success in crushing the dervishes would hasten its departure from Egypt.[88]

By the spring of 1896, therefore, relations between Britain and France appeared pacific if not altogether cordial. Because there did not seem to be any immediate threat to the Nile, Salisbury informed the British Consul-General in Cairo, Lord Cromer, that London was not considering a reconquest of the Sudan.[89] Two events, however, in the spring of 1896, compelled him to change his mind: the crushing Italian defeat at Adowa and the launching of the Marchand expedition.

The Italians, trying to expand their base in Ethiopia, came simultaneously under great military pressure from both the Mahdists at Kassala on the Atbara River and Menelik's forces in northern Ethiopia. They appealed to

---

[88]Andrew, 34-39; Pakenham, 453-468, 506-507, 511-522; Robinson and Gallagher, 300-304, 333-334, 342-344, 355; Peterson, 103; Sanderson, 316-317; Taylor, 137-138; 172-173; Wright, 58, 112-113.

[89]Bates, 45-48; Robinson and Gallagher, 340-346; Sanderson, 225-230; G.N. Uzoigwe, *Britain and the Conquest of Africa: The Age of Salisbury* (Ann Arbor: University of Michigan Press, 1974), 217-220.

London for assistance, pleading that the defeat of a European army by native African troops would endanger the position of all Europeans in Africa. Salisbury's initial reaction was to do nothing; to advance up the Nile would likely provoke the French. For the time being, he concluded, it was better to do nothing. On 1 March 1896, however, Ethiopian forces routed the Italians at Adowa and threatened to push the survivors to the sea. Yet, it was not until 11 March and after still some hesitation and disagreement that the British cabinet -- perhaps haunted by ghost of General Gordon -- formally authorized the Egyptian army, under its Commander-in-Chief ["Sirdar"] British General Herbert Kitchener, to advance up the Nile in relief of the Italians. Kitchener was ordered to advance to Dongola, beyond the third cataract, some 450 miles upriver from Fashoda. This operation marks the beginning of the Anglo-Egyptian effort to reconquer the Sudan and ultimately the British advance toward Fashoda.[90]

The extent of this Italian catastrophe in Ethiopia and its impact on British policy has generated varying interpretations among scholars. Many point to the Italian defeat as *the* pivotal event in the British decision to reconquer the Sudan. Some historians, most notably Robinson and Gallagher, argue that the crucial factor involved the balance of power *in the Nile valley* rather than the threat of other European interference. London had no intention to save the Italian position at Kassala, which was not worth saving; British assistance would not have helped the Italians quickly enough in any event. Before 1896, Salisbury had assumed that the Mahdists would decline slowly enough for the Sudan to be

[90]Bates, 48; Grenville, 114-118; Lewis, *Race to Fashoda*, 116-121; Pakenham, 468-469, 474-484; Robinson and Gallagher, 347-348; Taylor, 171-172; Uzoigwe, 220-227.

occupied and the Nile to be protected before any possible French challenge could ever materialize. The Italian defeat at Adowa, however, upset the British timetable because it altered the balance of power *within the region*; the Mahdists would be strengthened considerably if they were joined by the victorious Menelik. Moreover, if the Ethiopians turned out to be puppets of the French, their defeat of the Italians would indeed increase the French threat to the Nile.[91]

Other historians, principally G.N. Sanderson, argue that the Italian defeat launched the British up the Nile because Adowa upset the *European* balance of power. The collapse of Italy in Africa threatened the stability of the Triple Alliance, the instrument which maintained the balance of power against France and Russia. Moreover, in light of this obvious Italian ineptitude, Salisbury feared the possibility of an approach by Germany to Russia. Consequently, Sanderson argues that London entered into the reconquest of the Sudan as a gesture of solidarity with Italy (to insure against the possible disintegration of the Triple Alliance) and Germany (which maintained fears of an Anglo-French entente), and to prevent the emergence of new alignments less favorable to Britain, such as that between Germany and Russia. In doing so, Salisbury went to great pains to avoid provoking a French military advance toward the Upper Nile, a forward movement "to which Britain could make no effective reply." That plan, however, almost immediately began to be modified by African factors not yet foreseen.[92]

In either case, it appears that the British decision to advance up the Nile was made with little regard for the

[91]Robinson and Gallagher, 348-349. See also: Grenville, 107, 114-116, 118; Langer, *Diplomacy of Imperialism*, 284-287.

[92]Sanderson, 239-252, 396. See also: Barthorp, 138; Rolo, 67-68.

French. In London there was virtually no sense of impending crisis in spite of clear indications that the French were preparing operations into the Upper Nile. In early April 1896, Henry Howard, an official in the British embassy in Paris, advised that Marchand would proceed to Africa within the next month to take command of French troops on the Upper Ubangi, suggesting "an increase in French activity in that district."[93] A month later, in early May, *La Politique Coloniale* reported that Marchand was to depart from France by 16 May to lead an expedition on the upper Ubangi. The assessment of British intelligence, however, was that that there was "no reason to suppose that he will be accompanied by any Expeditionary Force, and [that] the present strength of the French in the upper Ubangi would not allow of any active operations to the North or the North-West." This analysis was produced on 18 May 1896, two months after the British had begun to take action in the northern Sudan. Consequently, whatever the reasons for the British decision to advance up the Nile, whether in response to balance of power concerns in the Nile valley or in Europe, apprehensions about securing the Upper Nile from French designs do not appear paramount or decisive.[94]

Still other historians, namely William L. Langer, argue that it was in fact the Marchand mission that pushed the British into pressing toward Khartoum before they were ready. Although talk of limited objectives and altruistic motives accompanied the British decision to advance into the Sudan, most observers suspected that the real purpose for the advance was victory over the French in the race to the Upper Nile. Salisbury admitted that French schemes for the Upper Nile had caused

---

[93]FO 27/3275, D.63, 9 April 1896, Howard to Salisbury.

[94]Rolo, 67-68; Sanderson, 239-252, 396; R. Taylor, 172.

anxiety for quite some time. He long believed that, in order to secure the headwaters of the Nile from the encroachment of other European Powers, the Sudan would eventually have to be reconquered. He had concluded that the most efficient plan would be to advance from the opposite direction; from the south -- to advance *down* the Nile, not up. This could occur, however, only after the construction of an 800-mile railroad from Mombasa on the Red Sea coast to Lake Victoria. But that was projected to take a minimum of two years. During the interim, Salisbury's nightmare involved the prospect of a string of French posts across north-central Africa from the Atlantic Ocean to the Red Sea as a direct and unambiguous threat to the British position on the Nile, a deliberate attempt to bisect London's design of an uninterrupted connection between Cairo and South Africa to say nothing of the greater direct threat to the headwaters of the Nile River. The paramount objective, therefore, was to get to the Fashoda before the French.[95]

In its overall design, the Marchand mission represented another effort by the French to effect the British evacuation of Egypt; to get a footing on the Upper Nile in order to compel London to begin serious negotiations. It was a stratagem of diplomacy rather than an enterprise of expansion.[96] In September 1895 Jean-Baptiste Marchand, a captain in the French marines, formally submitted to Hanotaux a proposal to establish French authority firmly on the Nile River. He produced a

---

[95]Langer, *Diplomacy of Imperialism*, 537-538. See also Giffen, 29, 82; Grenville, 107-108; Lewis, *Race to Fashoda*, 6-8, 154.

[96]For the genesis and early progress of the Marchand mission, see: Andrew, 36-39; Bates, 27-38, 50-68; Brown, 36-44, 50; Giffen, 211; Langer, *Diplomacy of Imperialism*, 537-538; Lewis, *Race to Fashoda*, 73-75, 84-91, 160-170; Pakenham, 467, 469, 509-510; Sanderson, 118, 271-285, 285-286, 307; Wright, 114-115, 127-129, 135.

map on which he drew two thick lines, one that ran from Cairo to the Cape, the other from Lagos in West Africa to Mombasa in the east; they formed what he labeled the "English theory of the African cross," its intersection in the Upper Nile valley. Marchand proposed taking a light mobile column of officers and men to proceed at speed and in secret to occupy Fashoda before anyone else. He intended to plant the French flag at the intersection of the cross, at Fashoda, and once and for all frustrate London's designs for an eastern Africa, British-controlled from the Cape to Cairo while also opening the way for a continuous belt of French territory from Senegal to the Red Sea. Most important, he hoped to force the reopening of the Egyptian question. His plan would ensure that French interests in the Nile River valley be respected and that its "eternal rival" would not be able to exclude France from a dominant position in Africa as it had done in the eighteenth century in India and North America. Hanotaux and the colonial minister Émile Chautemps both understood the implications of Marchand's proposals and thus chose to procrastinate, preferring to have neither the responsibility of saying 'yes' nor the odium of saying 'no.' They managed to avoid making a commitment until mid-October 1895, when the Ribot ministry collapsed and was replaced by a left-dominated ministry under Léon Bourgeois. Marchand and his hardline colonialist sponsors in the *parti colonial* quickly took advantage of Hanotaux's replacement, Marcelin Berthelot, an inexperienced left-wing academic; not only was Berthelot quickly confronted with the unaccustomed responsibilities of public office, he suffered a nervous breakdown following the death of his daughter soon after assuming office. By November, personally prostrated and easily misled, Berthelot agreed to the proposal. In part, Marchand secured Berthelot's consent through deceit.

The captain emphasized that the Nile regions belong as of right not to the British but to Egypt and its nominal overlord the Ottoman Sultan; the expedition, therefore, would only occupy land in these parts with the consent of its inhabitants or with the agreement of the Mahdist regime. It would be no more than a group of European travelers without a national flag or official instructions; they would make no treaties and the French flag would only be *displayed*. Thus, Marchand portrayed the mission as one without any military character whatsoever. Unknown to Berthelot, however, the actual instructions drawn up in February 1896 by the colonial ministry were far more provocative. Marchand indeed intended to fly the flag throughout; moreover, it *was* to be a military expedition, as Marchand would seek to make "serious alliances" and claim territory from local chiefs who would give France "indisputable title."[97]

Berthelot's reservations quickly disappeared amidst the outrage that swept through Paris in mid-March 1896, even among French officials hesitant to challenge London, at the news of the Anglo-Egyptian advance to Dongola. Berthelot complained to British ambassador Lord Dufferin that Kitchener's advance would "cause a considerable amount of excitement and irritation." Dufferin attempted to explain British actions as simply defense of the Egyptian frontier against "an outbreak of fanaticism . . . there may be trouble defending the Egyptian frontiers from the attacks which the Dervish forces will be encouraged to make." London, he added, hoped to "receive the concurrence of the French."[98] Berthelot, however, discounted Dufferin's explanation. After Dongola the reconquest of Khartoum would

---

[97]Bates, 32; Pakenham, 509; Sanderson, 285.

[98]FO 27/3266, D.318, 15 March 1896, Dufferin to Salisbury. See also: FO 27/3268, Tel.30, 12 March 1896, Salisbury to Dufferin; FO 27/3268, Tel.31, 12 March 1896, Salisbury to Dufferin.

certainly follow. Undoubtedly, it would prolong the British occupation of Egypt, "an arrangement peculiarly distasteful to French public opinion."[99]

Ultimately, Marchand and his colonialist allies benefited from the customary collapse of the French government. The Bourgeois government, which fell in late April 1896, was replaced by a new ministry under Jules Méline; Berthelot's replacement at the Quai d'Orsay was Hanotaux, returning for a third term as foreign minister. Hanotaux initially was distressed when he learned of Marchand's formal instructions. He did nothing, however, to significantly discourage the mission; it would have been political suicide otherwise. Hanotaux indeed increasingly found his policy under assault by the "fire-eaters" at the Ministry of Colonies. He had become, as Dufferin described him in March 1896, "more of a mouthpiece than a free agent." Besides, Hanotaux surmised, Marchand might not ever reach the Nile. After all, there were hundreds of miles of unexplored bush between the Congo and the Nile. Even if Marchand did reach Fashoda, his expedition was too small and too weak to do much damage. The more Hanotaux thought about it, the more he became reconciled to the operation. Allegedly he told Marchand, "You are going to fire a pistol shot on the Nile; we accept all the consequences!"[100]

In the spring of 1896, therefore, both governments began pushing slowly toward the Upper Nile. Marchand left Marseilles on 25 June 1896, arriving in the French Congo by late July. He dispatched the members of the expedition and their stores in four separate parties for the journey into the interior, initially up the Congo River.

---

[99]FO 27/3264, D.90, 17 March 1896, Dufferin to Salisbury. See also: FO 27/3264, D.82, 19 March 1896, Dufferin to Salisbury; FO 27/3264, D.83, 20 March 1896, Dufferin to Salisbury.

[100]Bates, 32; Lebow, 74; Pakenham, 509-510; Sanderson, 285.

He believed that they would reach Brazzaville, a distance of approximately 300 miles, by the middle of October. From the very beginning, however, numerous problems and delays burdened the expedition -- inadequate storage of provisions, the refusal of villagers to supply food and water to passing caravans, intertribal fighting, and indiscriminant outbreaks of rebellion by itinerant bands of marauders -- all of which required harsh pacification measures. Most serious, the mission could not make sufficient progress due to a shortage of river transport. Originally, French Congo authorities planned to make use of six steam driven river craft. In the end, only one steam-driven boat the *Faidherbe* was available for expeditious use. The only other vessels at the disposal of Marchand and his expedition included canoes and three simple steel boats powered by paddlers; the paddle-steamers were so small, however, and had such little space that they had to return, retrieve, and transport separately each of four parties of the expedition. As a result, Marchand reached Brazzaville on the Congo River by the end of 1896. Due to this shortage of transport, however, the mission could not proceed until mid-March 1897. They proceeded north along the Ubangi River, where they reached Bangui in early April and, in mid-May, the French outpost at Ouango at the confluence of the Mbomou and Uele rivers. The journey north and east to Tambura in the Bahr al-Ghazal took another five months because the rivers were generally impassable, the result of sandbanks, reefs, rapids, and waterfalls. Because the water level of the river system was so low during the dry season, the boats, baggage, and stores had to be unloaded, dismantled, and carried approximately one hundred miles over rough native tracks, which twisted and turned on the steep slopes of the Mbomou river. In the early fall 1897 they arrived at Fort Hossinger near

Tambura in the Bahr al-Ghazal and proceeded up the Sue River in December to Fort Desaix, from which Marchand would direct the tasks and movements of his mission for the next six months.[101]

Throughout the expedition, in addition to the many difficulties of supply and transport, the French lacked effective communications, either amongst themselves or with Paris. Marchand divided his party into sections, sending out individual members on reconnaissance missions. Although they established a series of posts they hoped would ultimately serve as administrative and military stations in the new French territories, all communications among them remained limited by the pace of their boats and African runners. Furthermore, all communications with Paris had to be conducted by mail and sent back through the French Congo. The French mission had access to telegraphic facilities in the Atlantic ports of Libreville, in the French Congo, and Dakar in Senegal, although these stations were owned and operated by British cable firms. The French government, unwilling to develop its own cable system for financial reasons, hired British firms to provide telecommunications to its colonies in west Africa.[102]

Hanotaux first raised the Egyptian issue with Ambassador Monson in January 1897. In spite of his farewell to Marchand, that France accepted the consequences of his "pistol shot," he was in fact quite

---

[101] Andrew, 36-39; Bates, 27-38, 50-68; Brown, 36-44, 50; Langer, *Diplomacy of Imperialism*, 537-538; Lewis, *Race to Fashoda*, 73-75, 84-91, 160-170; Sanderson, 118, 271-286, 307-309; Wright, 114-115, 127-129, 135. See also Monson's various reports in FO 27/3337, FO 27/3338, FO 27/3339, FO 27/3340, FO 27/3341, and FO 27/3342.

[102] Headrick, *The Invisible Weapon*, 64-65, 78-80; Daniel R. Headrick, *The Tentacles of Progress. Technology Transfer in the Age of Imperialism, 1850-1940* (New York and Oxford: Oxford University Press, 1988), 105, 111-112, 114-115; Wright, 11-12.

reticent about the enterprise. Monson had even written in December 1896 that Hanotaux was "becoming resigned to the Egyptian situation and that certain influential sections of French opinion, particularly in financial and commercial circles were really very satisfied with the status quo."[103] In early 1897, however, the foreign minister's disposition notably changed. In early January Hanotaux expressed vehement opposition to the Anglo-Egyptian push toward Khartoum and the British plan to reimburse the Egyptian treasury for Kitchener's advance to Dongola. When he pressed for clarification, Monson responded, not for the last time, that he had absolutely no information to give him but "thought that the newspapers which give currency to the report are very likely to be correct."[104] Several weeks later, when Monson on 3 February attempted to justify the British action, Hanotaux refused to discuss the matter, arguing that it would be "useless and barren of all results." Monson believed that France had secured a pledge of Russian support, while rumors maintained that German support would also be forthcoming. Monson also speculated that Hanotaux was simply uneasy "at finding himself involved in, and unable to extricate himself from, a policy which looks so much like systematically gratuitous obstruction to the beneficent efforts made by Her Majesty's Government on behalf of Egypt."[105] Days later, Monson's congratulations to Hanotaux following the latter's speech in the Chamber of Deputies on 8 February met with irritation and charges that London had increased the pressure over Egypt as a challenge to France. Hanotaux was in a "state of agitation,"

---

[103]FO 27/3367, D.388, 11 December 1896, Monson to Salisbury.

[104]FO 27/3314, D.15, 10 January 1897, Monson to Salisbury.

[105]FO 27/3314, D.73, 5 February 1897, Monson to Salisbury; FO 27/3314, D.76, 7 February 1897, Monson to Salisbury; FO 27/3314, D.82, 9 February 1897, Monson to Salisbury.

apparently over the recent speech in the House of Commons by Sir Michael Hicks Beach, Chancellor of the Exchequer. According to Monson, Hicks Beach's argument that French financial obstruction in Egypt would prolong the British occupation stirred up resentment and bitterness in France "even [among] those who have hitherto been friendly to England." The foreign minister complained that he was being reproached from all sides for weakness and that his position in the ministry had suffered, prompting Monson to speculate that Hanotaux's protests were mainly for domestic consumption and could be safely ignored.[106] Thereafter, Hanotaux abstained from raising the question with Monson, who believed that the foreign minister's attitude reflected a recognition that he had a weak case. In any event, the French government made no further serious attempt to raise the Upper Nile question, despite pressure from public opinion and the colonial lobby, until the fall of Khartoum in September 1898.[107]

Monson nevertheless began to note signs that the French would attempt to drive into the Upper Nile valley. In late January 1897 Monson reported the contents of a recent speech by Monsieur Deluns-Montaud, the president of the *Comité d' Égypt* and a member of the Chamber of Deputies, who criticized the British occupation of Egypt. As a result of their present policy in Egypt, Deluns-Montaud asserted, the British would not escape the necessity of heavy military burdens. After all, whoever holds Egypt, the connecting

---

[106]FO 27/3314, D.88, 11 February 1897, Monson to Salisbury. See also Monson's reports to Salisbury in FO 27/3314: D.89, 11 February 1897; D.90, 11 February 1897; D.96, 12 February 1897; Wood, 122-127.

[107]E. Malcolm Carroll, *French Public Opinion and Foreign Affairs, 1870-1914* (New York and London: The Century Company, 1931), 166; Uzoigwe, 246, 248. See also Monson's dispatches in FO 27/3275, FO 27/3276, FO 27/3337, FO 27/3338, FO 27/3339, FO 27/3340, FO 27/3341, and FO 27/3342.

link between Africa and Asia:

> [H]olds in his hands the passage, the historic route, definitely opened by French genius, by French capital, to the commerce of the world between the Mediterranean and the Pacific. Egypt is not only the gift of that Nile of which Herodotus tells us, but is, to speak the truth, the creation of France. [The French revealed its antiquity, educated its army and administration and have] inspired Islam itself, impenetrable as it appeared, with all that could be introduced of Western civilization. The English have misunderstood this.

It was impossible, Deluns-Montaud concluded, for Frenchmen "to abandon what may be called their historical situation, to surrender into the hands of their rivals the guardianship of what they have themselves created." Accordingly, Monson suggested, France's principal grievance involved the arrogance of the British, who "act as if they were the masters," their ambition, and unscrupulousness.[108]

In the meantime, Kitchener's expedition proceeded no faster than did the French. In part this was official policy. Salisbury insisted that the reconquest of the Sudan be exercised with caution and deliberation. While he never doubted that the ultimate outcome of the campaign must be the destruction of Dervish power, he also recognized that while Mahdist control was clearly in decline, the total destruction of its power could not be accomplished for a few years. For one thing, the advance was going to be expensive. It would require £1 million to £2 million, an undertaking the House of Commons would almost certainly hesitate to consider. Furthermore, Mahdist control must not be annihilated until Britain was

---

[108]FO 27/3314, D.60, 31 January 1897, Monson to Salisbury.

ready to act; otherwise, a dangerous power vacuum would be created in the Upper Nile. As a result, strategic and logistical realities required a two-pronged advance. On one hand, the British would advance from the south, pending the completion of the Mombasa-to-Lake Victoria railroad. On the other hand, Kitchener's army would advance from the north, the pace of which would similarly be dictated by the construction of a north-south railway along the Nile. Neither railway, however, were expected to be completed for at least two years.[109]

In addition to strategic and logistical realities, British caution was a result of political confusion. Although Kitchener easily captured Dongola on the Nile in September 1896, some members of the cabinet believed that the Egyptian army should wait two to three years before proceeding, while others (supported by Kitchener) pushed for an immediate advance, particularly as the Mahdist state apparently posed no significant military challenge. In November the cabinet authorized an advance to Berber, only 200 miles north of Khartoum on the Nile; in the spring of 1897, however, it backed away from any further advance. In Cairo Lord Cromer, reacting to delays and difficulties experienced by Kitchener, advised against a resumption of the advance on the grounds that the Mahdist forces were much more formidable than he originally believed. In London, Salisbury grew increasingly concerned about the French advance into the southern Sudan. By November 1896 British military intelligence reported Marchand's movement into the Upper Nile, possibly in conjunction with Belgian advances from the Congo and French expeditions from Ethiopia. Rumors even began to circulate in Paris that Marchand had indeed reached

---

[109]Bates, 41; Grenville, 120; Langer, *Diplomacy of Imperialism*, 537-538; Pakenham, 506-507; Sanderson, 249.

the Nile. Sir John Ardagh, head of military intelligence, pressed for immediate and substantial counter-measures in the Nile or resign itself to a French occupation. In response, Salisbury approved the Rodd and Macdonald missions. In the spring of 1897 he ordered Rennell Rodd to Addis Ababa for discussions with Menelik. Despite some minor commercial successes, Rodd failed to undermine the French position or shake the possibility of a Ethiopian-Mahdist combination. Salisbury also authorized an expedition under Colonel James Macdonald to strike at Fashoda from the south and thereby cut off Marchand. A serious mutiny and mass desertion by his Sudanese troops in the fall of 1897, however, rendered Macdonald's mission impotent.[110]

By the summer of 1897 the Salisbury cabinet, sufficiently encouraged by the Khalifa's failure to dispatch a large force to the north, decided to resume Kitchener's advance. Although Kitchener easily took Abu Hamed on 7 April and Berber on 31 August, his progress again stalled due to a disagreement over objectives. In October, General Sir Garnet Wolseley, commander-in-chief of the British Army, vigorously argued for the dispatch of regular British troops to Egypt; he proposed that Kitchener advance to Khartoum, destroy the Khalifa's army, and occupy the city and the White Nile before the arrival of the French. Salisbury, Cromer, and Lansdowne opposed the idea, contending that the pace of the campaign should proceed according to the military capabilities of the Egyptian Army and the financial resources of the Egyptian government.

Moreover, it did not seem in October 1897 as though there would be an encounter with the French in

---

[110]Barthorp, 139-141; Bates, 41-43, 74-75, 101-103; Brown, 71-72; Langer, *Diplomacy of Imperialism*, 537-538, 546-548; Robinson and Gallagher, 360-363; Sanderson, 252-260; Uzoigwe, 238-242, 248-249.

the Upper Nile in any event, much less a crisis. Ignoring recent reports detailing the movements of Marchand and Liotard, Salisbury wrote Cromer that "we have heard of no force moving up the Ubangi . . . still less of food and munitions." Part of the prime minister's confidence had to do with the logistical and geographical difficulty of actually *reaching* Fashoda -- from any direction, north or south. The problem for the French, he believed, was not merely to occupy Fashoda but to occupy it in strength, "sufficient to resist the crushing riposte from Omdurman which would be a mere routine operation for any power, Mahdist or Anglo-Egyptian." He was confident that even should the French move into the Upper Nile, the Mahdists would crush the small French expedition. Therefore, Salisbury hesitated to dispatch a more aggressive military advance against the Mahdists. By destroying Dervish power, he argued, "we are killing the defender who holds the valley for us now."

Through November and December 1897, however, concerns about Kitchener's position at Berber convinced the cabinet to commit itself finally and fully to a forward policy. In November *La Dépêche Coloniale* published a clearly authentic letter written by Liotard from Deim Zubeir in western Bahr al-Ghazal, making it certain that the French were indeed moving into the Upper Nile. It was also apparent that the Khalifa's power had not collapsed following his defeat at Berber, as Cromer and Kitchener had expected. The cabinet learned in mid-December that he was concentrating a large force at Kerreri, just north of Khartoum, apparently in preparation for a northward advance by the entire Mahdist army. Based on alarmist reports written by Major Sir Reginald Wingate, Kitchener's Chief of Intelligence, it appeared that the strength and fighting qualities of the Khalifa were decidedly greater than had been anticipated. Captured records after the fall of

Omdurman, however, showed that as a matter of fact the Mahdists had neither the means nor the intention of attacking Kitchener at Berber. Historian Darrell Bates suggests that this exaggerated crisis was engineered by Wingate and Kitchener in order to force London's hand.[111] These reports reached the cabinet at approximately the same time as reports from Monson in Paris, which suggested that Marchand had already reached the basin of the Nile and was presently acting in concert both with the Khalifa and Menelik. In fact, Parisian newspapers were reporting daily updates on Marchand's progress. In early January 1898, *France Militaire* wrote:

> It is beyond all doubt . . . that the expedition has already reached Fashoda, and that at this moment, the glorious French flag floats on the Nile. . . . [H]aving taken effective possession, there is henceforth established between the courses of the White and Blue Nile, between Khartoum and the great lakes, a zone secured from the clutches of England. . . . It means the miserable failure of a work in which England has persevered for years . . . the bankruptcy of her African policy.[112]

At the same time, it was clear that the Uganda railroad was nowhere near completion and that the Macdonald expedition had proven a total bust. Thus, under heavy pressure from Kitchener and Cromer, the cabinet on 26 January 1898 agreed to dispatch British reinforcements

---

[111]Bates, 80-83; Grenville, 114; Langer, *Diplomacy of Imperialism*, 549-551; Lewis, *Race to Fashoda*, 191-193; Sanderson, 260-265; Uzoigwe, 249-252; Wright, 107.

[112]FO 27/3410, D.16, 12 January 1898, Monson to Salisbury. See also: FO 27/3410, D.4, 4 January 1898, Monson to Salisbury; FO 27/3410, D.5, 6 January 1898, Monson to Salisbury; FO 27/3410, D.14, 12 January 1898, Monson to Salisbury.

and authorized Kitchener to advance to Khartoum.[113]

Salisbury remained hesitant about resuming the advance up the Nile although he was confident that the French would pose no substantive threat to British security. Nevertheless, he understood that the inevitable diplomatic engagements would be difficult even if the military challenge was not.

Relations between London and Paris indeed worsened during the winter of 1897-1898. They quarreled over all frontier questions particularly with respect to their positions on the Nile and Niger rivers[114] and began to anticipate the inevitable collision between Marchand's expedition and the Anglo-Egyptian advance up the Nile. In late November Monson reported a reawakening of public interest in the Egyptian question. News reports of difficulties to Marchand's expedition, although unconfirmed, had turned public attention again to "the efforts being made by France to reach the Nile basin from the west." For example, rumors reached Paris that Marchand and his men had met with disaster in the Congo and that everyone had been killed. At the same time, Hanotaux began making intimations that the French wanted to tie the Nile and Niger questions together. Monson, however, did not know "how far Her Majesty's present Government are prepared to endorse" Sir Edward Grey's statement of March 1895. His confusion prompted Sir Clement Hill, the chief clerk in the African department of the Foreign Office, to minute

---

[113]Langer, *Diplomacy of Imperialism*, 549-551; Lewis, *Race to Fashoda*, 191-193; Sanderson, 260-265; Uzoigwe, 249-250.

[114]For a complete discussion of the disputes over the Niger territories, see: Bates, 81-83; Grenville, 114-124; Pakenham, 516-522; Robinson and Gallagher, 403-408; Sanderson, 263-265, 320-323; Uzoigwe, 120-142. See also Monson's dispatches in FO 27/3276, FO 27/3337, FO 27/3338, FO 27/3339, FO 27/3340, FO 27/3341, FO 27/3342, FO 27/3410, FO 27/3411, FO 27/3412, FO 27/3413, FO 27/3414, FO 27/3415, and FO 27/3416.

that the ambassador had been instructed by Salisbury ten months earlier on 21 January 1897 that the present government adhered to the statement made by Sir Edward Grey but that Monson had been told not to make any statement on the subject unless Hanotaux raised the question. Salisbury agreed, adding that "it would be inopportune to bring it in" and thus risk compromising the pending negotiations over West Africa.[115] Monson got the point. In his most blunt and uncompromising communication of the British position thus far, he informed Hanotaux on 10 December that London "must not be understood to admit that any other European Power than Great Britain has any claim to occupy any part of the Valley of the Nile. The views of the British Government upon this matter were plainly stated in Parliament by Sir Edward Grey some years ago."[116]

By the spring of 1898, the prospect of war in West Africa began to appear very real. While the French occupied the contested villages of Nikki and Sokoto, Chamberlain embarked upon a "Chessboard Policy" in which British expeditions infiltrated behind and between French posts throughout West Africa. Both governments, therefore, endeavored to strengthen their diplomatic positions.[117]

France initially procured the support of King Leopold II, who agreed in 1897 to organize two expeditions that would assist Marchand against a possible attack by the Khalifa. Under the pretense of

---

[115]FO 27/3341, Africa 385, 22 November 1897, Monson to Salisbury. Minutes by Hill and Salisbury, 1 December 1897.

[116]Sanderson, 319-320. See Monson's reports to Salisbury in FO 27/3341: D.411, 9 December 1897; D.413, 10 December 1897; D.425, 12 December 1897; D.428, 14 December 1897; D.438, 16 December 1897. See Monson's reports to Salisbury in FO 27/3342: Africa 445, 18 December 1897; Africa 455, 26 December 1897.

[117]Sanderson, 320-321.

cooperation, however, Leopold sought to extend the dominion of the Congo Free State to the Upper Nile valley. The French also sought to secure the goodwill of the Khalifa against the British advance from the north and to revitalize their ties with Menelik. In March 1897 they promised to help Menelik establish his authority on the east bank of the Nile in return for his support of the French missions on the west bank.[118] In the meantime, Hanotaux sought the support of the other Powers for an international conference that would compel Britain to end her occupation of Egypt or at the very least to secure concessions from London. Although the convening of such a conference would be largely dependent upon the attitude of Germany, Hanotaux was confident that Berlin was willing to support an initiative to end the British occupation. Although relations between Paris and Berlin had been strained since the 1870s, recent efforts had been made on both sides to cultivate better relations. Wilhelm II assumed at times an attitude of rather theatrical generosity toward France, while in many French quarters the spirit of *revanche* began to wane particularly among the younger generation. Hanotaux understood that Franco-German relations would remain poisoned by Alsace-Lorraine. He nevertheless assumed that Germany, at a time when it was embarking on a policy of *Weltpolitik* and when mutual irritation over naval expansion and other colonial disputes generally strained Anglo-German relations, Berlin would share France's concern for the neutrality of the Suez Canal.[119]

Hanotaux also sought the cooperation of Russia. Initially, Paris was confident of Russian support on the

---

[118]Bates, 43-45, 72-80, 101; Langer, *Diplomacy of Imperialism*, 539-542; Lewis, *Race to Fashoda*, 93-98, 123-136, 198-199; Pakenham, 510-511, 524-532; Robinson and Gallagher, 360-365; Sanderson, 291-307; Wright, 115-119.

[119]Andrew, 46-48, 94-95; Langer, *Diplomacy of Imperialism*, 136-146, 184-186, 197-201, 492-532; Sanderson, 327-329.

Upper Nile. As early as March 1896 the anglophobic Russian foreign minister, Alexei Lobanov, gave seemingly unambiguous assurances to the French ambassador Gustave de Montebello that Russia had "an interest of first rate importance in Egypt – the neutralization of the Suez Canal." He offered to France "*l'appui le plus énergique*" [the most energetic support] in this question. These assurances undoubtedly carried weight with Prime Minister Bourgeois and Foreign Minister Berthelot when they approved the Marchand mission. By late 1897, however, Hanotaux had far less confidence in Russia. It became clear that Lobanov, for all his tough talk, was interested principally in preventing any rapprochement between London and Paris and so enable Russia a freer hand at Constantinople. Lobanov therefore evaded all hints at serious joint action with the French. Similarly, Lobanov's successor as foreign minister, Count Mikhail Muraviev, responded to French entreaties with formal but noncommittal platitudes. In fact Muraviev told the Italian ambassador in early 1897 that he "no longer intended to support the chauvinistic policies of France." Furthermore, it appeared that relations between Russia and Germany were beginning to warm. They cooperated in the Near East, where both favored the regulation of Turkish finances, and in the Far East, where both maintained interests in China. By mid-1897, therefore, the French grew increasingly resentful over the apparently one-sided nature of the alliance. It indeed appeared that Russian assurances of support came only with the French guarantee of further loans.[120]

Monson misread the situation and discounted any talk of coolness between France and Russia. In response to the description by German ambassador Count

---

[120]Giffen, 180-182; Sanderson, 278-280, 282-283, 314-315, 379.

Georges de Münster of an "unmistakable diminution of warmth" in Franco-Russian relations, Monson argued that the ambassador's conclusions were exaggerated "to an almost ridiculous extent.[121] Following the visit of President Faure to St. Petersburg four months later, he suggested that given Franco-Russian accord in negotiations over recent events in Armenia, Crete, and Greece, it was reasonable to "expect that Russian action in the Far East and French action in all those quarters in which it comes in contact with us will be proportionally bolder and more thorough-going."[122]

In London, Salisbury pushed forward the necessary diplomatic preparations. He understood that once British forces were committed to an all-out push up the Nile, there would be a showdown with the French at Fashoda. His primary objective, therefore, was to free his hands of complications elsewhere and to ensure French isolation at the moment of the clash. In spite of concerns among his colleagues that perhaps the prime minister's age and health had rendered him incapable of crisis management, Salisbury never lost sight of the overall picture. First, in February 1898 he temporarily resolved a potentially explosive situation in South Africa by using Joseph Chamberlain to restrain Sir Alfred Milner, the British High Commissioner, who wanted to move militarily against the Boers.[123] Second, he improved relations with Russia through efforts to partition their respective

---

[121]FO 27/3316, D.259, 8 April 1897, Monson to Salisbury.

[122]FO 27/3319, D.562, 27 August 1897, Monson to Salisbury; FO 27/3319, D.572, 31 August 1897, Monson to Salisbury.

[123]Continuing tensions between the Boers and the British government convinced Milner that unless President Paul Kruger and his oligarchy capitulated to British demands to give up Boer supremacy in the Transvaal, South Africa would be lost to Britain. Chamberlain, however, convinced the Commissioner that London was currently unprepared to go to war in South Africa. Grenville, 186-187, 237-238; Langer, *Diplomacy of Imperialism*, 606-608; Sanderson, 323.

spheres of influence in China and the Ottoman Empire. London's response to Russia's occupation of Port Arthur in March, moreover, was surprisingly moderate; the cabinet simply asked for compensation.[124] When his daughter and biographer Lady Gwendolen Cecil expressed surprise over the mildness of his reaction to the Port Arthur crisis Salisbury answered that, "In six months' time, we shall be on the verge of war with France; I can't afford to quarrel with Russia now." British moderation, he believed, would neutralize Russia's response to the Upper Nile question.[125]

Third, Salisbury improved relations with Germany, although not without some exasperation. Over the course of 1896 and 1897 relations between Germany and Britain had been marked by more or less mutual irritation, particularly as the restless ambitions of *Weltpolitik* began to inspire German foreign policy and challenge British colonial possessions in south and west Africa. Yet, the opportunity for agreement existed in the Far East, where they cooperated against Russian designs on China, and more significantly, in the African colonies of Portugal. In late 1897 Portugal sought a loan from London against its vast territories in Africa. The Kaiser and the foreign minister Bernhard von Bülow insisted that Britain make colonial concessions to Berlin in return for any rights it obtained from Portugal. If London did not respond favorably, Germany would cooperate with France and Russia against British interests in South Africa and by implication the Nile. Although Salisbury dismissed this as bluff, he came under pressure from his colleagues, particularly Balfour and Chamberlain, who wanted closer relations with Berlin. In the end, negotiations between

---

[124]Grenville, 136-197; Langer, *Diplomacy of Imperialism*, 492-532; Robinson and Gallagher, 366-367; Rolo, 72; Sanderson, 323-326.

[125]Andrew Roberts, *Salisbury: Victorian Titan* (London: Weidenfeld & Nicolson, 1999), 701.

London and Berlin were concluded to German satisfaction and the resulting Anglo-German Convention, signed on 30 August 1898, had some considerable influence on the attitude of Germany during the Fashoda Crisis.[126]

Finally, Salisbury worked to relieve British energies in West Africa by ending Anglo-French disputes there. Negotiations with Paris, which had resumed in late October 1897, produced an agreement establishing spheres of influence by late May 1898.[127] Salisbury was content to prolong the proceedings and left the discussions entirely in the hands of his delegates, Monson, Colonel William Everett of the War Office, and Martin Gosselin of the British embassy.

Monson's role in the resolution of the West African disputes was particularly instructive. While he generally conducted the negotiations without difficulty, Monson nevertheless betrayed some of the tendencies that would hinder his effectiveness during the Fashoda crisis, notably his excessive and almost fainthearted emphasis on the need to placate French concerns. In early September 1897, for example, Monson urged the cabinet to accept Hanotaux's requests to resume the West African negotiations, dormant since May 1896 and suggested that to do otherwise would risk a "marked deterioration in our relations with France." Although he plainly told Hanotaux that Britain had its own claims and grievances considered equally well founded -- "Britain is confronted with the problem that the French Government seems to expect that all the concessions should be made by Great Britain and that they themselves should give nothing in return. Negotiations on such a basis as this is clearly impossible" – Monson

---

[126]Grenville, 98-107, 150-173, 182-195; Robinson and Gallagher, 446-449.

[127]Grenville, 123-124; Robinson and Gallagher, 403-408; Sanderson, 317-323. For details of the Niger negotiations, see Monson's reports in FO 27/3339, FO 27/3410, FO 27/3411, FO 27/3412, FO 27/3413, and FO 27/3414.

encouraged London to show greater flexibility over West Africa. While appreciating the interests of the Royal Niger Company, the establishment of British forces into areas where the French title "cannot be disputed" would only produce a "very serious demonstration of resentment." British intransigence, moreover, might provoke a larger European combination against London: "It might even come about," Monson noted, "that on Colonial questions and indeed on all extra-European questions, a stronger combination than France and Russia might be found against us. M. Hanotaux has once hinted to me that proposals have actually been made from Berlin in this sense." Sir Clement Hill took exception to Monson's suggestion that the initiative was now London's responsibility:

> It is really the British government that has the right to complain and to expect explanations. Since the beginning of the year, London has made several proposals to resume negotiations . . . but never received any definite answer. Moreover, the French government continually allowed months to pass without answers to important communications relating to West Africa.[128]

Monson dismissed Hill's argument in a letter to Salisbury. Given the current temper of the French government, relations would be "most disagreeably, if not dangerously, prejudiced" if London rejected Hanotaux's invitation: "the representatives of the Republic throughout the world would receive every encouragement to thwart British policy by every kind of mischief which can be encompassed."[129]

---

[128]FO 27/3339, D.261, 5 September 1897, Monson to Salisbury; FO 27/3339, D.262, 5 September 1897, Monson to Salisbury; minute by Sir Clement Hill.

[129]FO 27/3339, 17 September 1897, Monson to Salisbury.

When negotiations resumed in late October 1897, and the British commissioners quickly concluded that many claims of the Royal Niger Company could not be established, Monson pressed for a conciliatory position. The French were firmly entrenched and their legal position was strong, he argued, and although Hanotaux was anxious for a peaceful solution, "I do not well see how [he] can give us what we want . . . without running the risk of being turned out of office."[130] In November Monson again warned that no progress would be achieved until London made concessions. Citing Colonel Everett's recent "Summary," which characterized several of the Royal Niger Company's claims as baseless, he was particularly furious that the British case was weaker than he had been led to believe. He complained to Sir Francis Bertie, Assistant Undersecretary of State for Foreign Affairs, that the Colonial Office "ought to have got up their case better" and that the Royal Niger Company had "grossly misled Her Majesty's Government both as to their rights and their measures of defending them." In London Chamberlain rejected Everett's conclusion and was shocked at the "sudden change" in Monson's attitude. Salisbury, who was becoming less and less sympathetic with the ambassador's uncompromising position, agreed: "I deplore the line Monson's views have taken. There is something fatal in the air of Paris. Everett goes in the same direction and Phipps in the former Commission was just as bad."[131]

Following Monson's blunt warning to Hanotaux of 10 December 1897, the discussions began to drag. As

---

[130]Sanderson, 391; Wood, 137-140.

[131]Uzoigwe, 127-128. In the summer of 1894, during discussions over colonial and diplomatic differences, London's representative was the deputy of the British embassy, Constantine Phipps. To his superiors in London, Phipps seemed too easily swayed by Hanotaux and appeared to project the French point of view with more enthusiasm than that of the British. Bates, 19; Pakenham, 456-458.

both sides continued their military activities and complained of treaty infractions, the British position became more rigid particularly as the cabinet remained steadfastly opposed to any compromise. On 20 January Monson suggested to Salisbury that, given "the indubitable strength of the case against us," the cabinet was overstating its case and needed to be more flexible:

> It appears to us that these instructions are of too stringent a nature to admit of any hope that the whole of the demands which are contained in them will be acceded to by France . . . [I]t may be said with reason that they are hardly such as any nation having regard for its dignity could accede to, except after war followed by defeat, for they involve the retirement of French troops on the east from territory which they have occupied for nearly a year, and on the west from territory which they have occupied for close upon a year and a half. . . . The instructions, as they stand, are so rigid in character as to leave but little room for negotiation.

As Hanotaux recently pleaded that the situation "could hardly endure much longer without a collision," Monson urged London to reconsider its case; otherwise, its uncompromising position could lead to war or to the loss of territories through arbitration."[132] A month later, Monson warned that, with the reemergence of the Dreyfus affair, certain elements within the French army and government might use these colonial disputes as an excuse to declare war against Britain, thereby rallying the nation and diverting public attention away from the domestic turmoil.[133] Chamberlain was incensed. He accused Monson and the other commissioners of blatant

---

[132]FO 27/3410, D.31, 20 January 1898, Monson to Salisbury; Pakenham, 516-517, 519-522; Sanderson, 318-321; Uzoigwe, 129; Wood, 142-152.

[133]See pages 112-116.

pro-French bias -- they were "excellent men to arrange an unconditional surrender . . . [they did not have] enough stiffening in the lot to hold up a paper collar" -- and rejected the ambassador's warnings that France might turn to war to escape the domestic agony of the Dreyfus affair. The French had fooled Monson, Salisbury, and most of the cabinet, he argued, and they were bluffing on both the Niger and the Nile.

Consequently, while Salisbury had endeavored to concede territory in West Africa in order to buy time for the Kitchener expedition, the colonial minister refused to compromise. Chamberlain and the jingoist press ascribed the prime minister's desire to reach accommodations over Siam, Tunis, Madagascar, and the Niger to appeasement. The apparent willingness of the British Colonial Ministry to fight ultimately persuaded Hanotaux, who was unwilling to fight and anxious to reach a settlement before the impending collapse of the Méline ministry, to give way in West Africa.[134] By early May London and Paris had resolved the main issues of contention; the British recognized the French title to most of the disputed Gold Coast hinterland, while the French agreed to flexibility in the tariff policy it intended to pursue in West Africa. Accordingly, the formal Niger Convention was signed on 14 June 1898.[135]

In the meantime, as the two governments devoted their energies to freeing their hands for a potential crisis, however, Marchand and Kitchener continued toward their showdown at Fashoda.

---

[134]See Monson's reports to Salisbury in FO 27/3413: AD.173, 15 May 1898; Tel. 61, 18 May 1898; AD.177, 19 May 1898; AD.178, 19 May 1898; AD.185, 23 May 1898; Roberts, 703.

[135]FO 27/3416, Tel.94, 14 June 1898, Monson to Salisbury; Pakenham, 516-522; Sanderson, 320-323; Uzoigwe, 133-142; Wood, 150-154.

Craig E. Saucier

Chapter Four

"SUCH CLAIMS ARE MORE WORTHY OF OPÉRA-BOUFFE"

From January to June 1898, Marchand's expedition remained stalled at Fort Desaix. The climate and geography largely dictated their pace; with the end of the summer rains in October 1897 the water level of the rivers fell, making river navigation particularly difficult. The French thus were forced to wait until the beginning of the rains in May or early June, when there was enough water in the river for the boats. Marchand split his forces; one party led by the captain himself set off on 4 June with the smaller boats for Fashoda; the rest of the expedition stayed behind, waiting for adequate water to bring the *Faidherbe* through the rivers. Marchand's group made slow progress due to the particularly thick and widespread *sudd*, the masses of floating vegetation that choked the watercourses and made navigation extraordinarily difficult. In addition, suspicious and hostile local tribes, particularly the Dinka and the Nuer, harassed the expedition.

At approximately 1700 on Sunday 10 July 1898, Marchand and his small force arrived at Fashoda. After nearly two years, it was a moment of great emotion for them all. On the morning of 12 July they formally raised the French flag over Fashoda. During the ceremony, however, the flagpole snapped and the flag fell to the ground just as Captain Charles Mangin gave the order to present arms. "A bad omen," remarked another French officer, Captain Emmanuel Largeau. "The Romans would have given up and run away!" The damage was soon repaired and a second attempt succeeded -- and Marchand took possession of Fashoda in the name of France. "The Grand Nile has truly become a French river," Captain Albert Baratier wrote.

For all the emotion of their arrival, however, they found themselves isolated and dangerously vulnerable. Fashoda itself was no more than ruins of a series of forts, which had been destroyed by the Mahdists. It was unbearably hot during the day and made pestilential by mosquitos at night. The French had very little military strength; their party consisted of six French officers and approximately 120 Senegalese soldiers equipped with light rifles and old fashioned muskets. They had little river transport and they had no news of their rear party. Information indeed proved difficult to obtain. Official dispatches from Paris took approximately nine months to arrive and information from local sources proved to be unreliable. They had no idea about the location of the British, other French and Belgian expeditions, or about their relationship with the Mahdists and the Ethiopians. The Khalifa's position moreover remained unchallenged. As soon as he heard that this French expedition had installed themselves at Fashoda, the Khalifa quickly announced that whatever their nationality, they were foreigners and infidels and would be attacked.

Nevertheless, there was sufficient cause for optimism among the French. They drove back attacks by Mahdist forces on 25 August and 29 August. Over the following week, on the strength of his victories over the

Mahdists, Marchand signed treaties with the nearby Shilluk and Dinka tribes. Furthermore, on 29 August, the day of the second attack, the *Faidherbe* arrived at the fort from the south, compelling the Mahdists to withdraw. The arrival of the *Faidherbe*, which again stirred great emotion, brought the French fresh supplies of ammunition, reinforcements, and other necessities.

By the middle of September, therefore, the French were confident that they had completed their aim of establishing French dominion in the Upper Nile valley. The French had not only gotten to Fashoda, they got their first; they had beaten the British. They had repaired and rebuilt the forts, planted gardens to grow vegetables and fruits, and established a market for local people to bring their produce for trade -- all of which established the French in a strong position. And now, they had made treaties with local tribes and established a chain of posts in the Bahr al-Ghazal and Upper Nile, which could presumably provide the basis for permanent occupation and administration by French authorities for years.

At the same time, however, Marchand and his men began to hear unsettling rumors about an advance from the north. First the British, then the Mahdists were said to have suffered defeat in a great battle. On 18 September, Shilluk messengers carried news that a huge Mahdist force with gunboats and thousands of soldiers, was advancing from Khartoum to avenge their earlier defeat. The French stood at arms for the remainder of the day. The very next morning at 0600, 19 September 1898, they received a letter from Kitchener, announcing the British arrival at Fashoda.[136]

By contrast to the French, the British advance had

---

[136]This description of the mission is based primarily on Bates, 84-100, 111-124; Lewis, *Race to Fashoda*, 206-222; Pakenham, 532-536; Wright, 137-158, 163-172. See also Monson's various reports in FO 27/3410, FO 27/3411, FO 27/3412, FO 27/3413, and FO 27/3414.

been quick and efficient. While Marchand had struggled through the swamps and bushes in the spring and summer of 1898, Kitchener proceeded up the Nile virtually unchallenged by either nature or enemies. Furthermore, Kitchener's force was much enlarged. Between 1896 and 1897, his Anglo-Egyptian army had consisted of approximately 11,000 Egyptian and Sudanese soldiers. By the spring of 1898, following the cabinet approval for an expansion of his force, Kitchener's army consisted of 17,600 Egyptian and Sudanese soldiers, supplemented by approximately 8,200 British soldiers and officers. Kitchener's advance, moreover, assumed greater impetus following a significant change in official British policy. After the Anglo-Egyptian force successfully assaulted the Khalifa's army at Atbara on 8 April, Salisbury shifted from a defensive strategy to one of total conquest. The British government previously regarded the Sudan as Egyptian territory that had temporarily passed into the hands of rebellious forces but, since 1896 was being recovered by the Egyptian army with military and financial assistance from Britain. In September 1898, however, it no longer seemed advantageous merely to restore the Sudan to Egypt. For one thing, the reintroduction of Egyptian institutions into the Sudan would handicap its future administration. For another, Egypt remained subject to international agreements; consequently, any commercial and financial benefits would have to be shared. Therefore, beginning in early June, the cabinet decided to treat the Sudan as an independent and sovereign "Mahdi state," not merely as *de jure* Egyptian territory temporarily dominated by rebels. The conquest of Khartoum would deliver the whole of this state into the power of the capturing army "by right of conquest." For the purposes of satisfying international opinion, the cabinet considered it necessary to display the joint nature of the operation -- British and Egyptian flags would fly side by side in the conquered lands. Because Britain had made a larger contribution, it would be entitled to a dominant position in the control and material benefits of the conquered territories.[137]

The cabinet approved the policy change in new orders dated 2 August 1898. After capturing Khartoum, Kitchener would send out two flotillas of gunboats, one up the Blue Nile and the other, under his command, up the White Nile. He was to do everything possible to avoid an armed clash with any *Ethiopian* forces he might encounter. The instructions for dealing with the French were less specific, leaving any course of action to his "judgment and discretion." If he happened to meet any French forces, he was to do all he could to convince their commander that their presence in the Nile valley represented "an infringement of the rights of both Great Britain and the Khedive."[138]

In August Kitchener's army left Atbara and made for Khartoum. On 2 September, one day after British gunboats bombarded the city, the Khalifa's forces attacked across the open Kerreri plain at Omdurman, where British artillery and rifle fire easily slaughtered vast numbers. At this Battle of Omdurman, Mahdist forces suffered over 12,000 casualties; the Anglo-Egyptian army lost forty-eight officers and soldiers. Kitchener's victory resulted not only in the thorough collapse of the Mahdist state but the almost total annihilation of the Khalifa's army.

A week later, on 10 September, Kitchener began the journey up the White Nile with five heavily armed

---

[137]G.P. Gooch and Harold Temperley, ed., *British Documents on the Origins of the War, 1898-1914* (London: His Majesty's Stationery Office, 1927), vol. 1, *The End of Isolation* (hereafter cited as BD) 195: 159-161; Bates, 108-110; Grenville, 218-220; Sanderson, 266-268.

[138]Bates, 125-127; BD 185: 159-161; Grenville, 222-223.

gunboats, a company of 100 Cameron Highlanders, two battalions of Sudanese infantry, which consisted of approximately 2,500 troops, a battery of Egyptian field artillery, and several Maxim machine guns. By 15 September they had covered approximately 500 miles and were closing in on Fashoda. Along the way, they captured two of the Khalifa's gunboats. Upon interrogating the Dervish crews, they discovered that there were indeed Europeans at Fashoda. Kitchener strongly suspected that the French had reached and occupied Fashoda and thus decided to give warning of his approach to avoid an accidental clash. He also wanted to impress upon their commander the point, in case he did not know, that the British had taken Khartoum, crushed the Khalifa's army, and were now masters of the Sudan. The Anglo-Egyptian force reached a point approximately 15 miles north of Fashoda on 18 September. The Sudanese and the artillery disembarked, set up a flagpole alongside the fort, fired a 21-gun salute, and hoisted the Egyptian flag at 1300. A letter to Marchand was drafted by Major Wingate and dispatched at 0600 on 19 September by two Sudanese NCOs.[139]

The captain's reply, delivered by approximately 0730, congratulated Kitchener on his victory. Marchand described his own spirited exploits in taking possession of the Bahr al-Ghazal and concluding a treaty with the local Shilluk tribe that, he emphasized, placed the whole area of Fashoda under the control and protection of France. Having thus established his own claim, he acknowledged Kitchener's "intention to visit Fashoda, where I shall be happy to welcome you . . . "au nom de la France." Kitchener proceeded up the river and at 1000 the first of his gunboats came into view of Fashoda. At 1030, accompanied by his second-in-command, Captain

---

[139]Bates, 130; Wright, 178-179.

Marcel Germain, Marchand boarded Kitchener's gunboat the *Dal* to pay an official call. The initial exchanges were formal and tense and conducted in French, as neither Marchand nor Germain spoke English. Both commanders were suspicious and allowed themselves to be upset by small matters of procedure and protocol. Kitchener explained that his orders were to reclaim Fashoda in the name of the Sublime Porte and His Highness the Khedive; Marchand replied that his orders were to occupy Fashoda and other parts of the Upper Nile abandoned by Egypt and therefore without any lawful owner. Kitchener drew attention to the preponderance of force at his disposal; Marchand replied that until he received orders to retire, he and his companions were prepared to die at their post before they would lower the French flag. Having relieved themselves of the awkward burdens of their official instructions and their prepared statements, both men began to relax. They agreed that the rights and wrongs of the British and French positions in the Upper Nile were outside their competence and should be referred to London and Paris. In the meantime, Kitchener would not demand the removal of the French flag and the retirement of the French, and Marchand would not object to Kitchener's hoisting the Egyptian flag at Fashoda and leaving a garrison. Wingate and Germain were sent ashore to settle the details, while Kitchener and Marchand opened a bottle of lukewarm whiskey and drank toasts to the Queen and the President of the Republic. Both men were soon observed leaning over the maps, describing their recent exploits and conquests, "patting one another on the back in a flurry of mutual congratulation." Marchand would later claim that to drink "this frightful" whiskey was one of the greatest sacrifices he ever made for his country.[140]

Marchand repaid Kitchener's hospitality that afternoon in a second meeting, conducted in equally good spirit in the French camp, with French champagne, green vegetables, and flowers. Kitchener handed Marchand the latest French newspapers, sent by express from Cairo. The generosity, however, was calculated; it was in fact contrived to undermine the morale and spirit of Marchand's men. As he praised the French for their remarkable achievement, Kitchener icily commented, "You know, the French government will not back you up. . . . France has other things to think about at the moment: the Dreyfus Affair." Up to that point, Marchand and his men had heard very little of it. The newspapers, however, described in exhausting detail the recent explosions caused by the Dreyfus affair, which had three months prior brought down the Méline ministry and had divided French society. Marchand wrote later: "An hour after we opened the French papers the ten officers were trembling and weeping. We learned then and there that the terrible Dreyfus affair had been opened with its dreadful campaigns of infamies, and for thirty-six hours not one of us was able to say anything to the others." Shortly thereafter, Kitchener ordered Wingate to deliver a sealed envelope to Marchand, a formal protest of his presence on "Egyptian and British soil." He departed before Marchand had time to read the letter and compose a reply. He then left a gunboat and a battalion of Sudanese infantry of approximately 600 strong under Major H.W. Jackson and, after steaming to the junction of the Sobat and the Nile rivers to raise the flags, returned straight to Khartoum. For good measure

---

[140]Bates, 128-134. For more details on the encounter at Fashoda, see also: Lewis, *Race to Fashoda*, 197-205; Pakenham, 539-548; Sanderson, 333-335; Wright, 94-105, 107-108, 173-181.

Kitchener notified Menelik, in language "more military than diplomatic," that the British were taking possession of both sides of the White Nile. Any claim Menelik may have made in the past to any part of the Nile valley had been forfeited by the discovery of evidence, in the records of the Khalifa captured at Omdurman, that while ostensibly a friend and ally of the Queen, he was in fact conspiring with the Khalifa.[141]

The decision by Kitchener and Marchand to defer the issue to their respective governments would prove significant in the ultimate resolution of the crisis. Among the most critical factors in the Upper Nile involved British control of information. At Omdurman Kitchener had a telegraph line to Cairo, which was connected to London by submarine cables. By contrast, Marchand had only two options; he could send messages back through the Bahr al-Ghazal and the Atlantic coast, which would take approximately nine months, or he could ask the British for permission to use their telegraph at Omdurman.

Immediately following their departure from Fashoda, Kitchener and Wingate drafted a report on 21 September while en route to Khartoum. The first part of the report described the meetings with Marchand. The latter half dealt with the position the French expedition currently held at Fashoda:

> A most anomalous position – encamped with 120 men on a narrow strip of land, surrounded by marshes, cut off from access to the interior, possessing only three small boats without oars or sails and an inefficient steam-launch which has lately been despatched [*sic*] on a long journey south, short of ammunition and supplies, his

---

[141]Andrew, 93; Bates, 133-135; Lewis, *Race to Fashoda*, 223-224; Pakenham, 548-549; Sanderson, 335; Wright, 180-181.

followers exhausted by years of continuous hardship, yet still persisting in his impractical undertaking in the face of the effective occupation and administration of the country I have been able to establish. . . . Our general impression was one of the utmost astonishment that a great nation like France should attempt to carry out a project of such magnitude and danger with so small and ill-equipped a force which, as the commander remarked to me, was neither in a position to resist a second Dervish attack nor to retire . . . The claims of M. Marchand to have occupied the Bahr el Ghazal [*sic*] and Fashoda provinces with the force at his disposal would be ludicrous did not the sufferings and privations his expedition endured during their two years journey render the futility of their efforts pathetic.

"Such claims," he concluded, "are more worthy of *opéra-bouffe* than the outcome of the maturely considered plans of a great Government."

When the two men arrived at Omdurman, they gave the report to Lord Edward Cecil, a captain in the Grenadier Guards and the prime minister's son, to take to Cairo for its dispatch to London. Although the report did not reach London until October, Kitchener wired two telegrams from Omdurman on 24 September and 25 September. The telegrams, which the Foreign Office received on 25 September, provided the first news to reach Europe about the meeting at Fashoda and the condition of the French expedition.[142]

This encounter at Fashoda set the stage for the

---

[142]FO 78/5051, Tel.244, 25 September 1898, Rodd to Salisbury; FO 78/5051, Tel.245, 25 September 1898, Rodd to Salisbury; BD 193: 167-168; BD 194: 168; Bates, 135-137; Headrick, *The Invisible Weapon*, 84-85; Sanderson, 336-339; Wright, 31, 56.

diplomatic crisis that brought Britain and France dangerously close to war. From Paris, Monson warned his government that the French were preparing to make trouble over Fashoda in spite of current appearances to the contrary. Late August and early September indeed was a period of relative calm for the British embassy in Paris; the Chamber of Deputies was not in session and most of the members were absent from the capital. Nevertheless, while all of Britain waited expectantly throughout the summer for news that Kitchener's Anglo-Egyptian forces had taken Khartoum, the ambassador had been following accounts of Marchand's progress via French colonial newspapers and reported growing excitement over the prospect of beating the British to the Upper Nile.[143] On 2 September, the same day as the Battle at Omdurman, Monson informed the cabinet that, according to *La Dépêche Coloniale*, Marchand reached the banks of the Nile in June and "may reasonably be expected to have arrived by this time at Fashoda."[144]

While the stories of Marchand's holy mission remained irresistible and riveting, however, French opinion in the summer of 1898 increasingly became diverted by dramatic developments in the unfolding Dreyfus affair. Monson observed in early August that -- although there existed a small but powerful colonial lobby, as well as their allies and agents in the Parisian newspapers and the Chamber of Deputies, which was "very noisy" and favored colonial expansion, even over British resistance -- the majority of French public opinion did not seem to care: "I do not believe that the country at large either cares much about such matters or knows anything about them."

---

[143]See extracts from the *Journal des Débats*' *France Militaire*, *Bulletin du Comité de l'Afrique Française*, and *La Dépêche Coloniale* in Monson's dispatches, January to June 1898 in FO 27/3410.

[144]FO 27/3415, A.D.285, 2 September 1898, Monson to Salisbury.

And yet, Monson could not help but speculate that news of an Anglo-Egyptian victory at Khartoum would be most irritating on French public opinion, and would "bring once more to the front that Egyptian question which France has recently allowed to slumber." It was after all a "sentimental grievance to which no French government had hitherto professed indifference . . . I need not remind your Lordship how easy it is to get up a popular cry in this country, which no Government, however strong its individual composition, could successfully resist."[145]

---

[145]BD 186: 161-162; Wood, 165.

Chapter Five

"AN UNEASY CONVICTION ... THAT JUSTICE HAS NOT BEEN DONE"

The encounter at Fashoda occurred at precisely the moment least conducive to a reasonable discussion by French and British representatives. In August and September 1898, the French government found itself engulfed by the sudden and dramatic reemergence of the Dreyfus affair. The impact of the "Affair" was twofold. First, it altered the setting in which the Fashoda negotiations were to be conducted; the French temper, both public and private, grew more explosive and unpredictable throughout the course of discussions. Second and more important, the Dreyfus affair made a profound impression upon Edmund Monson. In early September the ambassador believed that, so long as domestic pressures did not force Delcassé's hand, the French would resolve the Upper Nile dispute with "calmness." As the Fashoda negotiations dragged on without resolution, however, the French government began to lose control of the domestic situation. In particular, popular agitation over the revision of the original verdict triggered demonstrations, labor disruptions, newspaper rhetoric, and rumors of military plots, revolution, and war. Although Monson increasingly believed that the French government might attempt to divert public attention away from the domestic turmoil by a military confrontation with the British over the Upper Nile, he could never altogether decide what course of action France might take.

Prior to January 1898, the Dreyfus case was an interesting but generally inconsequential issue in French international politics. In late 1894 Captain Alfred Dreyfus, a Jewish officer assigned to the French general staff, was arrested for high treason. A military court-martial convicted and sentenced Dreyfus to imprisonment on Devil's Island although his trial was full of legal irregularities and the principal evidence against him was weak and circumstantial. In 1896 Colonel Georges Picquart, in charge of counterintelligence, noticed that despite the imprisonment of a traitor, the leakage of secret military information continued. Upon examination of the Dreyfus dossier, he became convinced that the captain was innocent and that the real traitor was another officer assigned to the general staff, Major Charles Ferdinand Walsin-Esterhazy, a "swashbuckler with expensive tastes."[146] Picquart's attempts to initiate proceedings against Esterhazy, however, failed due to the resistance of the general staff, whose members accepted the guilt of Dreyfus as an article of faith and who believed that challenging the findings of the court-martial would undermine public confidence in the army. By late 1897 rumors that Dreyfus was innocent and growing discomfort among leading generals on the General Staff forced the army to order Esterhazy before a court-martial. On 11 January 1898 seven military judges acquitted

---

[146]Robert and Isabelle Tombs, *That Sweet Enemy. Britain and France: The History of a Love-Hate Relationship* (New York: Random House, 2006), 426.

Esterhazy and thus reestablished Dreyfus's guilt. The acquittal of Esterhazy, however, and the mounting conviction of a cover-up in the General Staff prompted the publication on 13 January of Emile Zola's "*J'Accuse*," which transformed the case into an "affair" that divided the nation. The impact of Zola's open letter to the president of the Republic, in which he accused the highest ranking officers of the French army of knowingly acquitting a guilty man on orders from the War Office and of convicting and incarcerating an innocent man, was electric. The immediate result was an outbreak of anti-Semitic rioting in the provinces. The excitement, moreover, threw the government into turmoil as the Radicals in the Chamber, sensing an opportunity to overthrow the Méline cabinet, demanded that the government produce decisive evidence against Dreyfus.[147]

The Dreyfus affair was the first major crisis facing Monson as ambassador to France. During his first two years in Paris, he had dutifully reported the activities of the French government with respect to the pressing international questions of the day but had never been compelled to respond to any serious threat to peace or to British interests until the current discussions over the West African territories. Prior to January 1898, Monson knew no more about the Dreyfus case than what he had read in the newspapers. His first serious comments on the case described growing excitement in France of "an uneasy conviction . . . of the very great possibility that

---

[147]For background of the Dreyfus Affair, see: Jean-Denis Bredin, *The Affair: The Case of Alfred Dreyfus*, trans. Jeffrey Mehlman (New York: George Braziller, Inc., 1983); Michael Burns, *France and the Dreyfus Affair: A Documentary History* (Boston/New York: Bedford/St. Martin's, 1999); Guy Chapman, *The Dreyfus Case: A Reassessment* (New York: Reynal and Company, 1955); David L. Lewis, *Prisoners of Honor: The Dreyfus Affair* (New York: William Morrow and Company, 1973); Piers Paul Read, *The Dreyfus Affair: The Scandal that Tore France in Two* (New York: Bloomsbury Press, 2012).

complete justice has not been done."[148] Otherwise, Monson learned far more about the case from the British military attaché Lieutenant Colonel Douglas Dawson, who was much better informed through his many contacts in Paris, notably the German and Italian attachés, Colonel Maximilien Schwartzkoppen and Colonel Alesandro Panizzardi, two of the central figures in the case. In the wake of "*J'Accuse*" Monson further consulted the German ambassador Count Münster, who asserted that neither he nor any member of the German embassy had ever had any dealings with Dreyfus. When Monson asked about Esterhazy, however, Münster replied, with "a significant smile, 'Ah, the other gentleman . . . we know him well.'" The German ambassador also explained that during the original Dreyfus trial and for some time afterward, he called frequently on the French War Ministry and demanded to be put in a position to make an authoritative statement to the effect he knew nothing of Dreyfus, but that this had always been steadfastly refused.[149] Monson's initial reports on the case, therefore, proved relatively circumspect. A week after "*J'Accuse*" he discounted rumors involving a conspiracy within the French army and disregarded concerns about the potential for serious civil unrest:

> The demonstrations in Paris are almost entirely confined to the students of the Quartier Latin, who behaved very much as the undergraduates of an English university would do on the occasion of a Town and Gown Row. But their turbulence necessitates the constant employment of

---

[148]FO 27/3320, D.696, 19 November 1897, Monson to Salisbury. See also Monson's reports to Salisbury in FO 27/3320: D.698, 23 November 1897; D.703, 28 November 1897; D.718, 6 December 1897; D.730, 14 December 1897; D.733, 16 December 1897.

[149]FO 27/3393, D.19, 14 January 1898, Monson to Salisbury.

considerable bodies of police; and it is probably in
this that for the young men themselves the fun of the
whole thing consists.

Nevertheless, although he did not believe that the
political fallout from "*J'Accuse*" and the domestic
violence necessarily implied the coming of a fresh
revolution, Monson acknowledged that recent anti-
Semitic violence and unrest in the provinces had caused
many of his colleagues to report to their governments the
prospect of considerable danger.[150] He grew equally
concerned over the damnatory international press
commentary, which proved equally vicious in deploring
the acquittal of Esterhazy and the subsequent anti-Semitic
violence, while praising the courage of Zola. In London,
the *Daily Mail* wrote that France was "disappearing from
the list of civilized nations," while the *Times* described the
verdict as one of "really surprising perversity." Zola's true
crime, the *Times* wrote, "has been in daring to rise to
defend the truth and civil liberty." In Berlin, the *Tageblatt*
wrote that the Esterhazy acquittal represented for the
French army "its first victory since its defeat in 1870."
Even the Russian press was critical: "Paris is becoming a
large village in Asia or Africa . . . in which justice is
called the right of the strongest." Newspaper commentary
in Italy and Austria-Hungary was equally anti-French and
pro-Dreyfusard, and reports of revisionist sympathy and
protests came from areas as removed as Australia, Spain,
Denmark, South America, and the United States.
Hundreds of congratulatory telegrams poured into Paris
from all over the world, the great majority of which were
in praise of Zola and sharply critical of the French army.

---

[150]FO 27/3393, D.31, 21 January 1898, Monson to Salisbury. See also Monson's
reports to Salisbury in FO 27/3393: D.11, 12 January 1898; D.20, 14 January
1898; D.24, 16 January 1898; D.28, 18 January 1898; D.36, 23 January 1898;
D.37, 23 January 1898; D.46, 28 January 1898.

Furthermore, on 24 January the German Secretary of State for Foreign Affairs Bernard von Bülow categorically declared in the German Reichstag that absolutely no German agent had ever had relations with Captain Dreyfus; a similar declaration was made in the Italian Chamber of Deputies on 1 February. In Russia, while there was little sympathy for Dreyfus within government circles and at court, there did begin to emerge some apprehension concerning the reliability of France as an ally. From London, Courcel reported that public opinion was almost unanimous in proclaiming Dreyfus innocent and illegally condemned. The British, he noted, were "disposed to accept the most injurious judgments on the vices of the administration of justice in France, and on the dangers of the development of a militarist spirit."[151]

The principal concern for London, Monson believed, would be only the "effect which the sensitiveness of the public and the irritation of the Army" may have upon French diplomacy. After all, the esteem of the French army was vital to the stability of the country. While he condemned the mistakes made by the Ministry of War and ultimately came to accept the possibility of conspiracy within the French General Staff, Monson recognized the inherent esteem with which most French citizens held the army. The army was above politics; it represented the "greatness of France":

> It was the Army of Revolution, of Empire . . . It was the Army of Marengo, Austerlitz and Wagram, the *Grande Armée* that [French historian Ernest] Lavisse proudly called "one of the most perfect instruments of war history has ever seen"; the Army of the cuirasse and saber, of the képi and pantaloons rouge, of Sebastopol and the Malakoff,

---

[151]Bredin, 272; Brown, 62-65; Lewis, *Prisoners of Honor*, 209; Tombs and Tombs, 426.

of Magenta and Solferino, the Army that had made
France the greatest military power in Europe until
the rise of Prussia . . . Twenty years later, under the
never-absent shadow of Germany, the Army was
both defender of the nation and instrument of
revanche. It was the means of restoring, someday,
the national glory.[152]

As Monson came to understand, the problem was that as
a result of the General Staff's early and immediate
commitment to Dreyfus's guilt, the honor of the army
became synonymous with protecting the original verdict.
The army's resistance to revision was grounded in the
belief that to reopen the case was to discredit the army;
and a discredited army could not fight Germany and
restore the lost provinces. In the eyes of the army,
sympathy to revisionism was pro-German and
effectively treason.[153]

Throughout the spring, while he discounted rumors
of a military *coup d'etat*, Monson nevertheless suggested
that the French army, in view of these supposed attacks
upon its honor, might be inspired to vindicate itself "at the
expense of the perfidious Albion" particularly in light of
recent tensions in West Africa and the British cabinet's
recent decision to order Kitchener to Khartoum.[154]

Over the following weeks, Monson became more
disillusioned, even disgusted, with the behavior of French
leaders. On 23 January he described a fistfight that broke
out the day before during debate in the Chamber of
Deputies. After the socialist Jean Jaures condemned the
Esterhazy acquittal, the Comte de Bernis accused Jaures
of being the "lawyer of the syndicate." Jaures responded
by calling Bernis a "wretch and a coward." Pandemonium

---

[152]Tuchman, 175.

[153]Hoffman, 65-66; Tuchman, 175-176.

[154]FO 27/3393, D.31, 21 January 1898, Monson to Salisbury.

erupted and Prime Minister Brisson attempted to suspend the sitting, but disorderly proceedings, which extended to the lobbies, continued for twenty minutes longer. "Mr. Austin Lee of this embassy was present in the Diplomatic Box," Monson wrote, "and describes the scene as outrageous." Monson concluded: "A real leader of men might at this moment have a great opportunity, but France has no one to turn to for such a deliverance."[155] Three days later Monson met with Hanotaux, who complained about the harsh attacks of British newspapers on the French government, in effect intervening in "what is purely a French domestic question." Monson replied that while he had studiously tried to avoid the subject, it would be "perfectly impossible to prevent their discussing it, and vain to expect they would refrain from doing so." The ambassador's unsympathetic response left Hanotaux unimpressed and unsatisfied. In some respects, it reaffirmed the foreign minister's determination to defend French interests in the Upper Nile.[156]

Monson's attitude began to harden as well. Violent anti-Semitic street demonstrations continued throughout the country. As the trial and conviction of Zola in February aroused further excitement, petitions were signed and duels were fought daily. Monson grew increasingly concerned with the threat of instability and began to echo the fears of his diplomatic colleagues that France might pose a threat to the peace of Europe. On 26 February he wrote that following the international uproar raised by the slander trial of Zola, which concluded only three days before with the author's conviction, the French people sensed the indignation of European opinion over the absence of justice: "The Areopagus of Europe has . . .

---

[155]FO 27/3393, D.36, 23 January 1898, Monson to Salisbury; Bredin, 255-256; Chapman, 183-184; Lewis, *Prisoners of Honor*, 215.

[156]FO 27/3393, D.46, 28 January 1898, Monson to Salisbury.

judged France; and she stands condemned by the unanimous public opinion of every civilized people." He reports that in the opinion of his diplomatic colleagues,

> the present temper of France is a standing danger and menace to Europe . . . she is [returning] to the frame of mind of one hundred years ago, when she looked upon the rest of Europe as banded against her and when she had but one thought, with which she is now possessed, that between herself and destruction there stands only her army. There is a general wrongheadedness, which may be called madness . . . in France, which if dangerous to herself . . . is dangerous also to her neighbours.

A powerful conviction prevailed, he concluded, that the country would not much longer "escape an internal convulsion . . . in which the Army will play a prominent part, and which will equally be followed by a foreign war." Monson noted that while such opinions were probably exaggerated, the public temper was clearly and dangerously irritable, especially against foreign countries:

> In the flurry of excitement and under the influence of the irascibility of the Army, it might be a relief to France to pick a quarrel with the one Great European Power who cannot invade her, perennial jealousy of whom supplies almost as much ample ground for vindictiveness as is furnished against Germany by the memory of the last international struggle.[157]

It is possible that Count Münster and Count Giuseppe Tornielli, the German and Italian ambassadors,

---

[157]FO 27/3393, D.109, 26 February 1898, Monson to Salisbury; BD 172: 146; Wood, 155-156. See also Monson's reports to Salisbury in FO 27/3393: D.71, 11 February 1898; D.85, 15 February 1898; D.100, 20 February 1898; D.105, 22 February 1898.

influenced his attitude. Monson had close relationships with both men and sought their views on the possible impact of the affair on French policy. Münster and Tornielli tended to view France as intrinsically unstable. Both men were born in the 1830s, both had fathers who had fought in the Napoleonic wars, both had childhood memories of the Revolution of 1848, and both vividly recalled the chaos of the Commune. They undoubtedly saw in French instability a prelude to European instability. By the middle of February, they were trying to persuade Monson that the Dreyfus affair was producing in France a movement similar to Boulangism[158] and that this growing national defensiveness would soon destroy the peace of Europe. Despite their pessimistic assessments, however, Monson advised London that the alarm of his colleagues was merely "gloomy forebodings" to be taken as "conjectures for what they are worth."[159]

The excitement over the Dreyfus affair ultimately receded in the spring and summer of 1898 and Monson directed his energies and attention to the conclusion of the West Africa discussions. The respite from the Dreyfus agitation quickly ended, however, with the collapse of the Méline cabinet in June. The new prime minister Henri Brisson immediately declared the government's intention to get rid of the affair once and for all. Godefroy Cavaignac the new minister of war went before the Chamber of Deputies on 7 July to present evidence that

---

[158]Boulangism was a right-wing movement of extreme nationalism. Its adherents were inspired by the career of General Georges Boulanger in the late 1880s, and motivated by devotion to patriotism, the restoration of France to its former glory, and *revanche* against Germany. Following the example of Boulanger, who openly intrigued against the government and who sought to increase the strength and influence of the army, they looked forward to the overthrow of the Republic, which they considered too conciliatory toward Germany.

[159]Brown, 68-69. See Monson's various reports in FO 27/3393, FO 27/3394, FO 27/3395, FO 27/3396.

was intended to quiet Dreyfus's supporters and effectively bury the affair. Cavaignac, who was passionately convinced of Dreyfus's guilt, did not know that his predecessors had falsified several documents in order to strengthen the case against Dreyfus. Dreyfusard politicians, led by Jean Jaurès and Georges Clemenceau, publicly challenged several of the documents as forgeries. Fearful of a continuing polarization over the case, Brisson urged Cavaignac to have an expert, Captain Louis Cuignet, reexamine the Dreyfus dossier in order to be absolutely certain that the government's position was correct. In late August, however, Cuignet conclusively determined that the primary document on which the government's case rested was a blatant forgery. Caivaignac interrogated its author, Colonel Hubert Henry on 30 August and placed him under fortress arrest; the next day Henry cut his throat with a razor.

The reaction to Henry's suicide, similar to the publication of "*J'Accuse*," was electric. Public excitement soared. In August less than 2,000 people had attended pro-Dreyfusard meetings in Paris; by September, similar rallies drew over 25,000 people. Nationalist and anti-Dreyfusard journals such as *Le Temps* and *Le Matin* reversed their positions and demanded revision. Even army officers wanted the case reopened. Yet for the moment, nothing happened. Brisson, who had softened his previous hard-line position against revision, vacillated, apparently frozen with indecision. Minister of Justice J.M.F. Sarrien, while favorable to revision, wanted the initiative to come from the minister of war. Cavaignac, who believed that the discovery of Henry's forgery made no difference to Dreyfus's guilt, declared that he would not accept any alteration of the original verdict. Thus, when Madame Lucie Dreyfus formally petitioned the French government on 3 September for reconsideration of her husband's conviction, Cavaignac found himself outnumbered and resigned. The cabinet agreed that it should obtain some sign of official support from the army before reopening the Dreyfus case, largely to prevent any charge that revision would be directed against the army itself. On 5 September Brisson offered the Ministry of War to General Emile Zurlinden, the military governor of Paris, who was at best sympathetic to revision and at least willing to consider the case on its merits.

In light of these developments, and particularly in the wake of commotion aroused by Colonel Henry's suicide, Monson reported that public opinion was "rapidly veering round" in favor of revision and that the ministry "cannot much longer refuse to take this step." He did not believe, however, that the cabinet would collapse even if other ministers followed Cavaignac's example. Brisson was in favor of revision and public opinion would not tolerate any other view. What France needed was a "sensible and intelligent General" to take over the Ministry of War. The appointment of General Zurlinden, "so eminent and popular a General," would undoubtedly help the ministry to initiate the revision of the original verdict.

Whatever the merits of the case, Monson found himself exhausted and disgusted. The dragging length of this interminable affair, he noted, made it difficult "for an impartial foreigner not to look upon it without a sensation of pity very much allied to contempt." The more he had to give attention to it, the more he felt a "mental nausea." For the time being, he believed that revision was necessary to bring this disgraceful affair to an end.[160]

---

[160]FO 27/3396, D.434, 2 September 1898, Monson to Salisbury; FO 27/3396, D.436, 4 September 1898, Monson to Salisbury.

Chapter Six

DELCASSÉ

Within the Brisson ministry, one of the more impassioned and vocal advocates of revision was the new foreign minister, Théophile Delcassé, who took office when the Méline cabinet collapsed in June. In late 1894 Delcassé initially had been a committed anti-Dreyfusard member of the Dupuy ministry; in fact, as the new colonial minister, it had been his duty to select from among the French overseas possessions a place of exile suitable for the "traitor." His choice was Devil's Island. His unrelenting commitment to resist revision and to leave the case unaltered was a prerequisite for his inclusion in the ministry. When he learned, however, of Henry's arrest and the undeniable truth of the colonel's forgery, Delcassé immediately understood its significance and shifted his position; ultimately, he took the lead within the Brisson ministry to push for revision. In part Delcassé's change of heart was the result of remorse. He was disturbed immensely by the implications raised by the Henry forgery, that an innocent man had been convicted and condemned on the basis of forgery and calculated deceit. Once he came to doubt Dreyfus's guilt, his role in contributing to the severity of the prisoner's detention weighed heavily on Delcassé's mind. Beyond his sympathy for Dreyfus's innocence, however, he also favored revision out of consideration for his policy.[161]

Delcassé's foreign policy tended to follow the principles of his political guru, the ardent French republican and nationalist Léon Gambetta. As a disciple of Gambetta, Delcassé desired first and foremost the restoration of the lost provinces Alsace-Lorraine and the restoration of French national prestige. Furthermore, he favored an entente cordiale with Britain. As early as 1882, he had criticized Prime Minister Charles de Freycinet for allowing the entente with Britain to be broken and as recently as February 1898, he proclaimed that "however numerous or important might be the contentions between England and France, none was so vital as to justify a war." Unlike Gambetta, however, Delcassé vigorously supported the alliance with Russia. Gambetta always regarded the accommodation with Russia as an alliance of convenience; the two states after all had no common interests outside of their mutual opposition to Germany. Delcassé, however, considered the strength of the alliance to be their "lack of conflicting interests." He agreed with Bismarck's observation: "They alone, by reason of their geographic position and political aims, have the minimum causes for dissension."[162]

Delcassé's position toward Germany is harder to assess. While he is often portrayed as passionately anti-German and driven by the longing for *revanche*, there is evidence that he was in favor of some sort of rapprochement with Germany. The historian of Delcassé's foreign policy Christopher Andrew suggests that there was considerable moderation in his views toward

---

[161]Andrew, 59-60; Brown, 81-83.

[162]Andrew, 13-15, 22-23 Brown, 120-126; C. Porter, 8-15, 166-168; Frederick Schumann, *War and Diplomacy in the French Republic: An Inquiry into Political Motivations and the Control of Foreign Policy* (New York: Whittlesey House, McGraw-Hill Book Company, Inc., 1931), 160.

Germany. For example, several of his newspaper articles in the late 1880s indicate no trace of anti-German chauvinism. During the war scare and panic of early 1887 he wrote that, "We shall be very careful to do nothing which might lead to a fearful collision between France and Germany." During the Schnaebelé affair,[163] he wrote two articles; one demanded that Britain end its occupation of Egypt. The other addressed the crisis, insisting on the need for calm: "Whatever happens, let us maintain our *sangfroid*." Andrew notes furthermore that although Delcassé was never particularly fond of the German national character, he nevertheless lacked the deep anti-German prejudice that inspired many of his contemporaries. He had a lifelong passion for Wagnerian opera, which expressed the qualities of "*la grandeur et la noblesse*" more magnificently, he believed, than those of any contemporary French dramatists.[164] And yet, Delcassé's biographer Charles Porter argues that the foreign minister never considered seriously a possible rapprochement with Germany. In one respect, Delcassé wrote numerous times that Alsace-Lorraine made any prospect for an accommodation unfeasible, principally because Germany would never restore the lost provinces unless forced to do so. He also repeatedly warned that Germany was France's "mortal enemy," that it had "sworn the ruin of France," and that Berlin was planning to launch a "war of extermination."[165]

More generally, Delcassé's foreign policy was inspired by his imperial vision, the construction of French power in the Mediterranean. While he adhered to the contemporary justification for colonialism (i.e., the need

---

[163]In April 1887, a French frontier official, Guillame Schnaebelé, was illegally arrested by the German police after being invited onto German soil on official business. The "Affair" briefly provoked war panic in the spring of 1887.

[164]Andrew, 16-19.

[165]C. Porter, 40, 43-44, 117-118.

for markets and raw materials), the source of his own colonial ambition had more to do with the restoration of national prestige, tarnished by defeat in 1870-1871 and expulsion from Egypt in 1882. He considered the extension of a French empire around the shores of the Mediterranean with an African hinterland stretching southward to the Congo to be the primary means of restoring France to her former position in Europe.[166] If that meant crossing paths with the British then so be it. At all major points around the globe where London emerged as France's chief competitor, Delcassé proved far more eager than most of his cabinet colleagues to run the risk of confrontation. This is not to suggest that he did not still desire a rapprochement with London. He clearly favored some sort of entente with Britain but not at the expense of surrender in Egypt; his greater objective was to end British occupation of Egypt. While most of his compatriots remained obsessed with the return of Alsace-Lorraine, Delcassé adhered relentlessly to the advice of Gambetta, who wrote, "If we lose Egypt . . . we also lose our influence in the Mediterranean." France, Delcassé determined, would remain on the Upper Nile.[167] In his first speech in the Chamber of Deputies in November 1890, he used Gambetta's words to define his own attitude toward Britain: "I am, certainly, a sincere and enlightened friend of the English, but not to the extent of sacrificing to them the interests of France." The British respect as allies only those who, taking account of their own interests, make themselves respected.[168]

In temperament, Delcassé, who sported a grandiose mustache and was said to have worn lifts in his shoes, was serious and generally humorless. He allowed himself little

---

[166]Andrew, 86-87.

[167]Andrew, 21-23; 30-32; Brown, 19-25, 120-126; C. Porter, 34-36, 165-168; Sanderson, 119-120; Schumann, 160.

[168]Andrew, 3-4; C. Porter, 15.

relaxation. As foreign minister he became an infrequent visitor to the opera or to the *Comédie Française*, where in former times he had been a habitué. Unlike British foreign ministers, he never enjoyed either the long weekend or the long summer holidays. When business allowed, he went to bed at nine and rose at six. His recreation was restricted to an occasional morning ride in the Bois de Boulogne. In his conduct of affairs, therefore, Delcassé worked alone, took few into his confidence, and refrained from making known his purposes and methods. He was reserved and almost pathologically secretive. His colleague Joseph Caillaux wrote that the foreign minister did not lie, but "was capable of deception about his projects and intentions. He deceived by his silences and . . . by a flow of words behind which he concealed his carefully mediated designs." This secrecy was more often than not a critical necessity in Third Republic politics, a lesson he learned early in his career. In the early 1890s, while serving as undersecretary of state for the colonies, political opponents gained access to government records and in an effort to discredit him published several of Delcassé's confidential reports. As a result, he observed that, as often as not, a secret told to a French cabinet was a secret no longer. Consequently, when he later concluded treaties, Delcassé communicated only to the president of the Republic; he did not inform his colleagues in the cabinet about secrets of state. He developed the habit of giving verbal orders. His communications with his own ambassadors were always guarded and seldom contained any extended explanations of the rationale behind his policy decisions. While he himself remained reticent, he encouraged his ambassadors to make frequent trips back to Paris to consult directly with him. If that were not possible, he encouraged his ambassadors to write him long *personal* letters, as the contents of such letters need not be known to anyone except the sender and himself.

Such letters did not have to be filed at the Quai d'Orsay; hence, there was no danger of their contents leaking out to the public. In situations necessitating extreme security, he bypassed his own ambassadors and traveled to the foreign power himself. One of his close friends, André Mévil, quipped that Delcassé left the emptiest files of any French foreign minister. It should therefore come as no great surprise that he flatly refused to write his memoirs. Charles Porter indeed noted that one of Delcassé's last acts was to destroy a great many personal papers.[169]

His secret arrangements included the control of the *cabinet noir* and the press. The *cabinet noir* traditionally referred to departments of the French government that oversaw the clandestine interception and decipherment of private or diplomatic correspondence. Under Delcassé, copies of all telegrams sent by foreign diplomats and newspaper correspondents were passed on to the Quai d'Orsay as a matter of course by the French post office. Sufficient evidence survives to show that the *cabinet noir* possessed at least a partial knowledge of the diplomatic codes and ciphers used by Italy, Britain, Germany, the Ottoman Empire, and Japan, and probably also of those used by Spain and the United States. To most of the diplomatic corps in Paris, the knowledge of such an office was taken for granted; Monson would later write to Lord Lansdowne, British foreign secretary from 1900 to 1905, "I think it right to tell you that your recent letters by post have been palpably opened by the bureau noir." In addition to the cipher office, Delcassé also exercised great influence over significant sections of the press. A former journalist, Delcassé maintained close contact with friends and editors. He was too conscious of the power of the press to neglect to use it. Every evening he dictated items

---

[169]Andrew, 7-8, 59-74, 119-122, 129-131, 147-148, 151, 165; Brown, 10; C. Porter, 3, 76, 111-115; Schumann, 162.

to appear in the following day's newspapers, taking special care to vary his style according to the newspapers concerned. Therefore, certain Republican newspapers, such as *Le Matin*, *Le Temps*, and the *Journal des Débats*, tended to support official government positions and became recognized as semi-official mouthpieces of the Foreign Ministry. Delcassé also maintained a close relationship with *La Dépêche de Toulouse*, the most influential of the Parisian radical newspapers and whose correspondent, Louis Jezierski, was a close friend.[170]

As a result, unlike Lord Salisbury, Delcassé had extraordinary independence to conduct French diplomacy generally free from cabinet control. In one respect, this independence resulted from the preoccupation of successive French ministries with the internal crises caused by the Dreyfus Affair. Delcassé was impatient with the triviality of parliamentary debate and he generally confined his interest in domestic matters such as the Dreyfus case to their repercussions on his foreign policy. More important, however, the first three prime ministers under whom he served[171] all shared complete confidence in his ability while his final prime minister, Emile Combes,[172] took almost no interest whatsoever in foreign affairs. Consequently, for most of his seven years in office, he was very rarely called to account for any of his activities.

Not surprisingly, Monson found negotiations with Delcassé to be difficult. He often complained of the foreign minister's penchant for secrecy, his reluctance to engage anyone in straightforward discussions, his propensity if not preference for extreme ambiguity in language, and his disposition to avoid entering into

---

[170]Andrew, 7-8, 64-74, 168, 204; C. Porter, 111-115.

[171]Henri Brisson (June-October 1898); Charles Dupuy (November 1898-June 1899); Pierre Waldeck-Rousseau (June 1899-June 1902).

[172]Prime Minister, June 1902-January 1905.

detail.[173] He complained that the foreign minister was "undoubtedly more open to journalists than to diplomatists." Delcassé indeed preferred to avoid extensive conversations with foreign ambassadors. While communications with his own ambassadors were usually guarded and seldom included any extended explanations of the reasoning behind his decisions, he needed and was often very open to the advice of seasoned diplomats. Delcassé thus permitted several ambassadors a wide degree of latitude in carrying out their missions.[174]

In order to conduct an effective foreign policy, particularly one based on an assumption of competition with London, Delcassé needed freedom from the seemingly endless internal crises which always seemed to distract and break French cabinets. With the reemergence of the Dreyfus affair, he concluded that revision was inevitable and that the Brisson cabinet should take the lead in the process; otherwise, he feared, the government would collapse yet again. Delcassé's primary concern in the first week of September was to prevent any ministerial crisis that would disrupt his policy at the very moment when the government faced an impending confrontation on the Upper Nile, particularly as France found itself progressively isolated due to international outrage over the Dreyfus Affair.[175]

Delcassé indeed understood at this point that France was operating from a position of weakness and isolation. His predecessor Hanotaux, confronted with the impressive show of British force on the Nile in early 1898, had begun to reappraise French policy toward the Upper Nile;

---

[173]FO 27/3395, D.325, 1 July 1898, Monson to Salisbury; FO 27/3396, D.413, 18 August 1898, Monson to Salisbury; FO 27/3396, D.431, 1 September 1898, Monson to Salisbury.

[174]Andrew, 66, 68, 75-76; Brown, 10; C. Porter, 111-114.

[175]Brown, 83-85.

however, he managed to undertake surprisingly few effective expedients to improve France's diplomatic position. It is possible that Hanotaux missed an opportunity to cooperate with Germany on the question of the Portuguese colonies. In mid-June Count Münster advised his foreign minister Bülow that Hanotaux was "personally inclined to make common cause" with Berlin; Germany therefore should concert its policy towards Portugal with Paris. Bülow subsequently offered Hanotaux a proposal of cooperation. The German proposal, however, called for such an infringement of Portuguese sovereignty, it could hardly have been enforced without an ultimatum. Compounding the difficulty, the Méline cabinet collapsed shortly thereafter. As a result, Hanotaux, now an outgoing minister, took no action, leaving it instead for Delcassé. The new foreign minister likewise took absolutely no action upon the German proposal. On 30 June, two days after Delcassé took office, Anglo-Portuguese negotiations were broken off, thereby killing any incentive or opportunity for Franco-German cooperation.[176]

Moreover, Hanotaux did virtually nothing to secure the support of Russia. As Tsarist ministers had endlessly taken pains to emphasize that Russia was not prepared to support French adventures in Africa, Hanotaux never bothered to request Russian support in the Upper Nile. Roger Glenn Brown suggests that this lack of diplomatic preparation indicates that Hanotaux remained less than

---

[176]Delcassé would be criticized in the years following Fashoda for his inaction. Some, including Hanotaux, argued that he could have secured German support in the coming crisis. This hindsight was total nonsense. Bülow was at all times convinced that he could get a better deal by bargaining directly with Salisbury and he approached the French only as an additional means of exerting pressure on London. Once there was a fair chance of success in London, the idea of cooperating with the French was discarded. Andrew, 94-96; Brown, 76; Giffen, 148-152 Sanderson, 329-331.

wholeheartedly behind the Upper Nile scheme.

By the late summer of 1898, Delcassé obviously recognized that that Russian support for a new French initiative over Egypt would not be forthcoming. In addition to the habitual professions of Russian disinterest in African matters, on 24 August, six weeks after Marchand's arrival at Fashoda, the Tsar issued a manifesto in favor of a disarmament conference, without even consulting or forewarning Paris. While the reaction of most of Europe's statesmen was mixed -- publicly favorable and privately skeptical -- in France the reaction was one of "bewilderment." The Quai d'Orsay feared that the conference would seek to make permanent existing European boundaries and therefore make permanent the loss of Alsace-Lorraine.[177] Monson commented that it seemed "almost incredible that a step of such a nature should have been taken at St. Petersburgh [sic] without preliminary consultation with the professed ally at Paris." His diplomatic colleagues generally believed "that Berlin was treated in this respect with more confidence than Paris." The British ambassador to Vienna Sir Horace Rumbold echoed Monson's analysis. The German ambassador to Austria-Hungary Count Philip Eulenburg confirmed to him a certain satisfaction that the proposal "had been conceived without any regard to the feelings and calculations of Russia's would-be most intimate ally, and had cruelly dispelled what illusions may have been nourished in France as to the practical value of a much-vaunted understanding."[178] The implications of the Tsar's disarmament proposals of 24 August indeed defused any

---

[177]Andrew, 121-122; Brown, 75-77; Giffen, 161-170; Langer, *The Diplomacy of Imperialism*, 562-563; C. Porter, 136-137; Sanderson, 327, 327-331, 384.

[178]FO 27/3400, Tel.125, 29 August 1898, Monson to Salisbury; FO 27/3396, D.431, 1 September 1898, Monson to Salisbury; BD 262, 215-216; BD 267, 219-220.

lingering hope in Paris that Russia would stand unwaveringly with its ally.

At the same time, Delcassé also recognized that France would be without German support in spite of the Quai d'Orsay's initial confidence that Germany would oppose British policy in Egypt out of concern for the neutrality of the Suez Canal. French efforts to cooperate with Berlin always and inevitably broke down over the price: final renunciation of Alsace-Lorraine and acceptance of the Treaty of Frankfurt. Furthermore, throughout 1898 indications of détente between London and Berlin were unmistakable: the Kaiser's enthusiastic congratulations in April to Salisbury and Kitchener following British victories in the Sudan; a report of 2 August from the French *charge d'affaires* in Berlin that according to the British ambassador Sir Edward Malet, there was a feeling of confidence in London about the "attitude of the German Emperor on the Egyptian question"; the conclusion on 30 August of the Anglo-German Agreement over the Portuguese colonies; and a report of 5 September that the Kaiser, in a salute to the British victory at Omdurman, reminded an assembly of German troops of the historical "confraternity of arms between the English and the Germans" dating back to Waterloo.[179] Given such compelling evidence, Delcassé pressed Monson about rumors of an alliance between Britain and Germany, rumors that Monson denied.[180]

France's diplomatic isolation became particularly critical given British military successes in the Sudan. After Omdurman Britain unquestionably dominated the military balance of power in the Nile valley. The impressive show of British force had an unsettling effect

---

[179]Andrew, 46-48, 97-98; Brown, 76-77, 84; Sanderson, 327-331.

[180]FO 27/3396, D. 443, 8 September 1898, Monson to Salisbury; FO 27/3400, Tel. 128, 8 September 1898, Monson to Salisbury.

in Paris, and Delcassé worried that it would only be a matter of time before Kitchener encountered Marchand's troops. Moreover, he feared that Kitchener had received orders to eject Marchand by force and that such a collision would provoke a clash in which questions of national honor were raised.[181] After all, news of Kitchener's victory at Omdurman had already triggered a sudden arousal of chauvinism in British public opinion.[182]

Therefore, at a time when the British controlled the Nile river from its mouth to Khartoum, when British public opinion grew daily more chauvinistic, when the French government found itself rocked by the ongoing Dreyfus madness, and when France could not rely on any diplomatic support, Delcassé concluded that the moment was unfavorable for reopening the Egyptian question.[183] He had in fact become convinced that the Marchand mission no longer had any chance for success.

In early July he learned that news from Marchand finally had been received. In mid-June the Colonial Ministry received a letter, dated December 1897, from Marchand who insisted that action be taken on two matters of urgent importance. One was for the relief of the members of his expedition, including the replenishment of stores and equipment. The other was a request for explicit and up-to-date instructions on what he should do when he reached Fashoda. While the first request could be easily addressed, new instructions would require consultation between Delcassé and Georges Trouillot the Colonial Minister. Trouillot wrote on 4 July and again on 18 July for Delcassé's views and instructions. Delcassé, however, did not respond for almost two months.

When he finally did respond to Trouillot on 7

---

[181]Brown, 73-75; Grenville, 225; Sanderson, 312, 339.

[182]See pages 136-137.

[183]Brown, 73-75;Pakenham, 550-551; Sanderson, 312, 339.

September, the foreign minister wrote that circumstances had changed since the earlier years of the Upper Nile project. Kitchener's victory effectively eliminated the last military advantage enjoyed by Marchand and thus shifted the balance of power in the Upper Nile to the British. In light of the altered diplomatic balance in Europe, a confrontation with Britain was one in which France would be at a distinct disadvantage. Therefore, he would order Marchand to stop his advance at some point short of Fashoda but should instead establish himself in the vicinity of the confluence of the Sobat and the Nile. He further suggested that Marchand should concentrate on improving his communications in the Upper Ubangi rather than push forward. Delcassé went on to suggest that if Marchand did happen to encounter Kitchener, he should explain simply that he was protecting the approaches to the French possessions in the Congo basin and thus engaged, similar to the British, in a civilizing mission against the Mahdists. Finally, he should leave any and all questions of national rights, claims, and sovereignty that might arise for discussion in Europe.[184]

---

[184]Andrew, 91-92; Bates, 142-145; Brown, 85; Sanderson, 312.

Chapter Seven

"EMISSARY OF CIVILIZATION" OR "SCUM OF THE DESERT"?

The diplomatic crisis triggered by the confrontation at Fashoda unfolded in three phases. The first phase lasted from early September to early October 1898. In London Lord Salisbury preferred quiet diplomacy and conciliatory dialogue. In fact, he considered possible territorial concessions to the French in order to ensure Anglo-Egyptian control over the Upper Nile. British public opinion, however, proved inordinately chauvinistic, thus emboldening the prime minister's more belligerent colleagues in the cabinet to oppose any policy of compromise. Salisbury, therefore, assumed a firm and uncompromising position from which he would refuse to budge: London would not negotiate until the French government had formally ordered the withdrawal of Marchand from the Upper Nile. In Paris Delcassé proved equally uncompromising. Following Kitchener's victory at Omdurman he quickly came to understand the impossibility of the French military position in the Upper Nile and thus the inherent weakness of his bargaining position. He endeavored therefore to conciliate the British and hope for face-saving concessions to France in return for its recognition of British supremacy on the Nile. Mounting domestic pressures, however -- the insatiable demands made by the small but belligerent colonial lobby, as well as the growing public chaos caused by the unfolding Dreyfus affair -- compelled Delcassé to assume a more rigid and intractable position. He thus played for time in order to allow Marchand to consolidate his position at Fashoda while holding out for British concessions. Therefore, throughout September and early October, negotiations consisted simply of a reiteration by both sides of their uncompromising positions and arguments in support of them.

The formal diplomatic dialogue over concerns resulting from the inevitable encounter between Kitchener and Marchand began on Wednesday 7 September 1898, during Delcassé's regular diplomatic reception with Monson. After extending official congratulations to the British government for Kitchener's victory at Omdurman, the foreign minister speculated that the British flotilla would at once push up the Nile. He was anxious to state that the "explorer" Marchand might possibly be met before long, unless he had encountered difficulties with the Mahdists. In an effort to minimize the political significance of the captain's presence, Delcassé explained that Marchand had been instructed to "consider himself as simply an 'emissary of civilization' without any authority whatever to decide questions of right" and hoped that instructions might be sent to the British troops not to use force to expel him.

Since Delcassé mentioned the possibility of a meeting between the two expeditions, Monson asked where in fact Marchand was currently located and whether the French government had any recent news from him. The foreign minister replied that news of but not from Marchand arrived the day before but having been so long en route, it did not reveal exactly where the expedition was at present. Monson was skeptical and put forward several tentative questions "with the hope of eliciting something more definite, but without avail." He believed that Delcassé probably possessed more specific information but was unwilling to disclose it.

Nevertheless, Monson felt confident that France would admit British claims to the Egyptian Sudan without provoking a serious incident. Delcassé's calm and dignified manner, in contrast to Hanotaux's "petulance and hysterical susceptibilities on every occasion of contention," reflected a more reasonable French attitude toward Egypt. Indeed, Monson noted, the majority of his compatriots began to "recognise that there is nothing to be gained by blustering about Egypt and that it would be more dignified for them to accept the inevitable." While there would remain the usual abuse from the Parisian press, Monson believed that the French were going to discuss the question with "calmness." At the same time, he cautioned, Delcassé would remain conciliatory so long as domestic pressures did not force his hand.[185]

Misunderstanding emerged almost immediately. Both men's accounts of this conversation reflected a notable difference. According to Delcassé, there was no mention of his comment that Marchand had been given strict orders and that he was only an "emissary of civilization." While he stated that it was neither for Marchand nor Kitchener to infer the political consequences of their expeditions, he believed that the exploits of both men were "*au profit egalement de la cause de la civilisation.*" Accordingly, early the following week, Delcassé briefly questioned Monson about the

---

[185]FO 27/3400, Tel. 127, 7 September 1898, Monson to Salisbury; FO 78/5050, D. 441, 8 September 1898, Monson to Salisbury; BD 188: 163-164; Andrew, 92; Bates, 142-143, 145; Sanderson, 339-340.

"fidelity" of the ambassador's report.[186]

It is possible that Monson's rather optimistic assessment confirmed Salisbury's belief in the necessity of restraint. One of the prime minister's primary concerns from the outset was to temper the tone of the dialogue, particularly given that the initial response of the British press was contemptuous and abusive. In a remarkable outburst of enthusiasm and chauvinism following Kitchener's victory at Omdurman, the British public appeared to go "mad with the lust of fighting glory." Joseph Chamberlain declared that "[Omdurman] settles it for all time. Gordon is avenged." Within a week, however, when rumors began to circulate of a French "apparition" on the Upper Nile, outrage replaced celebration; in near unison the British press launched an assault on the audacity of the French. Numerous London daily newspapers published tastelessly abusive editorials and demanded that Her Majesty's Government refuse to consider negotiation. They referred to Marchand and his troops as "tourists," "irregular marauders," "scum of the desert," and a "French picnic party." Their mission betrayed undoubtedly "indubitable hostility" or "conscious antagonism" to Britain. On 12 September, the *Morning Post* urged the government to issue the French an ultimatum, supported by the mobilization of military and naval forces. The next day, the *Daily Mail* and *Evening News* called for ejecting the French if they refused to withdraw willingly "even at the cost of war." The *St. James' Gazette* advised the French government to avoid humiliation by immediately recalling their gallant "traveller" and the conservative *Standard* pointed out that public opinion was virtually unanimous:

Lord Salisbury has one overwhelming advantage --

---

[186]FO 78/5050, D. 449, 12 September 1898, Monson to Salisbury; Sanderson, 339-340; Wood, 168-169.

> he commands, on this occasion, the support of every
> class and section in the country. Liberals and
> Radicals are as enthusiastic as Ministerialists in
> inviting him to enforce the principles so admirably
> formulated by Sir Edward Grey.

The near unanimity of the British press matched the near unanimity and bloodlust of the politicians. Liberals, Conservatives, and Unionists alike fell over each other to line up behind the cabinet whether due to their own indignation with the impertinent French or the indignation of their constituents; they all insisted upon a firm and unyielding position.[187]

Concerned about the effect of this chauvinism in Paris, Salisbury initiated efforts to temper the tone of the dialogue. Leon Geoffray the *chargé d'affaires* in the French embassy in London reported to Delcassé that although the initial response of the British press was indignant, the *Daily Chronicle* -- the mouthpiece of the British Foreign Office -- proved rather conciliatory by comparison.[188]

Accordingly, the prime minister responded to Delcassé's initiation of dialogue by holding out the possibility of territorial concessions to France in the Upper Nile valley. On 9 September he instructed Monson to point out, if Delcassé reverted back to the subject, that in light of the recent military events all territories which had been "subject to the Khalifa" passed to the British and Egyptian governments by right of conquest. While

---

[187]T.W. Riker, "A Survey of British Policy in the Fashoda Crisis," *Political Science Quarterly* 44 (March 1929): 65-66. See also: Bates, 154-155; Wilfrid Scawen Blunt, *My Diaries* (New York: Alfred A. Knopf, 1921), 1: 296; James L. Garvin, *The Life of Joseph Chamberlain*, vol. 3 (London: Macmillan & Company, 1934), 227; Langer, *Diplomacy of Imperialism*, 552-553; Wright, 187-188.

[188]Langer, *Diplomacy of Imperialism*, 553; Peterson, 111; Riker, 66-67.

London did not consider that right to be open for negotiation, it was prepared to discuss in whatever manner suggested by Delcassé "any territorial controversies now existing in regard to those regions which are not affected by this assertion." Monson was to suggest that there were other territories in the Upper Nile valley which, not having been "subject to the Khalifa," could provide an opening for negotiation.[189]

The next day 10 September the ambassador received word from London that Kitchener would soon proceed upriver to Fashoda.[190] Without waiting for further instructions, he handed Delcassé a French paraphrase of Salisbury's telegram of 9 September as an *aide-memoire*. Delcassé expressed no immediate opinion but had difficulty with the phrase "territories subject to the Khalifa," which he thought vague. He had "no accurate knowledge of their extent." Moreover, because the paraphrase failed to include a French phrase corresponding to "by right of conquest," he maintained that if Marchand were indeed at Fashoda, his rights were exactly the same as those of Kitchener at Khartoum. Monson refused to address Delcassé's argument. Instead, he continued to press for details about Marchand's whereabouts, while Delcassé continued to insist that he had no idea of the captain's location despite newspaper rumors that he had in fact reached Fashoda. Aware of the foreign minister's influence with the press, Monson noted sarcastically in his dispatch to Salisbury that the cue had apparently been given to the newspapers "to profess incredulity as to the presence of Captain Marchand at Fashoda, qualified in some cases with an expression of indifference as to the risk of a collision."[191]

---

[189]FO 78/5050, Tel.57, 9 September 1898, Salisbury to Monson; BD 189: 164; Brown, 93; Giffen, 60-62; Sanderson, 340; Uzoigwe, 268.

[190]FO 27/3399, Tel. 131, 10 September 1898, Foreign Office to Monson.

[191]FO 78/5050, D.449, 12 September 1898, Monson to Salisbury.

Monson, however, had missed undoubtedly the subtlety of Salisbury's instructions and thus failed to convey the prime minister's offer to initiate negotiations over other disputed territories. Because he tended to read most of the prime minister's instructions in light of the 1895 Grey Declaration and the Note of 10 December 1897, both of which expressed Britain's uncompromising position that no other power had any claim or right to occupy any part of the Nile valley, Monson interpreted his orders as precluding any discussion at all. Throughout the course of the crisis, therefore, Monson never delivered Salisbury's intended carrot.[192]

Monson and Delcassé came to no conclusions, due to the lack of information from Fashoda and Monson's failure to convey Salisbury's offer of negotiations. This conversation, however, betrays indications of how ineffective Monson would prove to be during the Fashoda negotiations. With or without explicit instructions, the ambassador tended to answer evasively, elaborate on Salisbury's comments to Courcel, or defer the matter to London; this indeed became representative of discussions between the two men throughout the crisis. Moreover, Monson was never confident about how to interpret Delcassé's attitude. He clearly doubted the foreign minister's avowed ignorance of Marchand's location; yet he acknowledged that in other matters, Delcassé appeared anxious to avoid all difficulty with Britain. Delcassé followed up his numerous professions of desire for better relations by proposing one of his most trusted ambassadors, the Anglophile Paul Cambon, currently the French representative to the Ottoman Empire, to replace Courcel who had just announced his intention to retire.[193]

---

[192]Brown, 88-89; Sanderson, 340; Wood, 170.

[193]BD 191: 165-166; Keith Eubank, *Paul Cambon: Master Diplomatist* (Norman: University of Oklahoma Press, 1960), 62; C. Porter, 134-135; Wood, 120-121, 171.

Monson's ultimate ineffectiveness was also the result of his inability to navigate the growing internal insanity within France, which continued to intensify. He reported that while public opinion appeared largely uninterested in Egypt and the Sudan, the French press in mid-September began to respond to the impending crisis with increasing dissatisfaction. Several Parisian newspapers complained about their government's apparent inactivity. Many right-wing papers (i.e., *Le Soleil, Le Gaulois, L' Eclair*, and *La Patrie*) as well as moderate papers (i.e., *Le Figaro, Le Temps*, and *Le Matin*) argued that it was time to resolve the Egyptian question. Marchand's exploits, they contended, had given France a legitimate claim to the Upper Nile. They were incensed by continuing British insults and contemptuous demands for Marchand's unconditional withdrawal. Since Omdurman, argued the *Journal des Débats* (20 September), the French press had maintained an attitude of "perfect courtesy. . . . It has been answered from the other side of the channel by an explosion of rage and of hate." *Autorité* observed (23 September) that the current campaign in the British press began while France was absorbed in the Dreyfus affair: "They must have a pitiful idea in London of our government if they suppose that it is capable of cowardice in the face of such pretensions."[194] Monson, unceasingly sensitive to anti-British invective in the Parisian newspapers, reported that although the press reaction in early September to the British military victories was largely complimentary, French newspaper opinion remained censorious and sarcastic. Editorials made insinuations about the conduct of British troops in the field at Omdurman, that they were pitiless, refusing to "spare the weaker sex when occasion offers and their blood is up." Moreover, the Paris newspapers mocked the

---

[194]Brown, 86-87; Carroll, 167-168, 172-173; Peterson, 115.

British public for expressing regret, while rejoicing in a brilliant victory, at the "smallness of the 'butcher's bill.'"[195] By the end of the month, while most of the boulevard journals continued to indulge in their characteristically scurrilous attacks against London, anti-British sentiment had increased "even in the newspapers that may be called serious."[196]

In the meantime, the Dreyfus affair continued to take its toll on the cabinet. General Zurlinden, who accepted the War Ministry with the understanding that he be given time to study the dossier before agreeing to revision, concluded as did his predecessor Cavaignac that Henry's forgery was irrelevant to the ultimate question of Dreyfus's guilt. Therefore, Zurlinden regarded the charge of treason against Esterhazy to be baseless and joined those opposed to revision. When the Brisson ministry voted to submit the case to a judicial board for reconsideration, Zurlinden promptly resigned and was replaced by General C.S.J. Chanoine. Like his two immediate predecessors, Chanoine appeared sympathetic toward revision. On 26 September, however, when the ministry voted to submit Lucie Dreyfus's application to the Criminal Court of Appeal, the general abstained.

Throughout the balance of September, Monson continued to file dispatches concerning the Dreyfus case, most of which were numbing in length and detail. While he had been encouraged by the appointment of General Zurlinden, he grew ever more weary and ever more disgusted with the case. Monson correctly observed that the fundamental issue had become less a question of Dreyfus's innocence or guilt and more a question of

---

[195]FO 27/3396, D. 438, 6 September 1898, Monson to Salisbury. See also Monson's reports to Salisbury in FO 27/3396: D. 447, 12 September 1898; D. 456, 13 September 1898; D. 457; 14 September 1898; D. 465, 20 September 1898.

[196]FO 27/3397, D. 489, 30 September 1898, Monson to Salisbury.

confidence in the "legitimacy or illegitimacy in the proceedings of the Court-Martial." In other words, the key issue involved confidence in the French army. According to Monson, the French public began to believe that its government was in the hands of a "sinister conspiracy" ultimately aimed at the dismantling of the French military establishment. A week later, therefore, Monson reversed his earlier position and speculated that the Brisson cabinet could not remain in office much longer because "the majority of its members are openly revisionists."[197]

He became increasingly alarmed by the hardening of attitudes on both sides. Anti-Semitic violence continued to spread and rumors began to circulate of a military *coup d'état*, scheduled to occur with the reconvening of the Chamber of Deputies on 25 October. The belief in a "sinister conspiracy," magnified by the widespread condemnation of France by the international press, led to profound national resentment and defensiveness. The ministry came under increasing pressure from the Dreyfusard left for not acting quickly or resolutely enough in advancing revision and suppressing the continuing violence. At the same time, the nationalistic anti-Dreyfusard right was grouped around the *Ligue des Patriotes* and the *Ligue antisémitique*, both of which sought to provoke the military into overthrowing the cabinet in a *coup d'etat*. The two groups, although quite different, worked for the same objective. The *Ligue des Patriotes*, formed in 1882 by Paul Déroulède, had been dissolved when the Boulangist movement failed but reconstituted in September 1898. It represented a populist radical reactionary nationalism. It was fundamentally hostile to parliamentary government but was opposed to

---

[197]FO 27/3396, D. 453, 13 September 1898, Monson to Salisbury. See also Monson's reports to Salisbury in FO 27/3396: D. 459, 16 September 1898; D. 463, 18 September 1898; D.475, 23 September 1898; D.481, 27 September 1898.

royal government as well. Its rank and file consisted of approximately 60,000 members, the bulk of whom were in Paris, middle class, and lower middle class. The *Ligue antisémitique*, a particularly nasty and violent anti-Semitic organization, was formed by Jules Guérin in 1897. It consisted of anywhere from 5,000 to 10,000 members who operated not only in Paris but through active affiliates and branches in numerous other cities and towns. Its leader, Jules Guérin, received substantial support and very large secret subsidies on a regular basis from the main royalist pretender, the exiled *Duc d'Orleans* Prince Philippe who hoped that the anti-Semites would sufficiently disrupt the political situation that royalists could seize power and restore the monarchy. While the *Ligue antisémitique* tended to be more violently anti-Semitic and the *Ligue des Patriotes* tended to be more anti-Republic, both organizations made themselves loud and disruptive factors during the Affair, through street violence, public rallies and demonstrations.[198]

In the meantime, labor unrest in Paris began to spread. On 13 September excavation workers at the sites of the Paris International Exposition responded to calls for higher wages and voted to strike; within three weeks, over 30,000 construction workers had walked off their work sites. This labor unrest quickly intertwined with the politics of the Dreyfus affair and thus contributed to the continuing polarization of French society. Pro- and anti-Dreyfus politicians alike attempted to court the strikers. While the effort to recruit workers to the revisionist cause was only partially successful, right-wing nationalists

---

[198]FO 27/3396, D.453, 13 September 1898, Monson to Salisbury; Bredin, 348-349; Brown, 90-91; Maurice Larkin, "'La Republique en Danger?' The Pretenders, the Army and Déroulède, 1898-1899," *English Historical Journal*, C, 394 (January 1985): 91-92; Peter M. Rutkoff, *Revanche and Revisionism: The Ligue Des Patriotes and the Origins of the Radical Right in France, 1882-1900* (Athens & London: Ohio University Press, 1981), 1-3.

condemned strikers as part of a Dreyfusard conspiracy to weaken the nation. To most workers, however, whether Dreyfusard or anti-Dreyfusard, the quarrel over Egypt and the Upper Nile was irrelevant compared to the fight for shorter working hours and better wages. On several occasions revisionist speakers were shouted down when they tried to introduce politics into strike meetings. Many other workers' groups were openly anti-Dreyfusard. Right-wing groups nonetheless saw this as a suitably troubled background to conspire against the government. They spread rumors of a military *coup d'etat*, called meetings, and hired thugs to stir up excitement in the streets. Nationalist gangs disrupted several Dreyfusard demonstrations; those of 8 September, 15 September, and 17 September were particularly violent. When the government moved over 60,000 troops into Paris to keep order, the nationalists hoped that the soldiers might be inspired to divert their energies against the government that was supposedly failing to uphold the honor of the army against the Dreyfusards and the honor of the nation against the British at Fashoda.[199]

The atmosphere in Paris during the last two weeks of September seemed explosive. As a result, Delcassé met with Monson in a considerably more agitated frame of mind during their interview on 18 September. Although the foreign minister reiterated his desire for more cordial relations with London, he pressed his earlier argument that Marchand's rights at Fashoda were exactly the same as those of Kitchener at Khartoum. Assuming that the captain was already at Fashoda as the British newspapers were asserting, was the French government to understand that he had no right to be there? Monson simply repeated

---

[199]Bredin, 342; Brown, 101-103; Chapman, 234-235; Langer, *Diplomacy of Imperialism*, 553-554; Larkin, 87; Lewis, *Prisoners of Honor*, 251; Riker, 66-67; Rutkoff, 89-90; Sanderson, 359; Tuchman, 212, 251.

his previous non-response that Fashoda, a dependency of the Khalifate, had passed into the hands of Britain and Egypt by right of conquest and that any French advance into the Upper Nile basin would therefore be considered an unfriendly act: "Why, then, did they send this mission, when they must know what serious results its success in reaching this point must inevitably produce?" Delcassé reminded the ambassador that France had never recognized the British sphere of influence in the Upper Nile and that Hanotaux openly protested against it in the French Senate. Moreover, he argued, there never really was a "Marchand mission." The captain was in fact subordinate to Liotard, whose mission had been launched in 1893, long before the Grey Declaration made known London's uncompromising position. As Delcassé's assertion suffered from a selective recollection of facts,[200] Monson again resisted being drawn into a discussion of legalities and refused to consider Delcassé's line of argument. He agreed that the situation on the Upper Nile was dangerous; however, while London did not wish to pick a quarrel it would not consent to a compromise. He did not understand how the British position could cause any surprise in Paris "if we resent a step which we had cautioned France not to take."[201]

This would be the final meeting between the two men while they awaited information from the Upper Nile. In the interim Monson's attention remained consumed by the continuing deterioration in Paris. The strike activity continued to spread. As negotiations with the excavators

---

[200]First, the Monteil mission was launched in 1893; the Liotard mission was launched in late 1894. Second, the Marchand mission was approved in late 1895, several months after the Grey Declaration. Third, the status between Marchand and Liotard changed in November 1897. Bates, 152; Brown, 89-90; Giffen, 38-40; Sanderson, 8-9.

[201]FO 78/5050, Tel.137, 18 September 1898, Monson to Salisbury; FO 78/5050, D.471, 22 September 1897, Monson to Salisbury.

dragged on, the railwaymen's union announced that its members would stop work at the end of the first week in October. Tempers aroused by the Dreyfus affair continued to stir further anti-Semitic violence, mass demonstrations, duels, and cries to overthrow the French government.[202]

Faced with growing disorder and hopelessly divided over revision, the Brisson ministry appeared irresolute and weak. Nevertheless, Delcassé believed that the cabinet could be strengthened by both a vigorous suppression of domestic strife and a carefully staged diplomatic victory. Although he no longer believed that the Marchand mission had any chance for success, he chose to rely upon Salisbury's reputation for making graceful concessions. He hoped that London would make some territorial concessions in the Upper Nile that could be presented to the public and the Chamber as a diplomatic success. On 26 September, however, he learned from Monson that Marchand had reached Fashoda.

---

[202]Brown, 89-92; Rutkoff, 91; Sanderson, 340-341; Tuchman, 251.

Chapter Eight

"AS IMPOSSIBLE AS IT IS ABSURD"

On Sunday 25 September Salisbury received Kitchener's two telegrams from Omdurman. The telegrams, which provided the first news to reach Europe about the meeting at Fashoda and the condition of the French expedition, reflected the spirit and tenor of Kitchener's comprehensive report. They described the British arrival at Fashoda, the meeting with Marchand, the formal protest and departure. Kitchener's description, however, proved considerably more dramatic and apparently written with public consumption in mind:

> The position in which Captain Marchand finds himself at Fashoda is as impossible as it is absurd. He is cut off from the interior, and his water transport is quite inadequate; he is, moreover, short of ammunition and supplies, which must take months to reach him; he has no following in the country, and nothing could have saved him and his expedition from being annihilated by the Dervishes had we been a fortnight later in crushing the Khalifa.

Kitchener asserted that Marchand realized the futility of all his efforts and seemed "quite as anxious to return as we are to facilitate his departure." In transmitting Kitchener's telegrams, Rennell Rodd, the British Acting Agent in Cairo in the absence of Cromer, wrote the prime minister that if the French government would issue instructions for Marchand to withdraw from Fashoda, a special steamer could be dispatched immediately to bring out the expedition: "In view of the unpleasant position in which M. Marchand and his officers are at present placed, I am quite sure that no one would be more pleased at this arrangement for their release than they would themselves be."

In the meantime, Kitchener had ordered Major Jackson not to accept any letters from the French expedition nor to allow them to use the Nile route either for their official reports or personal letters. Furthermore, the British would not allow Marchand to use the telegraph at Omdurman. For the first crucial weeks therefore -- and in fact throughout most of the crisis -- the only accounts to be considered by the French and British governments were those of Kitchener. Because Marchand had no immediate or reliable means of communicating his version of events or his appreciation of the situation, Kitchener was able to present the situation in such a light that the French government would see no alternative but to order Marchand's withdrawal. Much of Kitchener's account indeed was misleading or blatantly untrue. There existed no evidence of illness. There existed no evidence of depression or indiscipline. The French had more boats than Kitchener asserted. Kitchener misconstrued Marchand's claim that the French could not resist another Mahdist attack or wished to retire from Fashoda (according to both Wingate and Cecil, the French had heard from the Shilluk that prior to Kitchener's arrival a large force of Dervish gunboats and soldiers were coming up the river to make a second attack and that "they were very naturally relieved when they discovered that the force was British"). Perhaps most misleading Kitchener claimed that the French were "short on ammunition and supplies." In fact, after the arrival of the *Faidherbe* in August, their stocks were replenished with four months of supplies and ammunition. Gardens planted at Fashoda supplied with fresh vegetables, while each soldier had his own groundsheet and mosquito net. When Marchand finally left Fashoda in December 1898, he handed over to Jackson fifteen tons of flour for which he had no further use. Kitchener's account, therefore, proved to be brilliant propaganda. British opinion saw in the Marchand expedition a hapless band of destitute explorers marooned in the darkest of Africa, saved from disaster only by the timely and fortuitous arrival of Kitchener.[203]

In London that afternoon, 25 September, upon receipt of Kitchener's telegrams, Salisbury immediately sent a private note to Queen Victoria reporting that Marchand was short of ammunition and supplies and "anxious to get away." That evening he sent copies of Rodd's telegrams to Monson with instructions to read them aloud to Delcassé on the understanding that the communication is a verbal one. He added, "you had better not leave a copy."[204]

Monson did not see the foreign minister until nearly 1600 on Monday afternoon due to a late meeting of the French council of ministers. He laid the telegrams before Delcassé, who was instantly relieved that no armed clash

---

[203]FO 78/5051, Tel.244, 25 September 1898, Rodd to Salisbury; FO 78/5051, Tel.245, 25 September 1898, Rodd to Salisbury; BD 193: 167-168; BD 194: 168; Bates, 136-141; Sanderson, 336-339.

[204]FO 27/3399, Tel.200, 25 September 1898, Salisbury to Monson; BD 195: 169; FO 27/3399, Tel.201, 26 September 1898, Salisbury to Monson; FO 27/3399, Tel.202, 26 September 1898, Salisbury to Monson.

had occurred. He expressed personal gratification at the dignified manner in which the meeting took place but would be unable to respond formally until after another ministerial council the next day. Delcassé therefore asked for something in writing to show his colleagues who would want something more definitive than his own recollections of those telegrams. Salisbury thus authorized Monson to communicate an *aide-memoire* which summarized the proceedings at Fashoda or to allow Delcassé to make notes for his own convenience. The foreign minister would be allowed to take these to his colleagues.[205]

On Tuesday 27 September, the Brisson ministry formally addressed the Fashoda situation for the first time. Delcassé described Marchand's position in terms of Kitchener's telegram and Monson's briefing of the previous day. He came under particularly strong pressure from Colonial Minister Trouillot, who was incensed by the implications in Kitchener's telegrams that Marchand was short of food and ammunition. He argued that in fact Marchand was well provisioned, with 130,000 cartridges and 18,000 kilograms of wheat, and that at least three relief missions would soon reach Fashoda from the French Congo and Ethiopia. The Colonial Minister asserted that Marchand could and should hold his ground. The principal problem for the ministry of course was its lack of accurate intelligence. The recent suicide of Colonel Henry, the chief of the General Staff's counterintelligence bureau, fell heavily on French intelligence operations, which had provided the Quai d'Orsay with regular and reliable military and political intelligence. Henry's death seriously disrupted the

---

[205]FO 78/5051, Tel.147, 26 September 1898, Monson to Salisbury; FO 27/3400, Tel.143, 26 September 1898, Monson to Salisbury; FO 78/5051, Tel.148, 26 September 1898, Monson to Salisbury; FO 78/5051, D.480, 27 September 1898, Monson to Salisbury;.

agency's normal routine of collecting and transmitting intelligence. As a result, the flow of vital information to the Ministries of War and Foreign Affairs was significantly reduced. Faced with this difference of opinion, the ministry decided to request a situation report from Marchand and to defer any decision until after it reached Paris. Given the lack of French communication facilities, however, this would not be an easy undertaking. The government could communicate with Marchand only via the British telegraph office in Cairo.[206]

Delcassé sent for Monson that evening and informed him that the Quai d'Orsay could not proceed until it received information from Marchand. According to Kitchener's telegram, reports sent by the captain from the French Congo and Ethiopia clearly would not reach Paris for some time. Because the French government "would be embarrassed to act without being made acquainted with the situation by their own agent," Delcassé requested permission to send a telegram to Khartoum "*en clair*, if wished." Marchand would be instructed to send a copy of his report to Cairo by one of the officers of his mission "so that the Government might be made acquainted with its contents as soon as possible."

Monson suspected -- correctly -- that Delcassé was playing for time and asked if he was to understand that the French government had decided not to recall Marchand until it received his report. Marchand's position appeared to be a disagreeable one and "he himself stated to be desirous of retiring from it; did [Delcassé] continue to refuse to recall M. Marchand at once?" Delcassé replied that he was ready to make concessions. If Monson pressed him for the impossible, however, "there could be but one answer." Preliminary discussions might begin without receiving Marchand's report but that was all he could do.

---

[206]Bates, 145-146; Brown, 88, 96-97; Peterson, 115.

When Monson again referred to Salisbury's prohibition of all discussion on such questions as Egypt's right to Fashoda, Delcassé retorted that "if there was to be no discussion, a rupture could not be avoided." The British position was vague, he argued. France should have some clear and explicit definition of what constituted Egyptian territory. Moreover, why was the French claim at Fashoda different or worse than those of the Belgians at Lado and the British at Wadelai? He begged Monson not to drive him into a corner by refusing to entertain his request for permission to transmit a message to Marchand. The Parisian press was already asserting that the captain had been abandoned by the government and was portraying Delcassé as the "author of national disgrace." Monson agreed to do so but only due to the foreign minister's "pressing appeal not to drive him to extremities."[207]

To be sure, public criticism of Delcassé began to mount. Immediately following the cabinet meeting of 27 September, Trouillot and his allies in the colonial lobby began to increase pressure on the Foreign Ministry by focusing public attention on Fashoda. Without the clearance of the Quai d'Orsay, he and Gustave Binger, the head of the colonial ministry's Africa bureau, briefed a journalist from the right-wing newspaper *Le Gaulois* on previously undisclosed facts about the Kitchener-Marchand encounter. The result was a series of sharply anti-British articles that not only enraged the *parti colonial* in the Chamber of Deputies but in turn inspired equally belligerent headlines in British newspapers. Conservative London journals, including the *Times*, the *Morning Post*, and the *Evening News*, regarded Trouillot's revelations as official French policy and demanded an immediate public clarification of British policy.

---

[207]FO 27/3400 and FO 78/5051, Tel.151, 27 September 1898, Monson to Salisbury; BD 196: 169-170; Rolo, 87; Sanderson, 341.

This new development, the waging of policy debates in popular newspapers, dramatically altered the framework of the dialogue. Salisbury and Delcassé had endeavored to keep their discussions on the level of cabinet diplomacy, largely because both believed that any public presentation of official points of view would arouse popular opinion and upset the flexibility of their negotiations. Heightened newspaper rhetoric on both sides of the Channel, however, brought both men under increasing pressure to make their official positions public. Just as Delcassé had complained to Monson that he was being hammered in the Parisian press, Salisbury also found himself under growing newspaper criticism. On 27 September the *Daily News* asserted that the "chief element of danger is to be found in the widespread belief prevailing on the continent that Lord Salisbury's squeezability is unlimited."[208]

Salisbury therefore decided to publish a diplomatic Blue Book. When Monson transmitted the French request for permission to send a telegram to Marchand, Salisbury sarcastically agreed to convey a message "to a French explorer who finds himself in a difficult position on the Upper Nile." He instructed Monson to point out that if the current situation was prolonged, "great uneasiness will be caused here, and some immediate publication of the facts by the Government will become necessary." The ambassador was to ask how much of Delcassé's recent communications on the subject London could consider itself at liberty to publish. Salisbury's stratagem represented a deviation from traditional diplomatic practice, in which the publication of selected diplomatic documents occurred only *after* a dispute was resolved. His objective was to put pressure on Delcassé. If Paris, he informed Monson, would announce the withdrawal of

[208]Brown, 97-98; Peterson, 115-116.

Marchand and his mission, further publication for the time being would be unnecessary.[209] Delcassé declared that if any such publication came from London, he would be compelled to make a communiqué of a similar nature. He appealed to Salisbury that "the prospect of conducting a Polemic in the press would be any more pleasing to Your Lordship than to himself." Monson suggested that the foreign minister was "evidently afraid" of the effect of any official publication on French public opinion.[210]

Without question, finding himself under growing pressure from the French colonial lobby and forced to assume a more belligerent public posture than he would have otherwise desired, Delcassé carried a heightened tone of combativeness into his discussions with Monson. During their interview of 28 September, the foreign minister was particularly contentious. While he regretted Trouillot's indiscretions, Delcassé vehemently maintained France's right to occupy territory "practically abandoned" by Egypt. He resented Britain's alleged right to warn off other powers that had not recognized London's claims of dominion or to declare the French advance an "unfriendly act." Furthermore, Delcassé audaciously insisted upon British concessions in the Upper Nile. He was willing to go far to secure a friendly settlement and added that he preferred London's friendship to that of Russia. He must not be faced, however, with impossible demands or there might be an explosion of French sentiment he would be powerless to control. While Delcassé acknowledged that national feeling was strong in Britain, he argued that Britons were not as excitable as the French and generally "felt sentimental considerations less deeply." Monson as always refused to entertain any discussion of British

[209]FO 27/3399, Tel.206, 28 September 1898, Salisbury to Monson; BD 197: 170-171; Brown, note, 98; Peterson, 111.

[210]FO 78/5051, Tel.156, 29 September 1898, Monson to Salisbury.

concessions and answered that it would be impossible to exaggerate the excitement in Britain, either on the part of the public or the government. The emotions currently aroused on both sides of the Channel, he admitted, caused him much apprehension. When Delcassé protested that "you surely would not break with us over Fashoda," Monson replied that it was "exactly that which I feared." In that case, Delcassé warned, France "would not stand alone," intimating the promise of Russian assistance.

Delcassé's frank and implicit threat of Russian support startled Monson and caused him to abandon his initial optimism that the French would be prepared to discuss and resolve the question with calmness. For the first time, he expressed the opinion that the French government would not back down from a confrontation. He wrote Salisbury: "Personally, I see very little hope of their sending M. Marchand an order to leave Fashoda."[211]

Like Monson, Delcassé began to fear the possibility of a military confrontation. He grew despondent, haunted by the prospect that London would formally demand France's withdrawal from Fashoda, to be followed by an ultimatum if necessary. His anxiety was heightened by a telegram from the Italian ambassador Tornielli to his government, intercepted by the *cabinet noir* on 30 September, which reported Monson's receipt of instructions from Salisbury to deliver an ultimatum demanding Marchand's immediate withdrawal. Although the information was false, Delcassé believed it to be accurate; when Monson called on him that afternoon, he believed that the ambassador was carrying a written ultimatum in his coat.[212]

Not surprisingly, Monson found the foreign minister

---

[211]FO 78/5051, D.486, 28 September 1898, Monson to Salisbury; FO 27/3399 and FO 78/5051, Tel.154, 28 September 1898, Monson to Salisbury; BD 198: 171; Sanderson, 342; Wood, 175-176.

[212]Blunt II, 123; Brown, 99.

in an emotional mood. Delcassé declared in language "more adamant" than usual that so long as London refused even to discuss the right of France to occupy Fashoda, it would be impossible for the French government to withdraw Marchand. They would consider any formal demand to retire as an ultimatum and would reject it: "Very well, Mr. Ambassador; France, through me, answers in advance: No!" While he professed his continuing desire for an understanding, Delcassé warned that France would accept war although reluctantly rather than swallow such an insult to national honor: "Whilst I may sacrifice material interests, the honour of the nation will remain intact as long as it is in my hands. No capitulation can be expected from the minister who stands before you." Monson, taken somewhat aback by Delcassé's abruptness, remained evasive. As in their previous interviews, he simply repeated the British position and refused to discuss the matter further. London had signified its point of view, he reminded Delcassé, "and for my part, I did not see how they could possibly retreat from it."[213]

Monson did not deliver any ultimatum, prompting Delcassé to believe that he had scored a diplomatic triumph. Moreover, as no ultimatum appeared over the next few days, Delcassé grew optimistic that the British were willing to negotiate.[214] In fact, he did achieve a minor success: Monson bought completely, at least for the moment, the foreign minister's threat of war -- that France would go to war rather than endure yet another affront to national honor. On 1 October Monson wrote a strongly worded dispatch devoted almost entirely to a statement of the French position. Similar to many of his warnings

---

[213]FO 27/3400 and FO 78/5051, Tel.160, 30 September 1898, Monson to Salisbury; BD 200: 172; Andrew, 98-99; Brown, 99; Sanderson, 342; Wood, 176-177.

[214]Andrew, 99-100; Wright, 185-186.

during the West African negotiations earlier in the year, Monson advised Salisbury that British inflexibility posed the most formidable obstacle to a resolution of the crisis. From the French point of view, London's unwillingness even to discuss the French right to be at Fashoda, the threat of humiliation, and insults to their national honor made a break inevitable. Delcassé's position remained hostage to the current public and political volatility, stirred by the Dreyfus affair and its accompanying demonstrations and strikes, all of which rendered the predicament of the government more than usually delicate. Given the irritation of the French army and a large portion of the public, the recall of Marchand was utterly impossible. "There is really no hope," Monson wrote, "that he will consent to send M. Marchand orders to retire." Such a step would involve the immediate fall of the ministry and would be disavowed by their successors: "Any symptom of weakness on the Fashoda question would be the signal for their downfall within twenty-four hours of the meeting of the Chamber."[215]

While Monson accepted wrongly Delcassé's promise that France would fight for Fashoda, he was correct nonetheless that the foreign minister had little if any flexibility in pursuit of anything other than a belligerent policy. Monson maintained from the beginning that so long as domestic pressures did not force Delcassé's hand the French would resolve the Upper Nile dispute with "calmness." By late September, however, as the Fashoda negotiations proceeded without any apparent prospect of resolution, the French government appeared increasingly incapable of maintaining control over its domestic unrest; hence, Delcassé's current defiance.

Delcassé understood the domestic and diplomatic

---

[215]FO 78/5051, D.491, 1 October 1898, Monson to Salisbury; Bates, 154; Brown, 99-100; Wood, 176-178.

realities that restricted his options. Above all, however, he sought to save France from humiliation and thus save the ministry. He realized that the best for which he could hope were some material concessions from London -- perhaps an outlet to the Nile River -- in return for the recall of Marchand. In spite of his failure to draw Monson into direct talks, Delcassé remained optimistic that Salisbury would negotiate along those lines. In one respect, he continued to rely upon the prime minister's reputation for making graceful concessions. Geoffray continued to report from London that while the press and public violently opposed any concessions, Salisbury continued to speak in conciliatory terms, apparently intent to avoid armed conflict. More to the point, he knew that Salisbury's interest in the Upper Nile valley was confined to the main course of the river between Lake Victoria and Khartoum -- and that he did not wish to assume the burden of administering and paying for what he once dismissed contemptuously as "wretched stuff."

The prospect of domestic turbulence convinced Delcassé that he had to make some definitive move before the arrival of Marchand's report. On 3 October he brought the Fashoda question before a ministerial council for a second hearing. Delcassé reviewed the details of his 30 September interview with Monson, in which he "prevented" the ambassador from issuing the British ultimatum, referring to their meeting as an "historic day." He explained to his colleagues that the recall of Marchand would be the only alternative to a pointless war. This action could be taken without injury to the national honor if France acquired territorial concessions in the Upper Nile. Accordingly, he sent Courcel back to London to press once again for such concessions.[216]

Delcassé's confidence in Salisbury's willingness to

---

[216]Andrew, 99-100; Bates, 152-155; Brown, 100-101; Wright, 111.

compromise, however, proved to be misplaced. In spite of Monson's ominous dispatch of 1 October Salisbury dismissed the foreign minister's declarations that France would go to war. Although he fundamentally remained willing to consider some token concession in the Upper Nile valley rather than embitter Anglo-French relations, Salisbury found himself under growing pressure from two directions to assume an intransigent position. First, he faced increasingly militant opposition within his cabinet to any compromise with France, particularly after Trouillot's disclosures of 27 September. Second, he understood that the British public simply would not stand for a policy of graceful concessions. This pressure compelled Salisbury to dismiss, albeit gracefully, the Queen's concern about the consequences of war. She telegraphed Salisbury on 2 October: "It seems a deadlock. The French Government do not telegraph Marchand to leave and he will be starved out and unable to remain for lack of water. Could we not delay till the French Government receive his report which can, I believe, come only through us?" While sympathetic to the Queen's frustration at the ongoing stalemate, Salisbury responded that her government was waiting and could do nothing further. "No offer of territorial concession on our part would be endured by public opinion here." Queen Victoria agreed to trust the cabinet. "Quite agree," she wrote Salisbury. "We cannot give way . . . If we wait, I think the force of circumstances will being the French to their senses."[217]

Therefore, in spite of his conciliatory words and gestures, Salisbury made it clear to Paris that Britain would not purchase a French evacuation of Fashoda with

---

[217]LQV, 289-290; Robert Massie, *Dreadnought: Britain, Germany, and the Coming of the Great War* (New York: Random House, 1991), 254; Peterson, 117; Sanderson, 342-343.

territorial concessions. In fact, he began to exert more pressure. After Kitchener had informed the cabinet that there would be "no great practical difficulty" in persuading Marchand to capitulate by cutting off all supplies, Salisbury instructed Rennell Rodd on 1 October to make Marchand's position "as untenable as possible." Until Paris expressed its intention of withdrawing the mission from Fashoda, no supplies were to be furnished to him "except in case of extreme necessity."[218] Salisbury instructed Monson to remain firm in upholding London's position; he should reiterate to Delcassé that whether in times of Egyptian or Mahdist dominion, "the region in which Marchand was found has never been without an owner" and that his expedition had absolutely "no political significance attached to it."[219]

Acting on these new instructions, Monson assumed a posture of nearly belligerent obstinance to Delcassé's line of negotiation. When Delcassé argued on Tuesday October that Salisbury seemed to imply that Fashoda had been under the rule of the Mahdists and that the French might therefore contend that they had not taken it from Egypt, Monson flatly refused to entertain any other interpretation. Salisbury's language, he countered, implied that Mahdist dominion had been extended only temporarily. Delcassé also expressed strong objections to Salisbury's intent to publish a diplomatic Blue Book and requested that its publication be delayed until around 23-24 October. Because French Yellow Books were usually not published during parliamentary vacations, Delcassé would have to wait three weeks in order to produce his own collection of documents. Otherwise, he feared that an earlier publication of a British Blue Book would whip up

---

[218]BD 201: 172-173; Grenville, 226, 230; Langer, *Diplomacy of Imperialism*, 553, 556; Sanderson, 342-343.

[219]FO 27/3399, Tel.213, 3 October 1898, Salisbury to Monson; BD 202: 173; Uzoigwe, 269.

excitement on both sides of the Channel and that the French newspapers would resent the inadequacy of the ministry's defense. Monson replied that although an increase in newspaper rhetoric would be regrettable, he believed it impossible for Salisbury to consent to a delay. He suggested that Delcassé in the meantime send a *communique* to the press, announcing the preparation of a Yellow Book by the opening of the Chamber.[220]

This interview brought Delcassé to a crossroad. After three weeks of unproductive and unsatisfactory conversations with Monson had thoroughly frustrated his efforts to work out a compromise with the British government. He needed a diplomatic victory even a minor one in order to defuse the growing resolve among colonial and army hotheads to stand firm against the British and thus to save, if only temporarily, the Brisson ministry. Specifically, he needed Salisbury to agree to concessions in exchange for Marchand's withdrawal. By early October, however, Delcassé had utterly failed to engage Monson in any serious discussion along those lines. Whether the ambassador was unable or unwilling to engage in any substantive negotiations, Delcassé concluded that it was now necessary to approach Salisbury directly through his own agent in Britain.

On Tuesday evening, following his meeting with Monson, Delcassé sent Courcel back to London. He ordered the French ambassador, who had been on leave in Paris pending his retirement, to persuade Salisbury that in return for the recall of Marchand, France should be allowed to keep a toe-hold in the Bahr al-Ghazal at least on paper as an outlet to the Nile. During their conversation the next day, Courcel asserted once again that the country bordering the White Nile, although

---

[220]FO 78/5051, Tel.163, 4 October 1898, Monson to Salisbury; FO 78/5051, D.498, 4 October 1898, Monson to Salisbury.

formerly under the dominion of Egypt, was *res nullius* by "its abandonment on the part of the Egyptian government." He added that in April 1895 Lord Kimberley (foreign minister in the Rosebery cabinet) had assured him that France as well as Britain possessed rights in the Upper Nile and had agreed to leave the matter alone so long as the situation there remained unchanged. The situation of course had now been modified by the British victory at Omdurman and the French occupation of Fashoda, two events that had, Courcel maintained, "precisely similar legal status." France therefore had as much a right to a position on the Nile as did the Germans, Belgians, and British.

Salisbury bluntly reemphasized that the British position was based on one overriding fact: Kitchener's preponderance of power *on the spot*. He conceded that although the Egyptian right to the Upper Nile had "certainly been rendered dormant" by the military successes of the Mahdists, that right was "entirely transferred to its conqueror." He reminded Courcel that 40,000 British and Egyptian soldiers with abundant stores and arms, a railway at their disposal, and a fleet of gunboats, faced eight French officers and 120 Senegalese soldiers. Even Delcassé clearly understood this fact; in a letter to his wife, he wrote that "all we have is arguments and they have soldiers right on the spot."[221] Moreover, Salisbury continued, there existed no grounds in international law for asserting that the controversy over rights between the Mahdists and Egypt, which could be settled only in battle, authorized a third party to "seize the disputed region as vacant or relinquished territory." The region that Marchand now claimed was in fact "territory already owned and occupied, and concerning which France had received repeated warnings that a seizure of

---

[221]Andrew, 100.

land in that locality could not be accepted."[222] Nevertheless, Paris sought to establish a title over the Upper Nile with such a small force that, were it not for Kitchener's timely arrival, Marchand and his men would almost certainly have been destroyed by the Khalifa. Therefore, France should not be surprised that their claim "would not be recognized by us."[223]

In the meantime, Salisbury pointed out that he could wait no longer to publish the diplomatic Blue Book about the crisis. British public agitation over Fashoda was growing more virulent and he himself was under increasing political attack. Continued public ignorance, he noted, would simply worsen the situation even more.[224]

The interview concluded without result. Courcel repeated the French offer to evacuate Fashoda in return for access to the Nile but made no definite proposition. Yet, he departed with an excessively hopeful assessment of the British intention to negotiate. In a lengthy and optimistic report, Courcel expressed confidence that Salisbury at the very least was beginning to soften his attitude. The prime minister had indicated that he wished to consult the views of his colleagues; he thought it preferable to wait and added that public opinion, once enlightened, "would regain its calm and moderation."

Courcel's dispatch raised Delcassé's hopes for a solution. On 5 October he noted, "the situation is still grave, but we are gaining time and time causes

---

[222]The warnings included the Anglo-German Agreement of 1890 (the "provisions of which . . . were never formally contested"); the Anglo-Congolese Agreement of 1894 (that the "rights of the Khedive over these territories were expressly asserted as still existing"); Sir Edward Grey's speech in 1895; and Monson's formal note in December 1897, which declared that the British government adhered to the statements made in Grey's speech. BD 203: 173-174; Sanderson, 344-345.

[223]BD 203: 173; Sanderson, 344-345.

[224]Peterson, 118-119.

reflection." He wrote to his wife that there appeared to be some growing "détente between England and ourselves," a détente he attributed to his own efforts: "My frankness and definitiveness, and the resolute, though perfectly courteous and moderate, tone of my language have made some impression. . . . I hope also further reflection has brought the conviction that England's real interest lies in fostering the friendship of France, and that for this friendship, a sacrifice of exclusive claims is reasonable."[225]

Salisbury, however, did not share Courcel's *optimisme*. In a letter to Monson, which the prime minister did not dispatch until 12 October, he wrote that nothing much was accomplished:

> We separated without coming to any conclusion; for I had no communication to make, except for the reiteration of our claim of right; and he made no suggestion of any arrangement by which that right could be reconciled with the present pretensions or desires of France.[226]

The prime minister, therefore, decided it would be safer to do nothing. For the time being, he would continue to apply diplomatic and military pressure on Delcassé. On 7 October, he authorized Major Jackson the British commander at Fashoda to blockade the French and prohibit all transport of war matériel on the Nile. Although Kitchener had formally placed the country in and around Fashoda under military law, Salisbury now authorized Jackson to take all necessary measures to enforce his orders. [227]

---

[225]Carroll, 173-174; Peterson, 119-120; Sanderson, 345-346.

[226]BD 203: 174-175; Wood, 180.

[227]BD 205: 176; Sanderson, 342-343.

Chapter Nine

GOLDEN BRIDGES FALLING DOWN

In early October the negotiations over Fashoda remained in stalemate. The crisis, however, entered a second and far more dangerous phase with the publication of the British Blue Book on 10 October. Until that point, Delcassé apparently had not fully comprehended the futility if not the absurdity of his diplomatic position. With the publication of the Blue Book, he finally began to appreciate that the French military position in the Upper Nile was untenable and that Marchand would have to be withdrawn. Continuing domestic turmoil, however, including the threat of a military *coup d'etat*, compelled him to pursue a somewhat contradictory strategy. On one hand, he attempted to mobilize French public opinion as an indication of the French willingness to fight. In this manner, Delcassé hoped to extract from the British the concessions he needed in order to appease those elements that favored resistance and therefore to retain political authority -- and political office -- at home. On the other hand, following the publication of the British Blue Book and the growing likelihood that he would not in fact obtain any concessions from Salisbury, Delcassé hesitated to make any further public statements that might so inflame public opinion as to render a French capitulation politically impossible. In London, Salisbury appreciated the precarious nature of Delcassé's political predicament; he continued furthermore to give indication that he favored compromise. The growing belligerence toward France, however, among the British public and within the cabinet, which included growing demands for preventive war, continued to circumscribe the prime minister's freedom of action. He thus withdrew from direct negotiations altogether, allowing the pressure to build until Delcassé reached the Rubicon in late October.

In early October 1898, Monson's role in the Fashoda dialogue began to change. Although he had been directly involved in discussions with Delcassé during the initial month of the crisis, the focus of the dialogue shifted in early October to London. When Delcassé initiated direct discussions with Salisbury through Courcel, Monson began to find himself on the periphery of the negotiations. Through the remainder of the month, but particularly during a two-week pause in the diplomatic dialogue, Monson endeavored to assess French policy and possible courses of action in the face of unfolding drama in Paris. Until the French decision to evacuate Fashoda in early November, the ambassador remained outside the principal discussions, his primary bearing on the crisis reduced to observation and the collection of information.

Monson's reduced role owed much to the personal styles of diplomatic conduct of Salisbury and Delcassé. Both men preferred to work through the French ambassador in London. Salisbury generally preferred to conduct British diplomacy in London with resident foreign ambassadors, particularly if these men enjoyed the confidence of their governments. He chose his own ambassadors carefully and usually allowed them a fair amount of independence, but he tended to ignore them.

Salisbury regarded them more or less as observers and reporters rather than as acting agents of British policy. Although he encouraged them to express their candid evaluations in private letters, his own contributions to this correspondence varied. The frequency of his letters often reflected the esteem in which he held a particular diplomat. Most representatives therefore rarely received more than three or four letters year a policy.[228] Delcassé, on the other hand, tended to avoid extensive conversations with foreign ambassadors altogether, preferring instead to conduct diplomatic business through his own representatives. He selected ambassadors who were highly capable, trusted, and sympathetic with his long-range goals, and he often gave them wide latitude in carrying out their missions.[229] Monson complained on a regular basis that Delcassé typically had little to say, even when he was not avoiding the ambassador outright. In June 1900, long after the Fashoda crisis, he wrote that the longer he dealt with Delcassé,

> the more I am persuaded by the correctness of the estimate made by my Italian colleague of [Delcassé's] method of doing business . . . that M. Delcassé preferred to have everything discussed with foreign governments by the French ambassadors accredited to them; and disliked conversing upon important questions with, or expressing any serious opinion to, the foreign ambassadors accredited to the French Republic.[230]

Monson's influence also suffered from growing dissatisfaction with his performance. Over the course of October, Salisbury and Delcassé both came to suspect the

---

[228]Grenville, 14; Steiner, 176, 178.

[229]Andrew, 66, 75-76; Brown, 10; C. Porter, 111-114.

[230]FO 27/3495, D.260, 5 June 1900, Monson to Salisbury.

ambassador's effectiveness and the reliability of his judgment. As a result, both men grew weary of dealing with him. Some of Monson's reports were inconsistent and inconclusive, and his nerves proved wobbly. When the situation appeared to drift toward war and revolution, Monson abandoned his previous caution and nervously warned his superiors in London to brace themselves for the worst. Salisbury had never shown particular confidence in Monson's abilities in any event. In 1888, for example, when Lord Lyons retired from the Paris embassy, Salisbury chose Lord Lytton previously the Viceroy to India as his successor. He reported to the Queen that there was no competition for the appointment. Even among other candidates, he noted, Monson did not possess enough ability. Similarly, in April 1893, when Rosebery sought to remove Sir Clare Ford as ambassador to the Ottoman Empire, the choice of the Queen and the Prince of Wales to replace Ford was Monson. Rosebery, however, had consulted Salisbury, who advised that "as there were no 'shining lights' in the service" he should appoint Sir Philip Currie of whom he had a very high opinion.[231] Salisbury considered Monson to be a mountain-out-of-a-molehill maker. In August 1899 the prime minister congratulated the Queen for her role in reducing anxieties between London and Berlin, noting that in France, "we have no such protection. Sir Edmund Monson is rather nervous, lest the extreme parties in France should see in a war with England the only refuge from disgraceful incidents in which France is now involved [Dreyfus]. But Sir Edmund always tends to be a prophet of evil; the danger does not appear to Lord Salisbury to be as yet of a serious kind."[232] Consequently, between September and December 1898, Monson

[231]Jones, 185-188; Uzoigwe, 12.
[232]LQV, 392-393.

received only two important letters from London. As a matter of fact, as Salisbury began to retreat from the dialogue and as the crisis had deepened, the prime minister wrote fewer and fewer letters to any of his ambassadors and virtually none to his cabinet colleagues. Cromer received only two letters while the Queen wrote more than she received. Nevertheless, when Monson complained that he had received no indication of Salisbury's views for more than six months, Sir Eric Barrington, the prime minister's secretary, wrote in November that Monson was "dreadfully hurt at never hearing from you, and he is not satisfied at being told that your silence is due to your perfect confidence in him." Salisbury replied with disgust: "What a plague his susceptibilities are. Writing to ambassadors generally does harm. However, I will try to put some verbiage together for tomorrow."[233]

In Paris Delcassé had become immensely frustrated by his failure to engage Monson in anything more than a superficial regurgitation of established positions. He suspected that the ambassador was only following orders but probably interpreting them more rigidly than Salisbury intended.[234] By early October he assumed that his own efforts to obtain concessions in the Upper Nile would produce more immediate results by ignoring Monson and approaching the prime minister directly.

Monson in the meantime continued to monitor the public excitement raised by the confrontation at Fashoda, warning London on 7 October that "we are within measureable distance of very dangerous excitement."[235] His renewed alarm was caused in large part by the

---

[233]Grenville, 13-14; Jones, 179-180; Uzoigwe, 260-261.

[234]Wood, 210-212.

[235]BD 204: 175; Peterson, 116.

headlines of the Parisian newspapers, most notably *Le Matin*, a journal widely regarded as a mouthpiece of the *Quai d'Orsay*. On 5 October its leading article stated that the government knew what it was doing and what it intended when it sent Marchand to Fashoda. France will consequently "return a categorical negative" to London's demand that Marchand be recalled without prior negotiations and without British concessions: "*NON! La Seule Réponse Digne de la France.*"[236]

Between 7 October and 10 October, however, Monson noted a "sudden and complete" change in tone among several newspapers, a shift toward moderation. *Le Matin* pointed out, for example, that the British press had modified its tone and that discussion between London and Paris "was now possible." Moreover, the Upper Nile was no longer worth the trouble:

> Whilst doing justice . . . to the energy, perseverance and indomitable tenacity of purpose which enabled Major Marchand to penetrate into the region . . . we must realize that it is most imprudent to saddle ourselves with useless and extravagant territories, practically inaccessible from the French possessions on the Atlantic coast, annexations in the mountains in the moon, which might, for all the good they do to us, as well be in the moon itself.

Le Matin went so far as to argue that Sir Edward Grey's speech of 1895, to which the French press had attached so much importance, was but a passing incident in the far greater question of the Upper Nile. Paris sought merely a commercial outlet on the Nile and "in no way [desires] to thwart English policy." From any point of view, a

---

[236]"NO! The Only Reply Worthy of France." FO 27/3399, Tel.164, 5 October 1898, Monson to Salisbury; FO 78/5051, D.499, 5 October 1898, Monson to Salisbury.

definitive settlement had to be made and the only means to that end was through calm and friendly discussion.[237]

Although Monson suspected that the source for the articles was Delcassé, he was uncertain about its possible impact on the Fashoda negotiations and the tenor of the debate: "If a hint from the Government has inspired this article . . . it will be interesting to observe whether this is but a solitary note, or whether the cry will be taken up by the whole pack."[238]

In spite of this apparent moderation in the French press, Monson remained anxious about the possibility of war. A widespread belief persisted in Paris that although the British government had made no formal demand on France that would justify an outburst, only a word from London would suffice. He also thought it likely that Fashoda would be made the subject for deliberation among the other powers. He believed as did many of his colleagues that it was Delcassé's goal to force Britain's hand by referring the question to an international conference, where France expected to find significant support. On more than one occasion, Delcassé had assured Monson that such a conference would be convened and that it would be difficult to oppose the "combined expostulations of all the Powers."[239]

In the meantime, Monson received no additional communications or instructions from Salisbury regarding negotiations with Delcassé. The silence from London complicated his already tenuous relationship with the foreign minister, who indeed began to grow impatient with the lack of response to his overtures. Within a week of Courcel's meeting with Salisbury, it was clear to Delcassé that the British attitude in fact had not softened

---

[237]FO 78/5051, D.504, 9 October 1898, Monson to Salisbury; BD 206: 176-177; BD 208: 178; Wood, 179-180.

[238]FO 78/5051, D.505, 10 October 1898, Monson to Salisbury.

[239]BD 204: 176; Bates, 152-153; Wood, 178-179.

at all. The Blue Book was published as promised on 10 October and, as Delcassé had feared, British newspapers loudly praised the cabinet's inflexibility. The next day, therefore, he sought to raise the prospect of an arrangement along the lines of the Salisbury-Courcel discussions. He told Monson that Paris would be prepared to evacuate Fashoda if given some assurances about the Bahr al-Ghazal. Probably anticipating the ambassador's usual vague non-replies, he pointed out that Courcel's report suggested that Monson had instructions to discuss some arrangements. Without any recent word from London, however, Monson continued to be evasive and uncompromising. He had not yet received Salisbury's account of the Courcel interview and thus assumed that his government had not abandoned its insistence that any negotiation with France be contingent upon an explicit French evacuation of Fashoda. He thus again reiterated that he had no authority to modify his previous attitude.[240]

Delcassé, wrote Monson three days later, "seemed despondent" and became emotional for the first time. He complained about London's intransigence and that his good intentions "seem to be disregarded, if not worse, by Her Majesty's Government." Delcassé complained that he was under attack for being weak and intimated the possibility of retiring from office. Another minister, he warned, would not be so accommodating. Monson, unaware of the hopes raised by Courcel's optimistic report of 5 October, thought that Delcassé's irritation was the result of "some unpleasant things said to him today at the Cabinet Council in regard to his having allowed such a clear intimation to be given . . . about the impossibility of the retention of Fashoda." Nevertheless, he suggested that after some negotiation Delcassé would be prepared to

---

[240]FO 27/3400 and FO 78/5051, Tel.169, 11 October 1898, Monson to Salisbury; BD 209: 179; Sanderson, 346; Wood, 182-184.

retreat from that position "if we can build him a golden bridge for that retrograde movement."[241]

Perhaps impressed by Monson's dispatch, Salisbury met again with Courcel on 12 October. The prime minister remained willing to consider the possibility of concessions. Following his previous meeting with Courcel, he instructed Kitchener to make suggestions for possible territorial concessions to the French. By 12 October, however, with the hardline chatter of his cabinet colleagues and the London dailies ringing in his ears, Salisbury reemphasized the British position regarding the Egyptian title to the Upper Nile, the Anglo-Egyptian right of conquest, and the impossible position of Marchand. No title or right to occupation could be created "by the secret expedition across unknown and unexplored wastes, at a distance from the French border, by Monsieur Marchand and a scanty escort," whereas Kitchener's victory at Omdurman had convincingly reestablished the Khedive's sovereignty over the Sudan. He suggested that the captain retire beyond the Nile watershed, while Paris protect its interests by a declaration that the French withdrawal would not prejudice any existing controversy. Courcel replied that Marchand would be withdrawn if Britain would concede a territorial delimitation that "would place France upon the navigable portion of the Bahr al-Ghazal, so that no frontier would intervene between our commerce and the [navigable system of the] Nile." Salisbury agreed to consider the French proposals. As he explained eventually to Monson, however, the "extreme indefiniteness . . . and the rhetorical character" of Courcel's language made it impossible to form or to express any definite opinion of his propositions. Therefore, rather than "entering upon a discussion which

---

[241]FO 78/5051, D.517, 14 October 1898, Monson to Salisbury; Sanderson, 346; Wood, 182-184.

under the circumstances would have been fruitful of misapprehension," Salisbury suggested that Courcel submit a precise written communication about the means of Marchand's retreat and "any other stipulations which it was his object to suggest."[242]

In spite of being presented with a real opportunity for progress, however, Courcel blew it. Perhaps encouraged by Salisbury's apparent willingness to negotiate and perhaps concerned that he had not fully carried out Delcassé's instructions of 4 October, he wrote the prime minister a private letter immediately after the interview. He stated that France *claimed* the entire region bounded by the Nile, the Bahr al-Ghazal, and the Bahr al-Arab, a region regarded as "*la continuation naturelle et le débouché necessaire de ses possessions du Congo.*"[243] The extent of the French demands took Salisbury by surprise. He responded in a letter the following day 13 October that without Courcel's note:

> I think I should have misunderstood the effect of the observations which you made during our conversation yesterday. The claim asserted in your instructions is quite new to me, and, as far as I know, has never been officially made on behalf of the French Government.[244]

Courcel immediately realized his mistake, but the damage was done. The prospects for a negotiated settlement and perhaps some compensation disappeared as Salisbury decided to avoid any and all further discussions as long as Marchand remained at Fashoda or until Paris proposed

---

[242]FO 78/5051, D.369, 12 October 1898, Salisbury to Monson; Bates, 155-156; Peterson, 125; Roberts, 706; Sanderson, 346.

[243]"The natural continuation and necessary outlet for its possessions in the Congo." BD 210: 180; Sanderson, 346-347.

[244]BD 211: 180.

some reasonable initiatives.[245] Courcel's departure from London on 13 October was followed subsequently by a two-week pause in the diplomatic dialogue. Discussions would not resume until after a meeting of the British cabinet on 27 October. While the newspapers on both sides of the Channel kept the crisis alive, Salisbury remained calm and uncommunicative; in fact, he spent much of his time on holiday. Consequently, in spite of Delcassé's intention to approach Salisbury directly, the prime minister's decision to retire from discussions until either the French withdrew Marchand or made some specific initiatives meant that official British communication with the French government would nevertheless remain in the hands of Monson.[246]

Official positions on both sides of the Channel in fact continued to harden and grow more bellicose. The escalation of French resentment owed much to Salisbury's decision to issue the British Blue Book on 10 October regarding London's role in the crisis. The publication of the Blue Book, issued largely in response to Trouillot's 26 September disclosure, particularly angered Delcassé. The Austrian *charge d'affaires* told Monson that Delcassé "showed considerable resentment" to the publication of the Blue Book, which he believed was intended to intimidate him by rousing public opinion in Britain.[247] A week later, therefore, Delcassé announced his intention to issue a Yellow Book relative to Fashoda, which would contain Courcel's account of his 12 October conversation with Salisbury -- although not the ambassador's private letters exchanged with Salisbury thereafter.[248] In response, Salisbury ordered Monson to inform the foreign minister

[245]Bates, 156; Brown, 101; Sanderson, 346-347.

[246]Ramm, "Lord Salisbury," 65; Uzoigwe, 260-261.

[247]FO 27/3400 and 78/5051, Tel.170, 13 October 1898, Monson to Salisbury; LQV, 294.

[248]FO 27/3400, Tel.174, 21 October 1898, Monson to Salisbury.

of London's desire to publish those letters in a supplementary Blue Book. Delcassé protested that he was unaware of this exchange of letters and did not see how their publication could be useful to Salisbury. Courcel also protested their inclusion because they were private and would certainly add to public irritation.[249]

As Delcassé had feared, the publication of these diplomatic books resulted in a significant increase in the public temper and a flood of political oratory in Britain. Politicians from all parties joined the public exaltation of British virtue and the denunciation of the French. Some of the strongest supporters of a firm and inflexible policy came in fact from opposition Liberals. Lord Rosebery, Sir Edward Grey, Sir H.H. Asquith, Sir Henry Campbell-Bannerman, and Sir William Harcourt all urged the cabinet to oppose any concessions to France in the Upper Nile valley. Much of this staunch Liberal support was based on political realities. Their enthusiasm for occasional colonial adventures and clashes with foreigners clearly attracted the cheers and votes of the masses.[250] Nevertheless, their speeches were as passionate, self-righteous, and indignant as the Conservatives.

Speaking at Epsom on 12 October, former prime minister Lord Rosebery declared that no British government "which showed signs of yielding would last a week." He added that if the nations of the world were under the impression that

> the ancient spirit of Great Britain is dead or that her resources are weakened, or her population less determined than ever it was to maintain the rights and honour of its flag, they make a mistake which

---

[249]FO 27/3400, Tel.179, 22 October 1898, Monson to Salisbury; FO 27/3400, Tel.180, 23 October 1898, Monson to Salisbury.

[250]Bates, 154; Blunt I, 298; Garvin III, 229-230; Giffen, 82; Langer, *Diplomacy of Imperialism*, 553.

can only end in a disastrous conflagration.

Chamberlain, the Liberal Unionist Colonial Minister, who feared that Salisbury would grant concessions thus raising the broader question of French claims in the Bahr-el-Ghazal region, claimed that if the British gave in over Fashoda the French would again try to link up with the Ethiopians in order to control the Upper Nile. It was essential therefore to stand firm. On 19 October Sir Michael Hicks Beach asserted at North Shields that the country had put its foot down and would go to war rather than yield: "If, unhappily, another view should be taken elsewhere, we know what our duty demands. It would be a great calamity . . . But there are greater evils than war." At Huddersfield on 28 October Sir Edward Grey claimed that the rights and necessity of Egypt, in addition to Britain's obligations to safeguard those rights on the Upper Nile, made it imperative for London to maintain its present position.[251]

The debate was excited further by the excesses of the British popular press, which loudly praised the cabinet's inflexibility and continued to indulge in an "orgy of scurrility." British newspapers regularly referred to Marchand and his expedition as "tourists," "irregular marauders," and a "French picnic party." The *Daily Mail* and *Spectator* both argued that Fashoda must be maintained "even at the cost of war." The *Times* warned (10 October) that "Lord Salisbury and his colleagues have taken a position from which retreat is impossible. One side or the other will have to give way. That side cannot . . . be Great Britain." The *Morning Post* noted (13 October) that "The British nation is indeed united in a way that it perhaps never was." *Punch* published (22 October) a highly offensive cartoon of an organ-grinder and his

---

[251]Garvin III, 227; Grenville, 228; Langer, *Diplomacy of Imperialism*, 553; Peterson, 124; Sanderson, 347.

monkey, which wore a French army uniform. The headline of the *Daily Mail* (26 October) exaggerated British military preparations: "Our Ships and Men Getting Ready for the Word 'Mobilize.'"[252]

Monson complained to Salisbury that the rhetorical excesses of British politicians and the London newspapers were having an adverse reaction upon public opinion in France. The Quai d'Orsay regarded the recent speech by Hicks Beach as particularly inflammatory. The patronizing and offensive language of the British politicians and newspapers, the ambassador warned, had rendered Delcassé's position very difficult. On 11 October the foreign minister told Monson that if the provocation continued on the other side of the Channel, "it would elicit response here, and make the preservation of peace difficult."[253] Ten days later, Delcassé complained about new accusations that he was too weak. He protested that he had all along been prepared to discuss Marchand's recall provided that it was "not forced upon him as an ultimatum." Monson, who had nothing but distaste for the Parisian newspapers, agreed that Delcassé's concerns were justified. Yet, he suggested to Salisbury, the French government "will be unable to maintain their contention as regards M. Marchand, but that, until they can announce that negotiations have begun on their claims to the west of the Nile, they will decline to withdraw him."[254]

Monson further warned Salisbury that in addition to the continuing domestic pressures on Delcassé, the chauvinism of the British press might easily provoke a dangerous reaction in France. Once again, there was talk in Paris of diverting public angst into foreign policy adventures, namely, war against Britain:

---

[252]Langer, *Diplomacy of Imperialism*, 553; Riker, 66-67.

[253]FO 78/5051, Tel.169, 11 October 1898, Monson to Salisbury; BD 209: 178-179.

[254]FO 27/3400, Tel.175, 21 October 1898, Monson to Salisbury; BD 214: 181.

> It cannot be denied that more than one of these London papers have adopted a style of invective and intimidation towards France calculated to provoke reprisals. . . . [Added to the] ostentatious criticisms and disquisitions [of the London papers upon the Dreyfus case] it might have been foreseen that a temper would be aroused here, even among people hitherto moderate in their language which would render the task of diplomacy . . . more difficult than ever. . . . [T]his has been the result, and I hear from every quarter that the spirit of resentment is rapidly growing.[255]

By the middle of October, therefore, Monson found himself unable to decide what course of action the French might pursue in the Upper Nile. In one respect he remained convinced that France was unprepared and unwilling to go to war over Fashoda; French public opinion was simply too divided over questions of revision and foreign policy objectives. And yet, at the same time, because the official position of the French government was growing increasingly belligerent and inflexible, Monson could never be altogether certain that France was in fact unwilling to fight for Fashoda.

---

[255]FO 27/3397, D.533, 21 October 1898, Monson to Salisbury; Brown, 110; Grenville, 228.

Chapter Ten

REPORTS OF REVOLUTION ARE "GROSSLY EXAGGERATED"

Monson continued to pay close attention to French internal politics particularly the ongoing drama of the Dreyfus affair. As the emotions of the case continued to divide French society, more popular meetings and demonstrations took place. On 25 September the *Ligue des Patriotes* sponsored a rally at the *Salle Guyenet*, attended by 3,000 to 4,000 people, while thousands more gathered outside on the streets. The rally was followed by a march of royalists and anti-Semites to the Place de la Concorde, where they demonstrated into the evening before they were dispersed by the police.[256] The socialists announced a public meeting for 2 October and appealed to the people of Paris to attend in support of Dreyfus and Picquart. Déroulède and Guérin subsequently urged their followers to protest outside what they called the "anarchist" rally. The night before the meeting the *Ligue des Patriotes* put up by posters throughout Paris, signed by Déroulède, who proclaimed, "The cosmopolitan anarchists who insult our soldiers have organized a public

---

[256]Brown, 91-92; Rutkoff, 91.

meeting . . . They have dared to convene the people of Paris to come and acclaim the TRAITOR DREYFUS & HIS FRIEND PICQUART. I will oppose the cries of the "Sans Patries" with our own triple cry of "*Vive la France, Vive l'Armie, Vive la République* . . ." Rumors quickly spread that up to 20,000 people would appear. The police took these reports so seriously that they ordered the meeting place, the *Salle Wagram*, closed to all parties. Both groups arrived and, finding the doors barred and guarded by police, descended upon the streets. The ensuing disorder, which lasted well into the evening, resulted in multiple arrests and fistfights between police and demonstrators.[257] The *Ligue des Patriotes* organized another major rally for 9 October in support of the army and President Félix Faure, an dedicated anti-Dreyfusard. It proceeded quite smoothly despite the concerns of police who, fearing more violence, called in an extra 200 men to guard the passage of the president.

In addition to the seemingly endless procession of Dreyfus-inspired riots and parades, the strike movement continued to expand. Union after union voted to join the protest until over 43,000 workers were on strike in Paris by 12 October. This continuing labor unrest, however, finally prodded the Brisson cabinet to action. In early October, as the excavators' strike expanded, infantry troops from the provinces arrived in Paris where they quickly occupied construction sites. Within a week, approximately 60,000 troops had moved into Paris, which began to resemble a city under siege. At night, campfires burned along the Seine and Champs-Élysées. When the leaders of the National Railway Workers Union of France, encouraged by the growing labor solidarity, ordered a nationwide strike for 14 October in the hopes of

---

[257]FO 27/3397, D.496, 2 October 1898, Monson to Salisbury; Hoffman, 177; Rutkoff, 92-93.

provoking a general strike, the government responded with great force in an effort to restore order and confidence. The threat of a railway strike under normal circumstances would have elicited a minor response from the government, which generally regarded the Railway Workers Union as one of the weakest in France. By mid-October, however, both Delcassé and Faure believed that the confrontation at Fashoda might lead to war as recent intelligence reports suggested that the British were engaged in extraordinary naval preparations. Under these circumstances, a nationwide railway strike capable of crippling troop movements represented a threat to national security. Therefore, on 12 October Edouard Lockroy French Minister of the Marine requested the immediate dispatch of regular troops to the port cities of Brest, Cherbourg, and Toulon. By the next day, the first of those troops were moving by rail to the coast, and by 14 October soldiers had occupied all the major railway stations in Paris and surrounding provinces.[258]

In spite of the government's efforts apprehension remained widespread. While the presence of the army was comforting to the nationalists, it exacerbated fears of a working-class revolution already entrenched in the minds of the middle class. Since the Commune in 1871 the bourgeoisie "trembled at the slightest unrest" and regarded striking workers as a threat to national security.[259] The presence of troops also aggravated existing concerns particularly among socialists and republicans of a royalist or military *coup d'état*. As soldiers began to move into Paris, reports began to circulate of a great nationalist and anti-Semitic demonstration for 25 October, the date on which the

---

[258]Brown, 103-105; Lewis, *Prisoners of Honor*, 251-252; Rutkoff, 90, 93-94; Tuchman, 212.

[259]Lewis, *Prisoners of Honor*, 251; Rutkoff, 89-90.

Chamber of Deputies was to reconvene, an event to be preceded by a series of mass meetings, marches, and demonstrations that would intensify as the date drew near. Rumors maintained that on the occasion of this demonstration, the troops massed in Paris would serve to encourage and abet rather than prevent the actions of the nationalists.[260] Daily headlines in *La Petite République* and *L'Aurôre* warned of a military plot to overthrow the government and heralded the arrests of leading revisionist agitators. The French security apparatus, the *Sûreté générale*, reported that a coalition of right-wing, nationalist, and anti-Dreyfusard groups, in concert with top generals of the French army, was planning drastic action to forestall complete revision of the Dreyfus affair. Mathieu Dreyfus, a leader in the movement to overturn his brother's verdict, wrote that the General Staff wanted street disturbances: "Grave trouble . . . would justify the proclamation of martial law. And once martial law was decreed, all power would pass into the hands of the military." So certain were the Royalists of "the day" that André Buffet, *chef de cabinet* for the *Duc d'Orleans*, telegraphed the Pretender that his presence in nearby Brussels on 24 October was "indispensable."[261]

A rumor to that effect was brought to Monson's attention by the British military attaché Lieutenant Colonel Dawson. According to Dawson, a group of dissident French officers and anti-Dreyfusards were said to be planning the arrest and impeachment of Brisson and all the Court of Cassation authorities on 16 October. While the names of persons implicated was a bit uncertain, Dawson was sure that General Cavaignac was the "organizer and leading spirit." Once the generals took over, the government would be replaced by an anti-

---

[260]Rutkoff, 83-84.

[261]Brown, 105-106; Lewis, *Prisoners of Honor*, 251-252; Tuchman, 212-213.

revisionist cabinet under Jules Méline, which would immediately declare war against Britain. As the day approached, there was considerable movement among Dreyfusards, many of whom temporarily assumed new addresses. Many socialists feared that the government would use the crisis to suppress the workers and crush the strike movement. As soldiers arrived and established positions in Paris this seemed to have already begun. Dawson warned Monson that although the troops appeared legitimately intended for the preservation of peace should the strike cause disturbances, there was no doubt that "the large force present was to be made use of, and most likely a considerable portion had already been tampered with." Moreover, he warned that five French army corps were under orders to prepare for the invasion of Britain. Several French admirals, Dawson wrote, bragged that London "need not count on a speedy termination of the war."

Monson did not take these rumors and alleged conspiracies seriously, at least at this point. In spite of Dawson's warnings, the continued arrival of troops in Paris, and the sudden rush of activity, he reported to Salisbury on 14 October that any intended *coup d'état* was prematurely divulged and that there was "no imminent danger of any disturbance."[262] The ambassador's confidence was borne out when nothing happened on 16 October except for the issuing of a socialist manifesto condemning the "state of siege." Monson attributed the rumors and apprehension to the sometimes overzealous and usually irresponsible excesses of the newspapers. While it was impossible to prevent much of the French public from believing some sort of plot was in progress, press reports that Paris was on the

---

[262]FO 27/3397, D.520, 14 October 1898, Monson to Salisbury; Bredin, 342-343; Brown, 110-111; Hoffman, 177; Sanderson, 359.

verge of revolution were "grossly exaggerated." While he did not wish to appear indifferent to the "grave possibilities latent under the undisturbed everyday aspect of the boulevards," he nonetheless admitted a concern over an extension of the strike, especially among railway employees, due to the weakness of the police and their inability to put down any serious disorder. Yet, he did not anticipate any disturbances at least until the reconvening of the Chamber on 25 October. It was regrettable, Monson noted, that the press should continue to indulge in such exaggerations as to portray Paris in a state of siege. The sight of a few soldiers wherever building work is going on "is no symptom whatever of an abnormal situation."

Monson also discounted speculation as he had in January that war would quickly follow a *coup d'état*. He acknowledged the possibility that the excitement might lead the French to embrace Fashoda as a *casus belli*. After all, a nationalist government installed through a military coup might be tempted to use Fashoda and French hatred of Britain to unite the nation and defuse the Dreyfusard agitation. French tempers would be stirred further when Delcassé published the French Yellow Book, which showed the British attitude "to be unalterable." He concluded, however, that France would never go to war. Any official effort to divert public attention away from Dreyfus and revision by focusing on Fashoda would ultimately fail because of the irreparable divisions in French public opinion. The French, he predicted, would prove less cohesive and less unanimous than the British "in the defense of what will be represented not only as the national interest but as the national honour also."[263]

French public opinion over Fashoda was almost as divided as opinion over Dreyfus. As Monson observed,

---

[263]FO 27/3397, D.524, 16 October 1898, Monson to Salisbury; Brown, 110; Grenville, 227-228; Lewis, *Prisoners of Honor*, 250-251.

there was no overwhelming sentiment in France of any kind in favor of war to defend Fashoda. Nothing existed in France that even remotely resembled the near unanimity of British public opinion and the British government, which was determined to go to war rather than tolerate the continued presence of the French flag at Fashoda. Monson noted on 7 October that the general feeling of the French public "upon the broad issues of peace and war, is universally pacific. There is no general desire in this country to run the risk of war with anyone." Wilfrid Blunt, a British poet and writer living in Paris, noted that several friends and acquaintances in Parisian society universally believe that France is unprepared for war and that "nobody wants to fight." The former foreign minister Gabriel Hanotaux, out of office but eager to return, complained to Blunt that the French public would never approve of a war over "such a trifle as Fashoda." The Egyptian question was one of small consequence for France, he asserted, and scathingly described the Bahr al-Ghazal as a "country inhabited by monkeys and black men worse than monkeys." No war would be popular in France because "nobody knew where Fashoda was or cared three straws about the Marchand Mission." A war with Britain over such a dispute, he exclaimed, would be "worse than a crime, a folly." Such a war would ruin both countries.[264]

The polarization of opinion over Fashoda and Dreyfus followed similar lines. The Dreyfusards were antimilitaristic, anticolonialist, internationalist, and favored conciliation with London. The anti-Dreyfusards were militaristic, colonialist, nationalist, opposed to any conciliation with Britain, and favored the retention of all territory annexed by Marchand. The Parisian newspapers reflected this division in opinion. The Dreyfusard press

---

[264]Bates, 155; Blunt I, 303, 304-305; Peterson, 121.

was generally moderate, conciliatory, and opposed to colonial expansion. They favored compromise over Fashoda provided London made minor compensations. The non-socialist *Le Siècle*, for example, condemned the entire Upper Nile project as "senseless" and demanded Marchand's immediate recall. On 21 October the socialist *Le Petite République* ridiculed the nationalists for their unconditional support of Marchand and their belief that the failure of the mission somehow threatened the "national interest." Because present policies were leading France to a possible war with Britain, they called upon the socialists of both countries to renounce the conflict on the Nile as an "unjust struggle between two capitalist minorities." The *Journal de Rouen* wrote on 22 October that "no one desires a war *à propos* of Fashoda." *Le Matin* asked on the same day, "Of what value is Fashoda to France in comparison to the price which England places upon it?" *Le Temps* argued (25 October) that France should clearly state its intention to evacuate Fashoda provided that "courtesy was observed toward her and that the question was not arbitrarily isolated from others." In *L'Aurôre*, Georges Clemenceau declared (25 October): "the brutal fact is that France cannot think of throwing herself into a war for the possession of some African marshes, when the German is camped at Metz and Strasbourg." The *Journal des Débats* maintained (29 October) that Marchand should withdraw even if France received no compensation.

Anti-Dreyfusard journals vigorously attacked the Dreyfusards for their unpatriotic views. In *L'Autorité* Paul de Cassagnac asserted (16 October) that the issue represented a more serious threat to France than the Hohenzollern candidacy that led to the Franco-Prussian War and (25 October) that London had "spoken to us as one would not speak to a dog. . . . England treats us with such complete hostility and insolence that we will be obliged at one time or another to go to war with her." Three days later *La Dépêche Coloniale* openly demanded war rather than the humiliation of withdrawing Marchand. *La Libre Parole, Le Figaro, Le Gaulois,* the Orleanist *Le Soleil*, Déroulède's *La Patrie*, Henri Rochefort's *L'Intransigeant*, and *L'Éclair* (generally regarded as the unofficial mouthpiece of the French army), all joined *L'Autorité* in unrestrained applause of Marchand and his heroic exploits. After all, wrote *La Nouvelle Revue* (23 September), Marchand "is the complete expression of our race, and he is our standard bearer." They deplored the damage to national prestige, weakened further by the internal quarrels over revision. Capitulation, it declared, was tantamount to treason. In late September *Le Gaulois* glorified Colonel Henry's forgery as a patriotic act. *L'Intransigeant* argued (22 October) that an international Jewish-Dreyfusard movement was manipulating the foreign ministry and French diplomacy. The nationalist journals also attacked Delcassé himself, particularly after his scheme to recall Marchand in exchange for concessions became public knowledge in the first week of October. In *La Patrie* Paul Déroulède ridiculed Delcassé as a traitor who completely sold out to Britain, the "hereditary enemy."[265]

Differences in public opinion also reflected a fundamental division between Paris and the provinces. The provinces reflected little of the bellicosity of the Parisian press. The provincial middle class generally opposed colonial expansion on the grounds that it endangered peace and profits. At the same time, the provincial newspapers particularly in the major commercial and industrial towns and seaports openly favored Marchand's evacuation from Fashoda.[266]

---

[265]Brown, 106-108; Carroll, 172-175; Sanderson, 359-360.

[266]Bates, 155; Brown, 9; Sanderson, 360.

This schism in French opinion convinced Monson that for the time being at least France would be unprepared to fight. While his diplomatic colleagues in Paris continued to maintain that "it needs but the whisper of a possible insult to the French flag to arouse a tempest of excitement," Monson was confident that the feeling throughout the country "upon the broad issues of peace and war is universally pacific." Below all the noisy agitation, the average Frenchman had a profound desire for peace and understood that no material interests were at stake in the Upper Nile valley. Four existing conditions, he believed, would guarantee French composure. First, the domestic condition was one of "unrest." Second, the turmoil of the Dreyfus case had grievously shaken the confidence of the French in their institutions, public men, and even the army. Third, French official circles lacked confidence in the prospect of Russian support. Finally, the government and the commercial and manufacturing classes looked forward to glory and prestige from the approaching Paris International Exhibition of 1900 and thus desired to free themselves from all damaging and embarrassing entanglements.[267] Even the mainstream Parisian newspapers, Monson noted, appeared conspicuously more conciliatory. On 11 October *La Dépêche Coloniale* maintained that France should receive some compensation (i.e., the Gambia) in return for a French withdrawal, while *La Politique Coloniale* noted with satisfaction Salisbury's willingness at least to discuss the rights of both countries in territories not previously subject to the Khalifa. When the extremes of the London newspapers and British politicians provoked heightened defensiveness and resentment in Paris, *Le Temps* wrote that while it often seemed that London's desire was not

---

[267]FO 78/5051, D.500, 7 October 1898, Monson to Salisbury; BD 204: 175; Sanderson, 359.

only to secure Fashoda but to "compel France to choose between gratuitous humiliation and calamitous rupture," it would be wiser, more dignified, and more patriotic to "make a rule of avoiding the utterance of anything calculated to embitter the discussion."[268]

And yet, Monson could never be certain.

---

[268]FO 78/5051, Tel.169, 11 October 1898, Monson to Salisbury; FO 78/5051, D.508, 11 October 1898, Monson to Salisbury; FO 78/5051, D.517, 14 October 1898, Monson to Salisbury; FO 78/5051, D.538, 22 October 1898, Monson to Salisbury.

Craig E. Saucier

Chapter Eleven

"I THINK SIR E. MONSON HAS BEEN FRIGHTENED BY THESE REPORTS"

Throughout the latter half of October, as military preparations were initiated and accelerated on both sides of the English Channel, Monson became consumed with two urgent questions: Would France go to war over Fashoda? If so, could it count on the support of Russia?

Monson could never entirely or satisfactorily answer the question of the French intention, preparedness, or will to fight Britain. On the one hand, he believed that whether the French government would go to war depended primarily upon the domestic situation within France which, he acknowledged, simply could not be predicted. Monson continued to maintain that opinion was too divided to justify a French concentration of resources to the Upper Nile. On the other hand, he reminded London of Delcassé's frequent declarations that France would accept war rather than submit to a national humiliation. Furthermore, as the French government continued its extensive use of troops to suppress labor unrest in Paris, he grew anxious over rumors of a military coup, followed by war, rumors he had previously discounted. Monson noted that a military government would be expected to place great emphasis on defending the national honor. Such a government, anxious to turn public attention away from domestic discord, would likely welcome a showdown with Britain.[269] Therefore, when Lieutenant Colonel Dawson reported rumors of a plot by dissident generals to seize power and initiate an immediate war with Britain. Sir John Ardagh head of British military intelligence ordered him to London on 16 October to brief the upper echelons of the British army and navy on the situation in France. Ultimately, Ardagh ordered Dawson to make the Channel crossing each evening, personally report on what he had learned that day, and immediately return for more firsthand information. During each of these nightly encounters, Dawson warned his superiors in London to prepare for the worst.[270]

The British government made it unmistakably clear that it was prepared to fight over Fashoda. The cabinet had already drawn up a scenario of military escalation. First, Marchand was to be neutralized by the dispatch of a superior force to the Sudan. Then, the reserve fleet was to be readied and the Home Fleet concentrated at Gibraltar. If France continued to resist and refused to back down, Kitchener would be ordered to engage and destroy Marchand. In case of war, the Royal Navy would attack and destroy the French Fleet.[271]

The British government remained supremely confident of its ability to manage the French military. Following years of ardent shipbuilding and ongoing naval increases, they knew that British supremacy at sea remained unchallenged. The Royal Navy had thirty-four battleships less than ten years old, each with a speed of at least sixteen knots. By contrast, France and Russia had

---

[269]Brown, 128-129; Wood, 189.

[270]Brown, 111; Lewis, *Prisoners of Honor*, 252.

[271]Langer, *Diplomacy of Imperialism*, 559-561; Lebow, 320; Robinson and Gallagher, 350-351, 357-358; Sanderson, 241-263.

only thirty battleships of varying quality between them. In the Mediterranean Sea, which would be the decisive theater, the British had eighteen battleships in active service and ten in reserve. France had fifteen battleships in active service and seven in reserve. One French critic, a "Lieutenant X," wrote that the British navy was "four times as strong as the French and stronger than all the fleets of Europe put together."

Nevertheless, the cabinet pushed naval preparations forward during the month of October. At Portsmouth provisions were made to enable the less mobile parts of the naval forces to take to sea at short notice. Channel squadrons cruised off the French coast, ready to blockade the French battleships at Brest. Another force watched the Straits of Gibraltar to prevent the French Mediterranean fleet from streaming into the Atlantic Ocean. In the Mediterranean, the Admiralty ordered a large squadron positioned between Malta and Gibraltar, ready to blockade the French at Toulon or to debark at Bizerta. Another force was dispatched to Alexandria to protect the Suez Canal. The ships of the Reserve Squadron were as quietly as possible supplied with coal and "full seagoing complements of officers and men." Crews speeded up repairs to ships in the dockyards and troop requirements hastened the return of army regulars from Capetown and Bermuda.[272]

In Paris, British naval preparations caused serious concern. Delcassé feared a naval war for which "we are absolutely incapable of carrying through even with Russian help" and admitted that if the French fleet challenged the British on the high seas, "it would be at the bottom of the ocean within a fortnight." The French fleet

---

[272]Giffen, 68, 83; Langer, *Diplomacy of Imperialism*, 559-560; Arthur J. Marder, *British Naval Policy, 1880-1905: The Anatomy of British Sea Power* (London: Putnam and Company, 1940), 321-322.

was by comparison pathetic. After years of neglecting naval spending and technological development, it fell to approximately one-half the size of the Royal Navy. In 1898-1899 France's total naval budget was 289 million francs compared to Britain's naval budget of 635 million [francs]. French construction of new ships totaled 86 million francs compared to British construction totals of 172 million [francs]. French naval tonnage was 565,388 tons to Britain's 1,074,266 tons.[273] The French Channel fleet consisted largely of battleships built before 1885. The ships were a collection of diverse and motley designs, a "fleet of samples," rather than a homogenous force. Moreover, there existed no workable contingency plans to meet the possibility of war with the British. Earlier ministries had drafted plans but never developed them in any detail. Their main proposal, a scheme for the invasion of Britain, appeared to both the chief of the naval staff Cavalier de Cuverville and the minister of the marine Edouard Lockroy completely unworkable. Naval ports at home and in the colonies suffered from a lack of manpower, reserves had been neglected, and arsenals were inadequately stocked. At Brest, Cherbourg, and Toulon, only one-third of the batteries could have been manned on the first day of mobilization. Lockroy told the Chamber of Deputies that the French fleet was no better prepared for war against Britain than the Spanish fleet had been for war against the United States. Moreover, the French had held no discussions with the Russian navy about possible collaboration in the event of war. Throughout Delcassé's tenure in office, all French proposals for an exchange of liaison officers between the French and Russian fleets had been rejected by the Russian ministry of marine. The best Russian ships in any event were in stationed the Far East, while its Baltic

---

[273]Andrew, 100; Brown, 125, 130; Sanderson, 348, 355.

fleet remained icebound from early November until late in the spring.[274]

The Quai d'Orsay feared that Britain might provoke a war to settle accounts with France once and for all. Although some French officials expressed a willingness to fight for reasons of national honor even if defeat was certain, there appeared to be general consensus that a naval war against the British would be virtually hopeless. This was obvious to Delcassé, who was briefed to that effect by Cuverville on 11 October. Further intelligence confirmed the futility of a fight against the British.[275] Nevertheless, through the remainder of October, Delcassé sought to play for enough time to make the most urgent defensive military preparations and to sound out St. Petersburg about possible Russian support.

Accordingly, with or without Russian assurances, the French government initiated a series of defensive preparations, along the French coasts. On the basis of Dawson's reports, Monson advised London that troops and ammunition were being rushed to Brest, where soldiers strengthened the forts, and to Cherbourg, where they hurriedly prepared ironclads, torpedo boats, and armored gunboats for sea. The French navy canceled all leaves from the fleet and marine,[276] moved contingents of marines to Ushant,[277] and continued preparations in port cities and along the coast.[278] Mayors of Channel ports were ordered to requisition churches for hospitals and to

---

[274]Andrew, 102-103; Sir Thomas Barclay, *Thirty Years: Anglo-French Reminiscences, 1876-1906* (London: Constable and Company, Ltd., 1914), 146; Marder, 323; Riker, 68-69; Sanderson, 355; Wright, 189.

[275]Andrew, 102; Keith Eubank, "The Fashoda Crisis Re-examined," *The Historian* 22 (February 1960): 152-153; Langer, *Diplomacy of Imperialism*, 561-562; Marder, 331-332.

[276]FO 27/3397, D.534, 21 October 1898, Monson to Salisbury.

[277]FO 27/3397, D.545, 25 October 1898, Monson to Salisbury.

[278]FO 27/3397, D.548, 25 October 1898, Monson to Salisbury.

report on beds and ambulances. At Toulon shipyards worked night and day preparing warships for sea duty, while work proceeded on the arsenal, preparations were made to lodge extra troops, and vessels of the squadron replaced their "*munitions d'exercice*" with "*munitions de combat*."[279] The Mediterranean squadron was reorganized and put under the authority of Admiral Ernest Fournier, one of France's ablest naval officers. Monson was highly concerned with the daily newspaper reports of active preparations at French ports and arsenals. When he tried to elicit some comment concerning such reports, Delcassé laughed at the question. He denied that France was currently making any extraordinary preparations for mobilization. While French consuls in Britain had been for several weeks reporting activity in British ports and arsenals, he was "quite unaware of any corresponding preparations in France." French forces were currently at their lowest effective strength, he argued, and denied that anything abnormal was going on -- even while Monson referred to detailed French newspaper descriptions of those very preparations. As Monson noted, the Havas news agency published reports denying any unusual warlike preparations in French ports, while newspapers continued to publish stories inconsistent with those assertions. In Toulon preparations for mobilization were reported to be in process of organization, while preparations were made for the city to receive fifteen hundred infantry of marine, six hundred artillerymen with armaments, and four battalions of the line.[280]

---

[279]FO 27/3397, D.551, 26 October 1898, Monson to Salisbury; FO 27/3397, D.552, 27 October 1898, Monson to Salisbury; FO 27/3397, D.556, 28 October 1898, Monson to Salisbury.

[280]FO 27/3399, Tel.245, 22 October 1898, Sanderson to Monson; FO 27/3400, Tel.181, 23 October 1898, Monson to Salisbury; FO 27/3400, Tel.183, 24 October 1898, Monson to Salisbury; Eubank, "Fashoda," 153-154; Langer, *Diplomacy of Imperialism*, 562; Sanderson, 348.

Monson did not attempt to interpret what these preparations suggested about French intentions; possibly he could not. During the final weeks of October, he limited his assessment of the military situation to the transmission of Dawson's numerous reports of French defensive preparations. With respect to his other urgent question, the ambassador could not easily address the question of Russian support for France. Throughout the crisis, given his limited access to information, he could never entirely ascertain whether in the event of a rupture Russia would actually come to the assistance of its ally. Five months earlier in May, Monson reported that Hanotaux betrayed some irritation with the Russians. At that time, Hanotaux showed an "entire absence of any enthusiasm for, or even defense of, Russian policy." The foreign minister was apparently "well aware that among the public at large there is a prevalent feeling that France's complete subservience to Russia in matters of foreign policy has been a little too patent."[281] Monson also noted the comments of some Russian diplomats abroad, particularly the language used to describe the French alliance, which is "almost always pitched in one key." Prince Lobanov had expressed himself as "nauseated" with the adulation heaped upon him in Paris; the new Russian ambassador Prince Lev Urusov on his arrival in Paris spoke of the Franco-Russian intimacy "almost with indifference." The Russians, Monson observed, "have not made these sentiments carefully concealed" and thus engendered growing resentment in Paris. His analysis changed, however, when he warned in early July that France would in fact be assured of support from Russia. He noted on 4 July that in spite of a recent waning enthusiasm in Franco-Russian relations, it would be "extremely dangerous were we to base our

---

[281]FO 27/3395, D.242, 19 May 1898, Monson to Salisbury.

policy in any controversy with France upon the assumption that we should be allowed to deal with her as our sole enemy."[282] And yet, the very next day, he again claimed that "the glamour of, and enthusiasm for, the Russian alliance, have faded away."[283] The question, however, assumed a far more serious sense of urgency when, on 15 October Count Mikhail Muraviev the Russian Foreign Minister visited Paris.

Russia had thus far not made much of an effort to assist France during the Fashoda crisis. On 1 September Delcassé telegraphed to Muraviev a recent dispatch from London warning of an imminent crisis on the Upper Nile. He had hoped for some public statement of Russian support to increase the pressure on Britain for a negotiated settlement. None, however, followed. After ten days he telegraphed a reminder, reporting London's intention to fly its flag alongside the Egyptian flag at Khartoum. In response to Delcassé's latest communication, Augustin Toutain the French *chargé d'affaires* in St. Petersburg wired on 12 September the uninspiring Russian response that "in this affair, as in all the questions related to Egypt, the Imperial Government would be resolved to march in agreement with us and to conform its attitude to that of the French Government." In the meantime, he passed along the Tsar's even less encouraging suggestion that a Turkish protest supported by the Powers might be useful. Muraviev departed the next day for a holiday, making Toutain's telegram the final official communication on the subject between France and Russia until Muraviev's visit to Paris on 15 October.[284]

The purpose of the visit by Muraviev, who was

---

[282]FO 27/3395, D.330, 4 July 1898, Monson to Salisbury; BD 184: 159.

[283]Andrew, 120.

[284]Andrew, 122; Sanderson, 356-357. Sanderson suggested that Muraviev deliberately disappeared from the diplomatic dialogue "perhaps to avoid further importunities."

accompanied by Finance Minister Sergei Witte and War Minister Alexei Kuropatkin, was as usual to negotiate a loan and to raise arms; events on the Upper Nile, however, were most certainly discussed. In fact the diplomatic community in Paris generally believed that Muraviev advised Delcassé to withdraw from Fashoda in return for Russian support in later negotiations over Egypt and other African frontiers. Monson made every effort to learn the result of the Muraviev-Delcassé discussions since he was never completely confident about the accuracy of that view. His subsequent dispatches revealed a decidedly unclear appraisal of the situation. On 21 October he wrote that there appeared to be "entire accord" between France and Russia on "every question of importance" including, presumably, the Egyptian question and the issue of Fashoda:

> [Muraviev's presence] will be found to have been encouragement to the French government in the attitude which they have assumed . . . it is argued that [Russia] has hitherto done so little for her Ally that it would have been difficult for [Muraviev] to decline to show some intention of giving his best support to France in the existing emergency.[285]

Later that same day, however, Monson informed London that according to the Italian ambassador Count Tornielli, Muraviev advised Delcassé to come to a "speedy understanding" with Britain. Monson argued that given the Tsar's recent proposal to reduce military and naval expenditures, such a view seemed correct: "It does not require the resources of divination to establish the probability of its having been tendered."[286]

A few days later, Monson reversed himself for a

---

[285]FO 27/3397, D.532, 21 October 1898, Monson to Salisbury; BD 213: 181.

[286]FO 27/3397, D.535, 21 October 1898, Monson to Salisbury.

second time. As military preparations continued in earnest, he noted that while Count Münster did not believe that Russia would support France militarily, "I differ from my German colleague on this point."[287] The next day, furthermore, he learned from an "entirely trustworthy" source that Muraviev had assured Delcassé of Russian assistance: "Do not give England any pretext for attacking you at present. At a later date, an opportunity will be found by Russia for opening the whole question of Egypt." Monson did not know how to interpret this information but was skeptical. Muraviev, he wrote, "neither categorically refused nor contingently promised, the support of Russia in the present emergency."[288]

By the end of the month, he was once again inclined to believe that Russia would support France in a war. On 27 October, recalling Delcassé's promise of 28 September that France would not stand alone in the event of a rupture, Monson reiterated "with positive assurance" his conviction that France could count on "more than moral support on the part of Russia."[289] Four days later Prince Urusov told Monson that he hoped that the incident would not lead to a rupture between London or Paris although he was certain France would probably yield over Fashoda.[290]

In London the routine shifting in Monson's views began to cause some frustration, especially since his reports at times conflicted with information received from other British diplomats. Frank Lascelles ambassador to Germany wrote that he did not believe the accuracy of Monson's report, which was "quite antagonistic" to what he had learned from other quarters. Ralph Milbanke secretary of the British embassy at Vienna reported that

---

[287]FO 27/3400, Tel.183, 24 October 1898, Monson to Salisbury.

[288]FO 27/3400, Tel.185, 25 October 1898, Monson to Salisbury; BD 215: 182; Andrew, 161; LQV, 299.

[289]FO 27/3400, Tel.189, 27 October 1898, Monson to Salisbury.

[290]FO 27/3397, D.572, 4 November 1898, Monson to Salisbury; Sanderson, 357.

Russian assistance would not be forthcoming. He noted that a few days after leaving Paris, Muraviev had told the Austrian Foreign Minister Count Agenor Goluchowski that Russia considered Egypt unimportant compared with her interests in the Far East.[291] Count Nicholas Lamsdorff the Russian assistant undersecretary for foreign affairs assured Sir Charles Scott the British ambassador at St. Petersburg that Russia had no intention of being dragged into a dispute in which it had no interest. Delcassé, Scott suggested, must have misunderstood Muraviev's "natural professions of sympathy."[292] The Queen, who feared the possibility of Russian support for France, urged Salisbury to find out if it was true:

> The news from Sir E. Monson about Russia's support of France in the event of war with us is most contradictory, and we ought to ascertain why Mr. Milbanke reported the very reverse of what Sir E. Monson now telegraphs. Ought we not to ask the Russians if such reports are true, and further get assurances of support and understanding with the other Powers?

The next day, she wrote that "I think Sir E. Monson has been frightened by these reports . . . I do not believe them." The Queen considered the ambassador excessively gullible and requested Salisbury to see Lascelles, "who leaves today and is so sensible and well informed." The prime minister himself did not trust the accuracy of Monson's reports and assured the Queen that there existed no reason to fear the possibility of any serious Russian assistance to France:

> If we asked Russia, she would give us an answer as

---

[291]Giffen, 161; LQV, 300-301; Sanderson, 358.

[292]Eubank, "Fashoda," 155; Sanderson, 358.

> should induce us to give way; that is to say, she
> would frighten us as much as possible. This would
> be quite consistent with her holding exactly the
> opposite language to the French; for a war now
> would be inconvenient to her. She wishes to stop it;
> but whether it is stopped by France yielding or by
> England yielding she does not care. .

Salisbury speculated that Monson was too disposed to accept the French view of events: "[He] does not tell us where he gets his information, probably he cannot. But I suspect it is somebody who has been put in his way by Russia or France."[293]

Without question, the ambassador's reports became increasingly alarmist toward the end of October as events within France intensified. Salisbury's suspicion that Monson was being deceived proved correct on at least one occasion. During Muraviev's visit to Paris, Delcassé attempted to obtain a public statement of Russian support. Until that point, he had received only one dispatch containing any suggestion of Russian assurance, the Toutain telegram of 12 September, which in response to Delcassé's reminder of 10 September expressed Russia's desire to co-ordinate its policy with that of France. The Russian suggestion that the concerted policy should be a Turkish protest supported by the Powers, however, diluted the impact of that telegram. When Muraviev agreed to the publication of the statement in the proposed Yellow Book, Delcassé wanted to strengthen it a bit, first by making it a simple statement of Russian support and then by making this support refer directly to the events on the Upper Nile. Such strengthening required not merely changing the text of the dispatch but also making it appear to be the reply to another dispatch to which it was actually unconnected and unrelated, Delcassé's initial telegram of 1 September. The

---

[293]LQV, 301, 303.

two dispatches that he proposed to publish as "question and answer" read textually as follows:

> At the moment when Anglo-Egyptian forces are advancing towards Khartoum, we cannot ignore the grave consequences which may shortly result from the events unfolding on the Upper Nile. I shall be obliged if you will call the attention of Count Muraviev to the possible eventualities and advise me of the manner in which they are envisaged by the Imperial foreign minister. [Delcassé to Toutain, 1 September 1898]
>
> I have acquainted the foreign minister with the information which you have communicated to me concerning the events unfolding on the Upper Nile. Count Muraviev has begged me to give you the assurance that in this affair, as in all the questions relative to Egypt, the Imperial government was resolved to work in agreement with us and to adopt the same attitude as the French government. Toutain to Delcassé, 12 September 1898][294]

President Félix Faure ultimately persuaded Delcassé not to publish these dispatches for fear of aggravating the situation. Delcassé, however, could not resist showing Monson the proof copy of the altered telegrams. He told Monson on 28 October that there were four other telegrams of a similar tone from Russia, which he offered to place before the ambassador. Monson at once accepted the legitimacy of the altered documents and the existence of the other four telegrams. He immediately wired London a "sensational telegram,"[295] reiterating his latest position that France could indeed rely on active Russian assistance. Delcassé had provided proof, he wrote, for his

---

[294]Andrew, 122-124.

[295]Sanderson, 356.

frequent claims that France would not stand alone in the event of a conflict but would have support behind her; that the Russians entirely approved of the French views and procedures in the Upper Nile and would associate themselves with any step ("*toutes les démarches*") that might become necessary in consequence. With respect to the other four telegrams, the foreign minister

> had suppressed them (the one I saw was scored out with red chalk) because, as he had stated to me before, he wished to make the publication conciliatory, and had thought that the appearance of such documents would rouse excitement here. He had done so to the loss of a certain amount of popularity, as he has been constantly attacked for not having been able to give actual proof of Russian sympathy and encouragement. He had, however, deprived himself of this opportunity . . . because he was desirous above all of keeping down excitement. . . . I must state, without reservation, that in the interest of peace I rejoiced that he had not published them, as they would have been interpreted in England as a menace, and would have been resented accordingly . . . Delcassé seemed somewhat surprised at the warmth of my rejoinder.

And yet, in virtually the next breath, Monson expressed misgivings about these Russian assurances, in spite of this provocative interview. Although he did not doubt the existence of other telegrams and never asked that they be produced, Monson noted that Muraviev had done all he could to persuade Paris "not to take any step which would provoke an attack from England and that his words have had their effect." He did not explain, however, how he arrived at this conclusion, which, like his previous dispatches, further confused his position.

By this point, Monson probably suspected that his views were being disregarded in London. He had become aware that several reports from other British diplomats had contradicted his warnings: "I have seen and heard from so many quarters that an entirely different view as to Russian sympathy and support has been submitted on excellent authority to your Lordship that, as I have always held another opinion myself, I am not sorry to be able to quote this confirmation of the conclusion to which I had already come."[296]

Monson was quite correct. His latest telegram met with immediate skepticism in London. Permanent Undersecretary of State Sir Thomas Sanderson suspected the ambassador had been deceived; Delcassé's dispatch, he noted, was founded on a report that the Russian government approved the French views and procedures in regard to the Upper Nile:

> It appears from this that Monson's sensational telegram of more than moral support from Russia is simply founded on a report from the French *Chargé d'Affaires* at St. Petersburg that the Russian Government approved the views and procedure of the French Government in regard to the Upper Nile and would associate themselves *avec toutes les demarches* which might become necessary in consequence.

London did not know, however, what views and procedures had elicited that statement. More important, in response to the Russian promise to support "*toutes les démarches*" that might become necessary, Sanderson pointed out that *démarches* are essentially diplomatic representations that did not necessarily imply military or material action. The expression could cover a broad base

---

[296]FO 78/5052, D.554, 28 October 1898, Monson to Salisbury; BD 221: 184-185; Andrew, 122-124; Eubank, "Fashoda," 155; Sanderson, 356-357; Wood, 193-195.

of activity such as Russian participation in demanding a conference.[297] Moreover, Salisbury was already convinced that Monson was becoming too willing to accept the French version of events and consequences. Monson's assessments concerning the impact of public opinion, the prospect of Russian assistance, and the likelihood that France would fight, had proved hopelessly inconsistent and subject to frequent change.

As confidence in the ambassador plunged rapidly during the last two weeks of October and as domestic pressures within France crescendoed to the dramatic collapse of the Brisson ministry, the nature of Monson's reaction and judgment yet again came into question.

---

[297]FO 78/5052, D.554, 28 October 1898, Monson to Salisbury; minute by Sir Thomas Sanderson, 29 October 1898; Ramm, 65.

Chapter Twelve

DOWN GOES BRISSON

The third and final phase during which the crisis reached its climax occurred over the final week of October 1898, as Delcassé concluded once and for all that the French position truly was untenable. By the middle of October Delcassé had determined that there was no alternative to the evacuation of Fashoda. He knew that unless France explicitly declared and demonstrated its willingness to fight, Marchand would have to be withdrawn; he also knew that France could *not* fight. Still, he continued to hope that France would at least be spared the humiliation of an unconditional withdrawal without even a promise of negotiations. Such a humiliation would be disastrous for the ministry at a time when French society remained hopelessly torn by the Dreyfus case and aroused by rumors of a military *coup d'etat*. Delcassé, therefore, sought to play for time until some respectable excuse could be found that would justify the withdrawal from Fashoda. Until that point, he would continue to meet with Monson, pledge his never-ending good will toward Britain, and attempt to impress upon Salisbury the need to cultivate French favor through concessions to France in the Bahr al-Ghazal. On 25 October, however, the Brisson ministry collapsed, exposing the full extent of the hopeless division within France. Two days later the British cabinet rejected Delcassé's final compromise proposal and placed the fleet on a full war footing. The French had reached match point.

Delcassé complained to Monson on 21 October that he was being widely criticized for his weak opposition to London. Reverting to previous arguments, the foreign minister asserted that France was entirely justified in its occupation of the Upper Nile because of its abandonment by Egypt, an abandonment confirmed by Britain's agreements with Germany, Italy, and King Leopold of Belgium. Monson predictably stuck to his talking points. He sought to sidestep the question of the French and British rights in the Upper Nile and adhered to his own previous argument that Britain held the entire region by right of conquest. Beyond that assertion he had no new instructions or authority to enter discussions of territorial rights. It was impossible to deny, Monson argued, that Marchand's mission had been nothing more than "a deliberate attempt to obstruct our advance up the Nile Valley, and to intercept our line of communication between North and South Africa, the establishment of which, as all Europe knows, is the object of our policy." The ambassador believed that Delcassé was playing for time and would remain obstinate although the foreign minister must recognize the weakness of the French government's contention that it had legitimate rights at Fashoda. Delcassé would therefore refuse to withdraw Marchand, Monson argued, until he could announce the beginning of negotiations on French claims to territories west of the Nile.[298]

The next day 22 October, Marchand's report, which

---

[298]FO 27/3400, Tel.175, 21 October 1898, Monson to Salisbury; BD 214: 181-182; Sanderson, 91-94; Uzoigwe, 189-194.

had been telegraphed from Cairo by his colleague Captain Albert Baratier, finally arrived in Paris.[299] Delcassé told Monson that the situation in the Upper Nile remained unclear. He had received only a portion of the report, which consisted principally of Marchand's telegrams drafted between July and late September. The description of the encounter at Fashoda and the summary of the French position were brief, confusing, and left huge gaps.[300] And yet at the very least, the report made clear that Kitchener's account was exaggerated. Even before all of the telegrams had come through, Delcassé ordered Baratier to Paris in order to supplement Marchand's report with verbal explanations. Although many in Paris hoped that Baratier would clarify the situation, it made little difference to Delcassé what the situation was at Fashoda except that it might provide a respectable excuse for withdrawing Marchand.[301]

In spite of his efforts to delay Marchand's inevitable evacuation until the necessary political preparations were complete, Delcassé understood that time was beginning to run short. He attempted to approach Monson the following day 23 October on the basis of Courcel's 12 October proposal to Salisbury. If France could be given firm assurances on the principle of access to the Nile, he

---

[299]The British cabinet permitted the dispatch of Delcassé's telegram to Marchand on 1 October. Kitchener forwarded the telegram on the gunboat *Kaiber*, which reached Fashoda on 9 October. Baratier left the following day with Marchand's report, arrived at Cairo on 21 October, and spent the evening telegraphing the report to Paris. Bates, 146-148.

[300]Darrell Bates argues that Marchand must have deliberately left gaps in his report "in the hope that he would be summoned to Paris himself for further questioning." This would have enabled the captain, Bates asserts, to stir up further support for his mission and to try and stiffen the wavering resolve of the French government. Bates, 148.

[301]FO 78/5051 and FO 27/3400, Tel.176, 21 October 1898, Monson to Salisbury; Bates, 147-148,155; Sanderson, 354-355.

would not hesitate to authorize Marchand's withdrawal. Monson, however, pressed him instead for clarification on French military preparations and refused to comment further. Finally grasping that nothing would satisfy the British short of an unconditional evacuation of Fashoda and recalling the captain's claim that the health of his men would suffer unless soon relieved, Delcassé wrote to his wife on 24 October that if London did not accept his proposal, he would "publish Marchand's journal and recall the heroic little band. I will not murder them out there with no gain to the country."

He ordered Courcel back to London to plead yet again with Salisbury. Since 5 October the prime minister had avoided seeing Courcel except for the brief encounter on 12 October. In the interim the ambassador had spoken with Sir Thomas Sanderson who preserved Salisbury's position by offering nothing. On 26 October Courcel proposed to Sanderson Marchand's "spontaneous" withdrawal if Salisbury would agree to a "spontaneous" discussion of frontiers that preserved French commercial access to the Nile. This new offer made no mention of the earlier territorial demands. When Salisbury refused to address the proposal until after the next day's cabinet meeting, Courcel feared that this cabinet "portended something in the nature of an ultimatum" to France.[302]

In Paris the domestic turmoil began to intensify once again as the Chamber of Deputies prepared to reconvene on 25 October. In anticipation of a nationalist attempt to overthrow the government in a military *coup d'état*, the newspaper rhetoric heated up on all sides. Right-wing newspapers called for the resignation of Brisson, who had become converted to the revision of the Dreyfus case. *La Libre Parole* called for "drastic action" to be the order of the day. *La Patrie* proclaimed (19 October) that

---

[302]Andrew, 102; BD 216: 182; Brown, 112; Ramm, 65; Sanderson, 348-349.

"Dreyfusism is in power . . . we must dislodge it." Left-wing newspapers warned of plots to overthrow the government, citing daily conversations among Déroulède, General Zurlinden, and General Cavaignac. *L'Aurore* (24 October) called upon all Republicans to demonstrate at the Place de la Concorde on 25 October to "foil the plot of the revolutionaries who have decided to seize power."

By 25 October more than sixteen organizations prepared to demonstrate outside the Chamber of Deputies in the *Palais Bourbon*, which by 1100 was surrounded by barriers. The police, anticipating a tremendous demonstration, were out in great force. Over one thousand officers took up positions along the streets leading to the Place de la Concorde, while regiments of cavalry waited nearby in the Tuileries gardens. Recognizing the foreign policy dimensions of the demonstrations, the police stationed special guards at the Ministry of Foreign Affairs and increased the protection for the British embassy. The vast and unruly crowds outside the Palais Bourbon were primarily supporters of Déroulède and Guérin; Guérin's supporters of the *Ligue antisémitique* were the rowdiest and most vociferous yelling "à bas les juifs" and provoking endless fistfights. The demonstrators marched on the Palais de Bourbon and after a clumsy effort to trigger a *coup d'état*, Guérin and three others were arrested in a bloody confrontation with police. Inside the Chamber the opposition from the center and right was determined to force Brisson from office over the issue of revision. To the surprise of everyone, however, Minister of War Chanoine marched to the tribune and without warning announced his resignation. In the subsequent bedlam and after prolonged and bitter debate, the government lost a vote of confidence 286-254, and Brisson was forced to resign. The crowds outside greeted the news of Chanoine's resignation and the fall of the government with cheers and several serious brawls that required the intervention of mounted police. The shouting of slogans and the waving of flags continued throughout the afternoon, and the demonstrators did not disperse until Déroulède appeared near 2000 in the evening. At no time, however, did the military or any nationalist group ever seriously attempt to seize control of the government. While the interim government was left to deal with police reports, the generals remained respectful, the nationalist deputies appeared more concerned with forming a viable constitutional ministry, and the striking workers continued to behave not as anarchists but as workers on strike.[303]

With the events of 25 October Monson completely abandoned his previous caution. Since September he had sought to play down rumors of a *coup d'état* in an effort to temper as much as possible the generally tense atmosphere between London and Paris. By late October, however, he had become increasingly exasperated by the rush of events in France. In the late afternoon of 25 October, as soon as news reached him of the dramatic events unfolding at the Palais Bourbon and of the massive demonstrations in the Place de la Concorde, he immediately telegraphed London that Chanoine's resignation was "an act of treachery to his colleagues which looks like the first step to a military *coup d'état*."[304]

Monson feared that this latest threat of revolution made war inevitable. In a long dispatch to Salisbury, he wrote that the events of the day presaged the "probable outbreak of a crisis which may have even revolutionary results" particularly in terms of French international relations. In light of the continuing naval and military preparations in the principal ports and arsenals of France, the French government placed itself in a position "from

---

[303]Bredin, 343-344; Brown, 106, 109; Chapman, 236-238; Hoffman, 26, 177-178; Lewis, *Prisoners of Honor*, 252-253; Rutkoff, 94-95; Tuchman, 212-213.

[304]FO 27/3400, Tel.186, 25 October 1898, Monson to Salisbury; Brown, 110-111; Lewis, *Prisoners of Honor*, 252.

which it will be exceedingly difficult for her to extricate herself peaceably without taking a step which will be inevitably considered by numbers of people, and especially by the Army, as derogatory to the national honour." Moreover, Monson feared that civilian government in France would not be able to survive against a "military domination which threatens to become a despotism." He believed that the establishment of a military government, or a nominally civilian government in the hands of the military, would clearly "render the settlement of our existing dispute far more difficult than it is at this moment." A government dominated by generals would welcome war with London if they could in that way stave off revision of the Dreyfus case. Thus, Monson concluded, while Brisson had been "honestly well-disposed" to Britain, the new ministry "whosoever may be its chief and whatever be its elements" would certainly abandon the previous conciliatory foreign policy, which would gravely endanger both France's "internal and external tranquility."[305]

Several observers shared Monson's view that London and Paris were at the threshold of war. Count Tornielli informed Monson that in the event of a rupture, Italy feared the outbreak of a general European war and wished to be in a position to defend its neutrality. On 26 October Italian authorities announced preparations to put the naval ports of Genoa, Spezia, and Madalena in a "state of defense at a moment's notice" at the first sign of war.[306] In Germany the threat of war also alarmed Kaiser Wilhelm II. On 29 October he urgently asked Count Münster for his opinion of the situation. In the margin of the ambassador's cautious reply of 30 October, the Kaiser

[305]FO 27/3397, D.546, 25 October 1898, Monson to Salisbury; Brown, 110-111; Sanderson, 349.

[306]FO 27/3397, D.535, 21 October 1898, Monson to Salisbury; BD 217: 183; Brown, 129; Lewis, *Prisoners of Honor*, 252.

wrote: "A *coup d'état*, therefore, is in sight. . . . I have informed Gossler and Schlieffen."[307] In London the cabinet authorized active naval preparations. On 24 October the Admiralty ordered the Reserve Squadron to be put in readiness. Following the collapse of the French government, they drafted war orders on 26 October for the Home, Mediterranean, and Channel fleets.[308] At the same moment, the telegraph to the French naval base at Dakar, operated by the British-owned West African Telegraph Company, suddenly fell silent for five days.[309]

Therefore, with the unsettling assessment of France on the brink of revolution and possibly war, the British cabinet met on 27 October to deal with the Fashoda question in an atmosphere charged with urgency. British public opinion, fed continuously with exaggerated press reports and inflammatory rhetoric, was overwhelmingly and eagerly in favor of settling accounts with France, particularly now when Britain clearly held the advantage. Salisbury sought to resist the pressures of the moment and presented to the cabinet Courcel's compromise plan -- of a "spontaneous" withdrawal in return for "spontaneous" concessions. Although he was not unwilling to grant France a commercial outlet on the Nile, the rest of the cabinet received the proposal quite coldly. Most members of the cabinet favored immediate and drastic action and therefore opposed any concession to France. They regarded a conflict to be ultimately inevitable and believed that it might as well come now as later. Colonial Secretary Joseph Chamberlain and Lord George Goschen first lord of the Admiralty pressed for an immediate

---

[307]Brown, 129. General Heinrich von Gossler, German Minister of War, 1896-1903. General Alfred von Schlieffen, Chief of the German General Staff, 1891-1905.

[308]Brown, 111-112, 129; Grenville, 229; Robinson and Gallagher, 375; Sanderson, 349.

[309]Headrick, *The Invisible Weapon*, 85; Headrick, *Tentacles of Progress*, 116.

preventive war against France to show the world that Britain was after all capable of responding in defense of its interests. The Admiralty confidently advised that the French navy would not have a "ghost of a chance" against the Royal Navy even with active Russian intervention. At the very least, most members of the cabinet favored an ultimatum coupled with a military show of force. Salisbury alone favored a peaceful and conciliatory settlement wishing to avoid provocation as much as possible. In this he was supported by the Queen, who loathed the prospect of a war over "so small and miserable an object" as Fashoda. "Not a stone should be left unturned to prevent war," the Queen wrote Salisbury.

The cabinet's ultimate decision was something of a balance between ultimatum and compromise. Marchand must be unconditionally withdrawn while Britain would make no promises about French access to the Nile. Only after the evacuation would it be possible to consider French claims. In the meantime, London would not dictate any specific date by which Marchand would be required to depart. The cabinet would thereby leave it up to the French to pursue any active measures that would "precipitate a conflict." Nevertheless, the war orders for the Royal Navy drafted only the day before were signaled to the Mediterranean fleet and on 29 October the Channel fleet was ordered to Gibraltar.[310]

Following the cabinet meeting, Salisbury finally saw Courcel. The contentious cabinet meeting actually strengthened the prime minister's hand as the militant sentiments of his colleagues lent credence to the British threat to go to war. He thus purposely exaggerated his difficulties in restraining the Chamberlain faction.[311] He

---

[310]Andrew, 100-101; Brown, 112-113; Garvin, III, 228-230; LQV, 298, 305; Marder, 323-327; Peterson, 124-125; Robinson and Gallagher, 373-374; Sanderson, 350, 355-356.

[311]Lebow, 323.

asserted that Britain would refuse to enter into any negotiation or compromise over frontier questions while the French flag continued to fly over Fashoda. To do otherwise would imply the legality of Marchand's position. He neither gave nor implied any promise of concessions even after the withdrawal and remained aloof with respect to the start of discussions. In his dispatch to Monson, Salisbury wrote that Courcel appeared to open a door for a resolution: "He said . . . that the reports received from [Marchand] seemed . . . to show that Fashoda could never furnish the outlet on the Nile which France might obtain; and that therefore it was of no use to her. He thought it therefore not improbable that M. Marchand would receive orders to retire."[312]

It was match point and Courcel knew it. The only expedient available was to bring about the evacuation with the minimal loss of face for France. He noted the change in Salisbury's tone after the Cabinet meeting[313] and informed Delcassé on 28 October that Salisbury's colleagues would not allow him to go any further; that this was London's final word. The next day, he forwarded Salisbury's unofficial *aide-memoire* which argued that "whatever was at present abnormal in the diplomatic relations between the two countries would cease" once Marchand was withdrawn. Only then would French claims be considered. At the ambassador's request, the cabinet provided written documentation that it had never formally demanded Marchand's withdrawal. Although he was convinced of Salisbury's goodwill, Courcel noted that no British minister would be able to withstand the public outcry caused by permitting a French presence in

---

[312]FO 78/5052, Tel.255, 27 October 1898, Salisbury to Monson; BD 223: 187.

[313]Others detected a change in the prime minister's tone as well. Blunt wrote in his diary, 25 October, that Salisbury clearly has been negotiating but that" he has allowed his back to be stiffened by the London Press and his colleagues' speeches." Blunt, I, 303.

the Upper Nile. The prime minister was stalling for time, to allow British passions to subside. He could not allow the public see that he was any more conciliatory than his colleagues. "We must deceive ourselves no more," Courcel argued. "We won't obtain any compromise on this point." Therefore, he urged Delcassé to withdraw at once from Fashoda while it was still possible for France to preserve its honor: "*avec honneur et la tête haute.*" The withdrawal of Marchand could be justified by referring to the "difficulties of the local situation."[314]

In Paris, Delcassé was now a *ministre démissionaire* following the collapse of the Brisson cabinet. Finding himself under unrelenting pressure in the face of the growing threat of war with Britain, he had counted upon his ability to extract concessions from Salisbury, which he could then present to the French public as a tangible diplomatic success. Instead of concessions, however, his reward was the British naval mobilization and Courcel's advice to evacuate Fashoda without delay. Compounding his difficulties, Delcassé came under growing pressure from the colonialists in the Chamber of Deputies to damn the consequences and refuse British demands to evacuate Fashoda. Baratier, who reached Paris on 26 October to a hero's welcome, attempted to convince Delcassé in their meetings of 27 and 28 October that contrary to Kitchener's account, the French forces at Fashoda were well-provisioned and well-armed. They could certainly remain in place until reinforcements arrived. It soon became obvious to Baratier, however, that far from wanting to know how long they could hold out, the foreign minister was in fact seeking an excuse to recall them. Delcassé indeed dismissed Baratier's arguments and began to discuss possible evacuation routes. He tried

---

[314]BD 220: 184; Eubank, "Fashoda," 156; Peterson, 127-128; Sanderson, 350-351.

to impress upon the captain the obvious lopsided nature of the military balance of power in the Upper Nile. Besides, he stressed, "You cannot desire the hostility of such a powerful State as England when we are still bleeding on our eastern frontier."

Finding the foreign minister unwilling to further support the Marchand mission, Baratier appealed directly to the leaders of the French colonial movement. The result was a series of newspaper attacks on Delcassé's position. On 28 October *La Dépêche Coloniale* openly demanded war rather than submit to humiliation. The next day most Parisian newspapers published a declaration, signed by several colonialist deputies, protesting the conclusion of any settlement without prior discussion in the Chamber. Further aggravating the irritation of the colonialists was the recent news that Marchand had departed without permission from Fashoda for Cairo. Although the captain's intention was to send a report to Paris, his departure was interpreted throughout France as the first step toward evacuation. The Parisian newspapers again attacked Delcassé, accusing him of having sent secret orders to Marchand to retire.[315]

Increasingly Delcassé began to show signs of strain. On 27 October he complained to Monson about London's rejections of all his conciliatory overtures. With great emotion he declared that if London rejected his current proposal, he could not continue in office. "It is you," he told Monson, "who make it impossible for me to remain." Delcassé was "much moved," wrote Monson, in his protests against the "humiliations which . . . we are desirous of inflicting on France." Monson casually replied that although there had been no intention to humiliate France and the situation was indeed embarrassing, Britain

---

[315]BD 224: 187; Bates, 149-151, 160; Brown, 113-115; Peterson, 123; C. Porter, 130; Sanderson, 352-353.

had done nothing to bring it about. Rather it was France's "own deliberate act which has brought her into difficulties, and I must repudiate all responsibility for England for the consequences which might follow."[316] Delcassé renewed his argument two days later, insisting that if London would not agree to negotiate at least a commercial outlet to the Nile, a humiliation would be inflicted upon France that he personally could not accept. The alternative would be war, which was "contrary to his avowed policy and repulsive to his principles." He seemed more than a little irate, Monson noted, by Marchand's unauthorized departure from Fashoda, which he described as "incredible and unpardonable" and promised that the captain would be ordered back to Fashoda at once. Monson attempted but without success to persuade Delcassé that there would be no humiliation in withdrawing an expedition that had no political mission and had advanced to the Nile only in an excess of zeal.[317]

Monson did not foresee any immediate resolution although he suggested that Delcassé's resignation from office might in fact facilitate the best chance for a solution. He often complained that Delcassé's "pertinacity was invincible" and that he always assumed that "his rhetoric is unanswerable . . . [he] has never chosen to content himself with my simple refusal to discuss anything beyond the deliberate illegality of the act committed by M. Marchand. As Your Lordship is aware, I have never succeeded in making the least impression upon him on this point." [318] Nevertheless, Monson predicted future complications because of the strength of

---

[316]FO 27/3400, Tel.191, 27 October 1898, Monson to Salisbury; BD 221: 184; Brown, 115.

[317]FO 27/3400, Tel.193, 29 October 1898, Monson to Salisbury; FO 27/3400, Tel.194, 29 October 1898, Monson to Salisbury; BD 222: 186; FO 78/5052, D.558, 29 October 1898, Monson to Salisbury.

[318]FO 78/5052, Tel.195, 30 October 1898, Monson to Salisbury; BD 225: 188.

the colonial lobby in the Chamber. Any eventual settlement of the Fashoda dispute in British favor might provoke a profound clamor, especially when the colonialists realized that London insisted on a "much further abatement of claim." Although the settlement itself might be effected without causing an actual rupture, "I am not alone here in thinking that such a settlement will for years place the relations between the two countries upon a footing so unstable and so full of offense to France that we shall have to count upon her active enmity in every quarter where she can exert it to our detriment."[319]

In spite of Courcel's communications of 28 and 29 October, Delcassé continued to maneuver for any concessions from London regardless of how minor or incremental. By this point hopelessly frustrated in his efforts to negotiate with Monson, the foreign minister considered approaching Salisbury via Courcel with yet another possible compromise. France would order Marchand's withdrawal if Salisbury would agree to a joint Anglo-French study over the delimitation of the Bahr al-Ghazal. This step would tie the French evacuation to the completion of provisions established by the West African Convention of June 1898 and give Salisbury the opportunity of making a promise without formally infringing upon the cabinet's refusal of negotiations over the Upper Nile valley unless Marchand was withdrawn.

Delcassé changed his mind, however, when the British Channel fleet sailed for the Mediterranean Sea on 29 October. As war seemed imminent Delcassé canceled Courcel's orders on 30 October, writing that it was useless at least for the moment to push much further. The foreign minister's new instructions horrified Courcel, who had begun unofficial discussions with Sir Thomas Sanderson on Marchand's probable route of evacuation. On 31

---

[319]FO 78/5052, D.566, 30 October 1898, Monson to Salisbury.

October he learned from Geoffray, who was currently in Paris, that Delcassé had proposed a plan calling for Marchand to withdraw from Fashoda and link up with the Ethiopians and other reinforcement missions. At a more opportune moment France would be able to challenge Kitchener's Anglo-Egyptian force. Courcel, convinced that Marchand had to be immediately recalled in the interest of peace, wrote to Geoffray: "*Cela me semble de la folie pure, de la folie dangereuse.*" He warned that although London had not yet decided on war and nonetheless appreciated Delcassé's efforts for peace, the British would in fact be ready to fight and would strike with maximum force when war appeared inevitable. He ordered Geoffray to see Delcassé repeatedly until his mind was changed: "Act [now], I beg you. . . . Straighten out these visionaries. Do not allow them to have their way . . . If you cannot see and enlighten [Delcassé], at least see [Nisard][320]. . . . If necessary I may ask you to go on my behalf to the Elysée. . . ."[321]

In spite of his last ditch efforts, by the end of October Delcassé too recognized that it was over. The decision by the British cabinet on 27 October effectively represented the last possible hope that France could retreat with its honor intact. British intransigence meant that the foreign minister's policy of incremental retreat from the crisis with the hope of securing even minor concessions had not just been impossible but in fact delusional. Instead of concessions, France was now confronted by the very real possibility of war.

The facts were simply indisputable. First, the British government remained completely inflexible and uncompromising as it had from the outset of the crisis.

---

[320] Armand Nisard, *Directeur politique* of the French Foreign Office.

[321] Brown, 115-116; Sanderson, 350-351; Taylor, 156.

Second, France was utterly unprepared for war. The government as always was in shambles. Jean Dupuy had just been entrusted with the task of putting together a new ministry and therefore reconstructing the government, amidst continuing fears of a military *coup d'etat*. The military likewise was in disarray. The army was currently demoralized by the Dreyfus affair, while the navy remained infinitely inferior to the Royal Navy. By contrast, the British made it unequivocal that they were willing, ready, able, and eager to go to war. British forces on the spot at Fashoda enjoyed vast superiority. Kitchener's army, which had just conquered the Sudan, numbered about 25,000, while the French forces remaining at Fashoda numbered seven officers and about 125 Senegalese soldiers. Moreover, Marchand's forces were isolated. For all of Baratier's protests to the contrary, they had only three small boats and the water level of the Bahr al-Ghazal, obstructed by *sudd* and difficult to navigate in any event, had been dropping since September. Communications, dependent on either the British route down the Nile or on their original route from the French Congo, remained dreadfully slow and unreliable. Therefore, the French possessed no practical force with which to bear against the British. Although Salisbury was personally reluctant to resort to war (as well as the Queen), he was prepared to do so if France did not agree to withdraw Marchand without conditions. Third, France was diplomatically isolated, without the support of its Russian ally or any other Power. Fourth, French public opinion was horrendously paralyzed and deeply polarized by the ongoing Dreyfus affair as well as its accompanying social unrest. The French were also deeply divided by the colonial expeditions in the Upper Nile. The majority of French citizens were opposed to a war for the "pestilential swamps of Fashoda," while significant elements of the press and the colonialist lobby continued to agitate for action against Britain. By contrast, British opinion was unified as never before. The British cabinet, the majority of British newspapers, and an overwhelming majority of the British public grew ever more abusive and supported preventive war against France at a moment when British advantage was greatest.

The intervention of the President of the Republic Félix Faure brought the crisis to a conclusion. It was manifestly clear to the president that France could not go to war. President Faure, decidedly impressed by the British naval mobilization and the immediate prospect of war, pressed Delcassé to order the evacuation of Fashoda. Although the foreign minister had no real alternative, it was not until Faure agreed to accept full responsibility for this decision that Delcassé gave his reluctant consent.[322] In bracing for the inevitable political assaults, he and his colleagues decided that the least hazardous line of defense lay in humanitarianism: that they would claim to withdraw Marchand and his men for their own well-being; that the expedition were short of food and ammunition, suffering from sickness and exhaustion. At approximately 2230 on 2 November 1898, Monson wired London that the French had decided to retire from Fashoda with the least possible delay and that Delcassé had ordered Marchand and Baratier back to Fashoda in order to carry out the decision. Salisbury announced the news on 4 November at a banquet at the Mansion House given in honor of Kitchener, recently arrived from Cairo: "I received from the French ambassador this afternoon the information that the French Government had come to the conclusion that the occupation of Fashoda was of no sort of value to the French republic." The *Times* reported loud

---

[322]Andrew, 101; Giffen, 46-49, 107-110; Langer, *Diplomacy of Imperialism*, 563, 576; Lewis, *Race to Fashoda*, 224-225; Robinson and Gallagher, 371, 375; Sanderson, 353-354, 360-361; Uzoigwe, 261.

cheers and some laughter. "And they have resolved,"
Salisbury continued, "that the occupation must cease," at
which there was more cheering.[323]

[323]FO 78/5052 and 27/3400, Tel.199, 2 November 1898, Monson to Salisbury;
FO 78/5052 and 27/3400, Tel.200, 3 November 1898, Monson to Salisbury; BD
226: 188; FO 78/5052, D.570, 4 November 1898, Monson to Salisbury; BD 227:
188; Roberts, 707-708.

Chapter Thirteen

FRENCH HEARTACHES CONTINUE

The French withdrawal from Fashoda did not mark the end of the crisis. From November 1898 until the following spring relations between London and Paris remained tense. Despite a vast array of political and colonial disputes, the primary problem involved the delimitation of their possessions from the Sudan to the Congo and the settlement of French claims in the Upper Nile valley. Although Paris anticipated that these matters would be taken up at once, the British government showed no disposition to embark upon negotiations. On the contrary London continued its military and naval activities to such a degree that until the conclusion of the Upper Nile question in March 1899, the threat of war dominated relations between the two states.

In November 1898 the decision to evacuate Fashoda generated a profound depression in France. The most important source of French unhappiness involved the British unwillingness to negotiate the settlement of the Upper Nile territories. Following the announcement of the French withdrawal, Courcel cautiously sounded out Salisbury about discussions over territorial claims. The prime minister, however, politely refused to consider such talks until public excitement had died down. Considering the continuing anti-British hostility in French opinion and the continuing British chauvinism about Fashoda, Salisbury regarded any resumption of discussions relating to the Upper Nile as imprudent and therefore declined to enter any direct negotiations, explaining that he needed further geographical information. Courcel agreed and informed Delcassé that Salisbury could not make concessions to France in the Upper Nile while the "fighting words of Rosebery and Grey were still fires in the public mind." Therefore, they agreed to delay revisiting the question until after the prime minister's speech of 9 November at the Guildhall. After the toasts and a wide-ranging overview of the international situation, he addressed the recent confrontation over Fashoda. The prime minister paid tribute to the "great judgment and common sense displayed by the French Government in circumstances of unusual difficulty." French prudence, he argued, had "relieved Europe of a very dangerous and threatening storm." While Salisbury rejected the idea of a British protectorate over the Sudan, his speech received a decidedly mixed reception in the French newspapers. The *Petit Journal* feared his "simple opportunism," which made him more dangerous than Chamberlain. *Le Matin* worried that the ongoing British naval mobilization, which the prime minister took pains to justify, remained directed against France. In light of Salisbury's decision to defer negotiations, Courcel left London for good on 11 November. Substantive discussions would not begin until Paul Cambon took the initiative in January 1899.[324]

Even beyond British obstinance, French officials were particularly bitter that the alliance with Russia had

---

[324]FO 78/5052, Tel.273, 10 November 1898, Salisbury to Monson; Grenville, 231-232; Roberts, 708-709; Sanderson, 354; Uzoigwe, 280-282.

proven so worthless. St. Petersburg had offered little more than professions of sympathy during the critical weeks of the crisis. Monson observed that Russia's indifference contributed to the current vindictiveness against Britain "whose action has revealed to the public, not only of France but of the whole continent, the amount of value which hitherto the Russians have attached to the 'alliance.'" The bitterness over this revelation would have been even stronger, he noted, had the French public known that to a great extent their government's original refusal to recognize "the untenable nature of their position at Fashoda" followed direct encouragement from Russia, which was not dissipated until Count Muraviev's visit. In contact with the reality in Paris, Muraviev became convinced "that it would be too dangerous to continue to buoy up the courage of France by allowing her to trust . . . her ally for material aid."[325] The French press was more direct. On 13 November the *Soleil* wrote:

> We sent our sailors to Kiel on the occasion of the opening of the Baltic Canal in order to please Russia; we consented after the Chino-Japanese War to pull the chestnuts out of the fire for Russia, and she thereby gained Manchuria and obtained a preponderating position in the China Seas without spending a single rouble and without risking the bones of a single Cossack . . . In the Fashoda Affair, Russia has not lifted a finger to defend us. She doubtless considers that the services we have rendered her are sufficiently repaid by some telegrams which have flattered the vanity of M. Félix Faure and some decorations which have pleased M. Hanotaux.[326]

---

[325]FO 27/3397, D.580, 7 November 1898, Monson to Salisbury; FO 27/3397, D.598, 11 November 1898, Monson to Salisbury.

[326]Andrew, 122; Langer, *Diplomacy of Imperialism*, 563.

The French government faced another problem in Marchand's initial defiance of the cabinet's decision. Although the captain eventually withdrew from Fashoda on 13 December, Delcassé's concern was that Marchand, already a national hero, embraced by the anti-Dreyfusards as a gallant soldier who defied the perfidious Albion only to be betrayed by politicians -- would portray himself as another perhaps more satisfactory Boulanger.[327]

The government's final trouble of course remained the seemingly endless Dreyfus case. The Court of Criminal Appeal on 29 October ruled Lucie Dreyfus's appeal for reconsideration of her husband's conviction well-founded and declared that it would proceed to a further investigation of the original verdict. Monson described the recent revelations as extremely "damnatory" and conclusive against the military authorities. Nevertheless, he fully expected a second court-martial to confirm the original verdict: "The solidarity and '*espirit-de-corps*' in the French army are evidently as powerful for evil as for good." He warned that should the verdict be overthrown, no other resource would be open to the military party other than violence, which would "practically entail the suppression of all constitutional guarantees and subvert the existing Republican system." He concluded: "Never in this century, and that is say much, has France given more occasion for that pity which is allied to contempt than she does at this present moment."[328] Through November into December, Monson continued to express disgust with the hypocrisy and injustice of the case "so repulsive as to render criticism superfluous." He found "regrettable" members of the Chamber of Deputies and the Senate, who "while

---

[327]Bates, 160-162, 183-185; Eubank, "Fashoda," 157-158; Lewis, *Race to Fashoda*, 224-226; Wright, 201-202. See Monson's reports on Marchand's withdrawal from Fashoda in FO 78/5052.

[328]FO 27/3397, D.561, 30 October 1898, Monson to Salisbury.

deploring the actual condition of affairs, have surprised me by the pertinacity with which they espouse the anti-semitic [*sic*] cause, and the credulity with which they swallow stories of corruption" alleged against the Court of Cassation, while at the same time inveighing in the strongest of terms against similar charges brought against the General Staff. He thus believed that it would be quite impossible to make any forecast of "the turn which affairs will eventually take" and feared the continuation of parliamentary disorder in the coming session. True to form, anti-Dreyfusard gangs again undertook street demonstrations to intimidate the Chamber of Deputies, while in the Chamber itself the case provoked angry outbursts, recriminations, and challenges to duels. The prospect of continuing disorder, Monson noted, was disquieting not only for most Frenchmen but also for their foreign neighbors "whose relations with a country seething over with the effervescence of political passions, cannot but be . . . rendered still more uncertain and difficult." He had been informed by the German ambassador Count Münster, tongue firmly in cheek that it was the desire of Germany that the Dreyfus scandal be allowed to sink into oblivion, "in order that the incapacity, the truculence and the corruption of the French general Staff may continue to have their due effect in sapping the military strength of France."[329]

The French, Monson concluded, appeared "staggered [and] humiliated." While the members of the new Dupuy ministry impressed him with an outward display of courtesy and a sincere desire to be on the best possible terms with London, "there is no doubt that this country

[329]FO 27/3398, D.649, 27 November 1898, Monson to Salisbury; FO 27/3398, D.690, 16 December 1898, Monson to Salisbury; See also: FO 27/3397, D.608, 15 November 1898, Monson to Salisbury; FO 27/3397, D.613, 15 November 1898, Monson to Salisbury; FO 27/3398, D.689, 16 December 1898, Monson to Salisbury. Bredin, 344-346; Lewis, *Prisoners of Honor*, 255-256.

has been intimidated by the attitude" of Britain:

> Frenchmen had not realized what their position
> would be if their neighbour across the Channel
> whom they had been used to flaunt with comparative
> impunity, suddenly gave them to understand that the
> limit of toleration had been reached. . . . They were
> quite unprepared both for the speedy exhibition of
> British force and for its apparently crushing
> supremacy.

Delcassé, deeply wounded by the Fashoda withdrawal, retreated into a "sulk." He complained that although it had cost him much to continue in office as foreign minister in the Dupuy ministry, he accepted the decision "knowing that he exposed himself to a certain loss of popularity, and foreseeing also that he should have a very disagreeable experience in defending in the Tribune the policy upon which the Cabinet had decided."[330] By late November Delcassé remained profoundly depressed and tended to avoid all references to Fashoda; he "evidently dislikes having to discuss the evacuation question at all."[331] When Monson asked his opinion about recent proposals for the situation on Crete,[332] he answered that in order to maintain the accord between the powers, Paris would agree to anything to which the others assented. After all,

---

[330]FO 27/3397, D.585, 8 November 1898, Monson to Salisbury; BD 228: 189; BD 230: 190; FO 27/3397, D.598, 11 November 1898, Monson to Salisbury; BD 233: 191-192.

[331]FO 78/5052, Tel.213, 24 November 1898, Monson to Salisbury; FO 78/5052, D.643, 25 November 1898, Monson to Salisbury; BD 234: 192.

[332]In September 1898 Muslim garrisons attacked a British force on Crete and in the ensuing violence, several hundred Christians were killed. After London threatened to act alone if the other powers refused to cooperate, the powers invited the sultan to withdraw his troops in exchange for the guarantee of his suzerain rights and the well-being of Christians and Muslims alike.

he bitterly asked, "what is the use of France having an opinion of her own about anything now-a-days?"[333]

By late 1898 Monson was discouraged by the lack of progress in strengthening relations between the two countries. While he hoped that their resentment would be transitory, he feared that the French would use the coming two or three years' respite afforded by preparations for the International Exhibition to increase her naval strength. On 11 November he reported that Edouard Lockroy Minister of the Marine had held a council of French admirals, which considered "not only measures for present defense, but a programme of necessary shipbuilding."[334] Monson gloomily portrayed France as "depressing, even for those who have the greatest faith in . . . recuperative powers." Its internal dissensions were "repulsive" and "ferocious"; the Parisian press "unscrupulous and unbridled"; religion was used for political ends to justify "forgery, perjury . . . tyrannical oppression," and anti-Semitism. This turmoil, moreover, held dangerous implications for Britain:

> The seeds of hatred toward Great Britain are scattered . . . The rising generation is brought up in the faith of the perfidy of Albion and of her treacherous animosity towards France; and the eradication of the sentiments thus implanted would be no easy task, even in the improbable event of a thorough change of tone on the part of those who educate public opinion. But of such a change, I confess that I see no present symptom.[335]

For good reason, Monson had cause to fear the possibilities inherent in French domestic instability.

---

[333]FO 27/3397, D.599, 11 November 1898, Monson to Salisbury.

[334]FO 27/3397, D.598, 11 November 1898, Monson to Salisbury; BD 233: 191-192.

[335]FO 27/3398, D.716, 29 December 1898, Monson to Salisbury; BD 239: 197.

Despite the evacuation of Fashoda, the prospect of war did not disappear.

Chapter Fourteen

WAR SCARE, 1898-1899

The most serious source of tension between France and Britain remained their continuing military and naval preparations. From November 1898 until February 1899, throughout the continent many observers believed that war would break out, although at London's discretion. In France resentment seethed over Britain's "gratuitously provocative" behavior. In Britain public opinion, fueled by offensive and abusive London newspapers, remained chauvinistic and provocative even after the announcement of Marchand's recall. "Homemade Humiliation," wrote the *St. James Gazette*; the French, because of her meddling and hostility toward British imperial ventures, got what they deserved. France was a nation with "feminine impulses and a man's strength and infinitely difficult to deal with" wrote the *Spectator*. "We suppose we must fight in the end, but let her begin it." Monson complained that the patronizing tone of the British press amounted to "a pedagogue lecture to a flogged schoolboy -- let this be a lesson to you not to be naughty again." British arrogance found its loudest voice in Joseph Chamberlain, who sought at least a public display of France's humiliation. On 4 November shortly after the French decision to withdraw Marchand was made public the colonial secretary declared that this would not end the conflict: "The time has come where England and France have to settle their differences once and forever." While Salisbury continued to advocate concessions, Chamberlain questioned the prime minister's resolve:

> I am afraid Lord Salisbury himself has not got the strength of mind to bring about the necessary crisis and choose the right moment to strike like did Bismarck at Ems. You may be certain, however, that all my colleagues, even Mr. Arthur Balfour, are of the same opinion as I namely that Lord Salisbury's policy "peace at any price" cannot go on any longer and that England has to show to the whole world that she *can* act. I consider that the present moment is very favourable for us and you will see what is going to happen as soon as our war preparations are finished. . . . [A]s soon as we are ready we shall present our bill to France *not only in Egypt* but all over the globe, and should she refuse to pay, *then war*.[336]

Similarly, at Manchester on 15 November he attacked the system of pushing and prodding that French ministers had ceaselessly pursued at every point in the world where the two nations came into contact. He denounced this policy of "pin-pricks" and argued that all the posts established by Marchand in the Bahr al-Ghazal must be renounced: "Fashoda is only a symbol; the great issue is control of the whole valley of the Nile."[337]

Nearly as offensive was Kitchener's offer to purchase the *Faidherbe*. In an offer forwarded to Delcassé, Kitchener helpfully pointed out that its transport by French troops in the Bahr al-Ghazal to the French

---

[336]Garvin III, 234; Peterson, 128-129.

[337]Garvin III, 233; Grenville, 230-231; Riker, 73; Sanderson, 363-364; Uzoigwe, 279-281.

territory in the Upper Ubangi would be "attended by great difficulty and delay and might even cause loss of life to those employed in the work." In order to facilitate their departure from Fashoda, Kitchener proposed that the British take over the Faidherbe "at a fair valuation, when Major Marchand has no longer any use for her on his journey up the Sobat."[338]

Most unexpected, however, and nearly as insulting was Monson's "Pin-Prick" speech to the British Chamber of Commerce in Paris on 6 December. Two days before, *Le Temps* published a letter by a well-known and active member of the *parti colonial* in the Chamber of Deputies J.L. Deloncle who proposed the establishment of French schools for the "education of natives" at Khartoum and Fashoda. Because the schools would exist in competition with the Gordon Memorial College, Monson regarded the proposal as an act of defiance aimed at British influence in the Sudan. At the annual Chamber of Commerce banquet, he took up Chamberlain's thesis. Although he denied that Britain had any "aggressive designs that need inspire fear in any nation that would deal with London honestly," he asked the French government:

> to abstain from the continuance of that policy of pin-pricks which, while it can only procure an ephemeral gratification to a short-lived ministry, must inevitably perpetuate across the channel an irritation which a high-spirited nation must eventually feel to be intolerable.[339]

Monson's comments provoked a storm in Paris and

[338]FO 27/3399, Tel.293, 28 November 1898, Sanderson to Monson; FO 27/3400, Tel.217, 29 November 1898, Monson to Salisbury; FO 27/3400, Tel.218, 2 December 1898, Monson to Salisbury.

[339]FO 27/3398, D.668, 6 December 1898, Monson to Salisbury; Monson MSS, c.1290; Langer, *Diplomacy of Imperialism*, 263-264.

many, including President Faure, regarded his remarks arrogant and improper: "The Fashoda incident is closed, but because the government [intends to organize] some schools in the Sudan, Monson gives it an impudent lesson, and tells our Ministers what they must do." His mistress, Marguerite Steinheil responded, "Yes, the Marquis of Dufferin was a different man."[340] The adverse reaction to his speech took Monson by surprise. The day after, he wrote that "the remarks I made yesterday . . . on the relations between France and England have been well received in official circles." Two days later, however, he learned that several outraged deputies asked Delcassé for "information as to an expression of mine which had been interpreted by [the] Chauvinist Press as an unwarrantable comment upon the internal affairs of France."[341] The *Journal des Débats* described his reference to "pin-pricks" as especially disquieting. While the newspaper praised Monson for his good intentions and courtesy during the recent crisis, "a speech must not be separated from the man delivering it."[342] Many in Paris believed that his words had been authorized by London. Although this was not the case, the French considered the comments to be representative of British policy and remained convinced that London was preparing for war.[343]

British naval preparations indeed continued. The Admiralty maintained the regular navy at maximum preparedness and did not halt the commissioning of the Reserve fleet, which had been initiated on 24 October.[344]

---

[340]Steinheil, 101.

[341]FO 27/3400, Tel.222, 7 December 1898, Monson to Salisbury. FO 27/3400, Tel.224, 9 December 1898, Monson to Salisbury; FO 27/3398, D.675, 9 December 1898, Monson to Salisbury.

[342]Monson MSS., c.1290, Monson to Salisbury, 8 December 1898.

[343]Barclay, 157-159; Garvin III, 234; Langer, *Diplomacy of Imperialism*, 564-565; Sanderson, 364; Wood, 199-203.

[344]Sanderson, 364.

In early November Monson reported that the continuation of British naval preparations and the "flaming accounts" of those preparations by the London newspapers were causing anxiety in Paris. The French government had assumed that once Marchand was withdrawn, there would be a cessation of British armaments. Instead, it appeared that when the British build-up reached maximum strength, London would present Paris with a list of unacceptable demands, then declare war when those demands were rejected.[345] Monson also noted that while the commentary of the boulevard press remained contemptuous, even the more serious newspapers began to insist that the British were imposing upon France a humiliation they would never forget and for which, "however long she may bide her time, she will eventually retaliate."[346] *Le Figaro* published on 21 November an article entitled "*Le Péril Anglais*," written by an "Admiral of Distinction." The admiral argued that the British, having revived all her traditional hatred, must be regarded as the "persistent enemy" of France. War would be inevitable and France should be prepared to fight an industrial war, waged with the intention of starving Britain, using battleships to protect French harbors and coastlines, while attacking and destroying British seaborne supplies of food.[347]

Throughout November and December the French nervously watched London's naval activities, convinced that British interests required the total defeat of France as a maritime foe as soon as they found a pretext for declaring war. Both Courcel and Cambon warned that French naval weaknesses, unmistakably exposed during the Fashoda crisis, might tempt Britain to attack and that the danger would pass only when France was strong

---

[345]FO 27/3400, Tel.204, 7 November 1898, Monson to Salisbury.

[346]FO 78/5052, D.583, 8 November 1898, Monson to Salisbury.

[347]FO 27/3398, D.629, 21 November 1898, Monson to Salisbury.

enough to offer serious resistance. These warnings made a profound impression on Delcassé, who told Monson on 9 December that he was deeply disturbed about the continuing British naval preparations. London had not modified but maintained those activities on the same footing, a circumstance which "gave some countenance to the report that there is a strong party, not unrepresented in the Cabinet, which wants war at any price." Monson quickly reminded him that when the crisis began to look serious, Delcassé repeatedly maintained that France would not stand alone, that she would be backed up by Russia. "Wouldn't it have been an act of culpable negligence," he asked, if Britain did not prepare "at once against the combined attack of two powerful nations?"[348] A week later Monson reported that more than at any time during the Fashoda crisis, the French believed that they would be attacked, that the British would seize the first opportunity, or even make one, for crushing France as a maritime foe.[349]

The British justified their naval preparations as a response to corresponding activities in France. They minimized French concerns about a British attack. Instead, they claimed that the French were carrying out their own vigorous preparations with the intention of attacking Britain. Their argument was not without some justification as the French government clearly intensified its own preparations in late October, November, and December. Torpedo boats were readied for sea at Bordeaux and Dunkirk. Civilians were drafted to man forts at Brest and Cherbourg. In Tunisia coastal defenses were strengthened. On 3 November the Lille garrison received orders to prepare to move at short notice. All

---

[348]FO 27/3398, D.677, 9 December 1898, Monson to Salisbury; BD 238: 197; Grenville, 231; Marder, 334; Sanderson, 364.

[349]FO 27/3398, D.689, 16 December 1898, Monson to Salisbury.

leaves and furloughs were canceled in the French navy, army officers belonging to the military ports were recalled, and the naval reserves were called up on 7 November. Rumors circulated that the French fleet would attempt to tie down the British fleet while troops drawn from interior garrisons would be transported across the Channel in a single night.[350]

Throughout the war scare, Monson transmitted Dawson's numerous and detailed reports involving ongoing coastal and colonial defensive preparations, the movement of troops and reserves, the preparations of new torpedo stations, new infantry tactics, the completion of a new battery at Dolmard, target practices by the French navy, the creation of new companies of marine infantry, and regulations for protecting lines of communication. While most of these reports afforded little more than collected statistics and details, Monson appeared to have regained his composure. He clearly did not take the French naval preparations very seriously.[351] He even betrayed some irritation with the French government. He deplored their failure to "profit by the lesson of Fashoda [and] to appreciate the friendly consideration with which they had been treated." As Paris appeared determined to put British forbearance to the test, the time had come, he wrote, for Britain to show France that the limit of her patience had been reached.[352]

The consensus throughout the rest of Europe, however, was that war was inevitable. Philip Currie, transferred to Rome in 1898, reported uneasiness in Italy over Anglo-French tensions and added that French and Russian representatives had approached Admiral Felice

---

[350]Eubank, "Fashoda," 156; Grenville, 231; Marder, 329-320, 332, 335; Sanderson, 365.

[351]See Monson's reports to Salisbury from November 1898 to February 1899 in FO 27/3397, FO 27/3398, FO 27/3455, and FO 27/3456.

[352]FO 27/3398, D.633, 21 November 1898, Monson to Salisbury; Wood, 198.

Napoleone Canevaro the Italian foreign minister about Italy's position in the event of war.[353] Horace Rumbold British ambassador to Austria-Hungary reported in early November that French officers were in Austria to purchase 3,000 horses and that Foreign Minister Goluchowski "seemed much impressed by the serious preparations" being made by the British government.[354] Sir F.R. Plunkett British minister at Brussels wrote that Baron Lambermont expressed "earnest anxiety as to what the near future might have in store for the world."[355] At the same time, there even appeared to be renewed hints of Russian assistance for reopening the Egyptian question. Currie reported that Alexander Nelidov the Russian ambassador at Rome sought information about British armaments and stressed to Canevaro the necessity of obtaining security for the Suez Canal. On 7 November the semi-official Russian newspaper *Novoye Vremya* declared its support for the "convening of a new international congress to reopen the question of Egypt." Salisbury remained convinced, however, that Russia would not intervene. Rumbold reported from Vienna on 5 November that Goluchowski, who confirmed that Muraviev's advice to Delcassé was strongly in favor of conciliation, did not believe that France could be assured of much backing in any event. Based on his own discussions with Muraviev on St. Petersburg's "absorbing interest" in the Far East, Rumbold argued that Russia was "indifferent as regards Egypt and the Suez Canal."[356] Sir Charles Scott added that "all reports, however apparently well authenticated, of any encouragement given by Russia to France or hopes held out of Russian assistance in raising general questions

---

[353]BD 229: 189; BD 232: 191.

[354]BD 231: 190-191; Eubank, "Fashoda," 156.

[355]BD 235: 192-193.

[356]FO 78/5052, Tel.50, 5 November 1898, Rumbold to Salisbury; Andrew, 161; BD 229: 189; BD 232: 191.

of Egypt may be received with utmost caution," reiterating his earlier assertion that such an opinion could only have arisen from a "serious misunderstanding or misinterpretation of the Tsar's views." Referring to Monson's dispatches of 25 October and 28 October, he noted that Count Lamsdorff positively assured him that Russia had no direct interest in Egypt or the Suez Canal and referred to the Marchand mission as "reckless and ill-timed." The only possible advice that Russia could give to France, Scott intimated, was to retire from that "utterly untenable and ridiculous position."[357]

The most dangerous rumor involved the possibility of German assistance to France. During and immediately following the Fashoda crisis, the French government, which had become desperately frustrated with its Russian ally, began to look elsewhere for support. As hatred for Britain intensified, support for some sort of rapprochement with Germany grew steadily in November and December. Several Parisian newspapers, even within the moderate republican press, began to tone down their standard anti-German invective while many younger right-wing extremists and Germanophobes began to downplay feelings of *revanche*; they began to replace Sedan with Fashoda as the object of French disgrace. Even Delcassé discussed the possibility of some accommodation with Berlin. He had mentioned to Monson on a number of occasions that France would secure an alliance with Germany. Relations between Paris and Berlin did indeed appear far more cordial when in November, two German warships put in at Algiers. The officers and their men were well received by French authorities and the Germans made a splendid impression. The Kaiser was sufficiently moved to send a message of thanks to the French President for the reception accorded

---

[357]FO 78/5052, D.373, 17 November 1898, Scott to Salisbury; LQV, 312.

his ships and intimated that he would confer decorations upon the French officers who participated in the courtesies at Algiers. The publicity generated by this most uncharacteristic display of Franco-German cordiality contributed to the spread of rumors that the German ships had been dispatched to support France in an eventual war with Britain.[358]

The most significant overture took place in early December. Arthur von Huhn a correspondent from the *Kölnische Zeitung* visited Paris, where he was invited to a breakfast arranged by a confidential agent of the French government Jules Hansen, a Dane who since 1871 had served as an unofficial intermediary between Germany and France. Von Huhn met a company of men from the French Foreign Office whose sentiments he found strongly colored by aversion to Britain. Hansen came to the point: France was dissatisfied with Russia's lack of support and was seeking some sort of reconciliation with Germany. The preponderance of British influence in Africa lay in the fact that Germany and France were at loggerheads; a Franco-German rapprochement could put an end to British hegemony there. Hansen added that the *revanchist* mood was on the decline and that the ministry could cleverly push an understanding through the Chamber. Alsace-Lorraine, the major point of contention, could perhaps be overcome by an exchange of the lost provinces for a French colony. Although receptive, Von Huhn was understandably skeptical.

He met days later with Delcassé, who expressed great indignation at the way in which he had been treated by the British. Every day, he complained, they made him "swallow a toad frog" and the end was not even in sight. France and Germany ought to pursue a common policy in

---

[358]Jamie Cockfield, "Germany and the Fashoda Crisis, 1898-1899," *Central European History* 16 (September 1983): 266; Giffen, 195-197.

the face of British encroachments, he argued. By a mutually friendly attitude, the gulf that separated the two counties could be overcome. A simple and practical means to this end could be found in colonial policy. France, Delcassé argued, was already over-supplied with colonial territory and hence would look kindly upon German expansion, particularly in China. Von Huhn, however, reiterated his utmost lack of confidence in French overtures. First, the ultrachauvinists and their press would have to be placated and that would be impossible. Second, the German government had concerns over the stability of the French government and the cohesion of French policy. After all, Berlin could have no assurances that the policy of one ministry would be that of another. Third, the German government simply could not believe that the French would or *could* merely dismiss *revanche* or that any French minister would dare go before the Chamber of Deputies and ask for the ratification of such an alliance. Delcassé tried to minimize the reservations of the German agent; he claimed that chauvinism was rapidly dying, that one minister was more or less bound to follow the policies of his predecessor, and that he would go personally to the Chamber "tomorrow, if you like!" To maintain the appearance Delcassé dined very ostentatiously at the German embassy several days later.[359]

Delcassé's motives remain a subject of conjecture. Some historians maintain that his overtures to Germany were intended as a tactical move designed to make London pause before it launched a preventive war.[360] Others argue that Delcassé took reports of British military preparations seriously enough that he genuinely sought

---

[359]Cockfield, 267-269.

[360]Sanderson, 378.

the assistance of Germany.[361]

In Berlin the official German position throughout the Fashoda crisis was one of strict neutrality. German statesmen and the press avoided taking sides in the question; after all, Germany claimed no territory in the Upper Nile and had no treaty commitments to either side. In response to French overtures, the official German response was cordial but skeptical. Several outstanding factors explain why Germany was hesitant. First, German ties with Britain were in fact currently quite warm and the Kaiser did not care to antagonize London – or his grandmother the Queen. Second, Berlin had very little faith in French motives. They regarded French interest as inspired by nothing more than a fear of Britain. As soon as the danger passed France would turn her back on Germany at the earliest opportunity. Third, they had little trust in Delcassé himself, the "most tenacious and skillful of the protagonists of *revanche*." Germans disregarded Delcassé as unprofessional, a mere politician who knew nothing about diplomacy and who should have disavowed Marchand from the beginning. He had created difficulties for himself and for his country by "climbing up on a high horse." Fourth, Berlin also recognized that any cooperation with France was bound to be limited. Germany relinquished its interests in the Upper Nile valley in July 1890 and kept its actions there subordinate to general foreign policy. German leaders were willing to cooperate with France but only where there was a clear balance of tangible advantage to Germany.[362] The most important factor, however, remained Alsace-Lorraine. No German government could take seriously any suggestion

---

[361]Andrew, 112; Brown, 123; Carroll, 177.

[362]Bernhard Heinrich Martin Karl, Furst von Bülow, *Memoirs of Prince von Bülow*, vol. I, *From Secretary of State to Imperial Chancellor, 1897-1903*, trans. F.A. Voight (Boston: Little, Brown, and Company, 1931), 318; Cockfield, 259, 267-269; Sanderson, 384-386.

that even alluded to them. Arthur von Huhn's paper the *Kölnische Zeitung* wrote on 15 December: "The possibility of a Franco-German rapprochement can only arise when the word Alsace-Lorraine shall have disappeared from the vocabulary of French statesmen and of the French press." German officials simply could not believe that Paris would renounce the "Lost Provinces" for the psychological satisfaction of seeing the British ejected from Egypt. Consequently, most German officials viewed the French interest with either suspicion or casual indifference.[363]

At the same time, Kaiser Wilhelm II could not resist taking advantage of the situation in order to drive a wedge between France and Britain, believing that tensions between London and Paris inevitably would drive the British "into the arms of Germany." Historian Jamie Cockfield asserts that although no document or memorandum exists in the archives of the Wilhelmstrasse that explicitly describes the course of the Kaiser's thinking after early November, the available evidence strongly indicates that he made a conscious if amateurish effort in the months that followed to rekindle Anglo-French antagonism and bring the two nations to war, convinced that such a war would benefit Germany. He did so apparently without the knowledge of either his chancellor or his foreign minister.[364] He believed he had great influence over the British through his grandmother and the support of certain British statesmen, such as Joseph Chamberlain, who were decided advocates of an Anglo-German alliance. The Kaiser therefore began to advise the British at every turn, even while the French were courting the Germans, to take advantage of a

---

[363]Andrew, 112; Bülow, 318-319; Carroll, 168, 175-178; Cockfield, 259-260, 264-269; Giffen, 154-158; Langer, *Diplomacy of Imperialism*, 567-568; C. Porter, 205-206; Sanderson, 377-378, 385.

[364]Cockfield, 260, 264.

magnificent and unrecoverable opportunity to settle accounts with France once and for all.[365]   In mid-December the Kaiser invited British ambassador Frank Lascelles to a dinner, in which Wilhelm came dressed in the uniform of his honorary British regiment. He stated his promise to support Britain in a war with France in the event of hostilities. On 21 December Lascelles wrote Salisbury that even six weeks after the French had yielded at Fashoda, the Kaiser considered that the danger was by no means past and that it was probable that war would break out in the spring. The Kaiser noted that from a military point of view, the moment was ideal for Britain to settle accounts once and for all:

> France was by no means the equal of England at sea, and she would receive no assistance from any other Power. In fact, if the war took place it would be conducted at sea and the other Powers, even if they desired to assist France, would be unable to do so effectively. The English fleet was immensely superior to all others, and the German and Russian fleets were mere pigmies in comparison. England would, therefore, have an excellent opportunity of settling accounts with France without any fear of the interference of other Powers, and it was doubtful whether so favourable a combination for England would ever again occur.

Lascelles told the Kaiser that he did not understand the arguments on which this idea was based and that the British government certainly had no desire to force a war upon France. In spite of Lascelles's arguments to the

---

[365]Cockfield, 256-257, 260, 264, 270; Michael Balfour, *The Kaiser and His Times* (Boston: Houghton Mifflin Company, 1964), 214; E. F. Benson, *The Kaiser and English Relations* (London: Longmans, Green and Company, 1936), 138-140; BD 124: 102-104; BD 127: 107-108; BD 129: 109-110; Garvin, III, 231-232; Grenville, 159-160; LQV, 300; Sanderson, 363.

contrary the Kaiser persisted, asserting that if Britain ever were in serious danger, "he would certainly come to her assistance" and believed that Britain would do the same under similar circumstances.[366]

Other German diplomats followed the Kaiser's lead. In Paris, Monson reported that Count Münster was "much impressed" with the continuation of naval preparations and with the "plain-speaking of public men" in Britain. He observed that there was a general expectation in Europe that London would not shy away from a war with France, which was "notoriously unprepared to encounter the British naval forces" and when the weather conditions in the north would prevent any assistance from its Russian ally.[367] The German ambassador in Vienna Count Eulenburg congratulated Horace Rumbold over the British success at Fashoda but said that it was a pity London "had not taken advantage of the excellent opportunity . . . of giving the French a well-deserved lesson." Eulenburg observed that Anglo-French differences were far from settled and hoped that London "would not let them off another time." In London, however, Salisbury and Queen Victoria regarded German professions of support with much suspicion. Salisbury told Arthur Balfour earlier in the year that the Kaiser's main objective "since he has been on the throne has been to get us into a war with France," while the Queen was incensed by the Kaiser's "systematic and hardly concealed attempts" to set Britain against the Dual Alliance. She wrote the Tsar in March 1899 that Wilhelm "takes every opportunity of impression upon Sir F. Lascelles that Russia is doing all in her power to work against us . . . I need not say that I do not believe a word

---

[366]BD 124: 102-104; BD 127: 107-108; BD 129: 109-110; Cockfield, 270.

[367]FO 27/3398, D.633, 21 November 1898, Monson to Salisbury; BD 123: 101-102.

of this, neither do Lord Salisbury nor Sir F. Lascelles. But I am afraid William may go and tell things about us to you, just as he does about you to us . . ."[368]

In the meantime, while assuring London that Russia would never support the French, Wilhelm in fact began chastising the Russians for *not* supporting the French. The Kaiser worried that if tensions reached the level that it had in October, the Russians might act to defuse the war scare. The best way to prevent that was to shame the Russians into support of their ally in any new crisis. In the middle of December, he chided the Russian ambassador Count Nicolai von der Osten-Sacken for not supporting France, implying that Russia had let the French down. The Russians ultimately proved as skeptical of the Kaiser's sabre-rattling as the British. When he realized therefore that his efforts to foment an Anglo-French conflict were proving ineffective, the Kaiser began in early 1899 to encourage belligerence on the French side. In a meeting on 8 January with the French ambassador the Marquis de Noailles Wilhelm expressed "shock" at the belligerent attitude of the British. Early in February, as rumors spread that Germany would support France in any Anglo-French war, the Kaiser told Noailles of a meeting (alleged and unlikely according to Cockfield) between Lascelles and Bülow, in which the German foreign minister accused the British of bribing French newspapers to attack Franco-German rapprochement in order to "put a stick in the wheels" of their progress toward an understanding. On 19 February on a hunting trip with Noailles, the Kaiser again told the French ambassador in no uncertain terms that Germany would not let France be crushed in a war against Britain.[369]

---

[368]Benson, 142-144; Paul M. Kennedy, *The Rise of the Anglo-German Antagonism, 1860-1914* (London: George Allen and Unwin, 1980), 237; LQV, 340-341, 343.

[369]Cockfield, 271-272.

From the beginning, Monson regarded German provocations and promises of support for Britain or France as implausible. Delcassé on occasion had suggested that, as France felt driven to cultivate the assistance of other powers who would be only too glad to cooperate against British colonial policy, an understanding with Germany was a real possibility. Monson believed, however, that the spirit of *revanche* would prevent any rapprochement with Germany.[370] Whatever Delcassé's motives, he considered the prospect of a Franco-German entente "a most improbable suggestion." The French people would never consent to "such a condonation [*sic*] of the injuries inflicted by the war of 1870 for the purpose of gratifying what is really nothing but a comparatively petty jealousy."[371] Similarly, when Delcassé promised on 9 December "for about the twentieth time" that in the event of war France would obtain the support of Germany, Monson concluded that he had probably been listening to "mischievous and prejudiced politicians" and is misrepresenting the opinion of the large majority of his countrymen.[372] A week later he reported that the court being paid to Germany was led by members of the press, politicians of the colonial group, and younger officers of the French army, "those who only know by school teaching of the Franco-German war, and whose comparative youth renders them more susceptible to the outcry of the present than to the Tradition of the past." Although most Frenchmen would welcome warmer relations with Germany, the older generation would never consent to any proposal which abandoned *revanche* for "so doubtful a chance as the aid of their most recent

---

[370]FO 78/5052, Tel.554, 28 October 1898, Monson to Salisbury; BD 221: 184-185.

[371]FO 78/5052, D.604, 13 November 1898, Monson to Salisbury.

[372]FO 27/3398, D. 677, 9 December 1898, Monson to Salisbury; BD 238: 196-197; Andrew, 112; Rolo, 95-96; Sanderson, 378.

enemy in the endeavor to cripple a Power against whom their grievances are rather sentimental than practical."[373] Monson regarded with great surprise therefore the Kaiser's persistent declarations, as late as February 1899, that war between France and Britain was inevitable. He did not believe that Delcassé had communicated anything to Count Münster to warrant that view. Monson suggested that Berlin probably desired to "keep up the panic" in France, although he incorrectly attributed German intentions to the Kaiser's fear that France was trying to woo Italy away from the Triple Alliance. Monson speculated that the Kaiser's views were likely strengthened by Münster, who was probably influenced by the openness with which the Parisian newspapers reported French military preparations.[374]

Although German professions of support were ultimately disregarded in London and Paris, the Kaiser's schemes clearly contributed to the continuing tension. Throughout November and December, the British and French governments remained entrenched in a series of colonial disputes that fueled the anticipation of war. First, London continued to protest the levying of tariffs in Madagascar, complaining that France had imposed higher duties upon British goods than was justified and had tried to dissuade the natives from buying British merchandise. Although Delcassé and Cambon both tried to be conciliatory, they found themselves bound by the Chamber of Deputies' protectionist policies. In January, Cambon feared that the dispute might lead to war, particularly after London's publication of a Blue Book on Madagascar, which publicized a string of broken French

[373]FO 27/3398, D.689, 16 December 1898, Monson to Salisbury; FO 27/3398, D.716, 29 December 1898, Monson to Salisbury; FO 27/3455, D.6, 6 January 1899, Monson to Salisbury.

[374]FO 27/3455, D.67, 3 February 1899, Monson to Salisbury; BD 243: 200-201.

promises and caused "considerable irritation in Paris."[375] Second, they made no progress in resolving their dispute over French fishing rights in Newfoundland. The prolongation of the problem was largely the result of a misunderstanding. Cambon apparently misinterpreted Salisbury's lack of interest as a disinclination to negotiate, when in fact the prime minister wished to pursue further discussions. Third, they quarreled over spheres of influence in China. In early 1898 when France demanded the extension of a concession that it already possessed at Shanghai, the British government encouraged China to resist and even promised "material support." Fourth, a quarrel arose in February 1899 over a projected lease of a coaling station to France by the sultan of Muscat. Although Muscat was never a formal British colony, it was under British influence. Lord Curzon Viceroy of India sent three warships on his own initiative to Muscat waters and ordered the sultan to withdraw the lease under the threat of bombardment by the Royal Navy.[376] Although each of these incidents ended with negotiations undertaken and resolutions reached in London, Monson was not directly involved and not always kept informed. On 2 March Delcassé informed him that the basis of an "agreement respecting a coal depot in the Muscat territory [was] practically arrived at."[377]

At no time, however, did Monson seriously believe that war would break out. Despite continuing military preparations and continuing nervousness in Paris, he remained confident that France would remain pacific and unconcerned that any external assistance for France might

---

[375]FO 27/3455, D.12, 8 January 1899, Monson to Salisbury; FO 27/3455, D.21, 13 January 1899, Monson to Salisbury; Andrew, 114; Riker, 75; Rolo, 96; Sanderson, 364; Stuart, 32-33.

[376]Andrew, 114-115; BD 255: 209-210; BD 256: 210; BD 257: 211; BD 258: 211-212; BD 259: 212-213; BD 260: 213-214; Giffen, 187-188; Stuart, 32.

[377]FO 27/3456, D.131, 2 March 1899, Monson to Salisbury.

come from "continental countries which . . . have no particular reason to be tender about her, and who certainly do not find themselves in sympathy with her in regard to her domestic attitude at this moment." His dispatches reflected a prevailing sense of detachment from the anxiety he previously observed in Paris. He reported, for example, a recent conversation with the editor of the *Temps* who pointed out that London was very likely to take this opportunity to settle affairs with France by force and that no one doubted what the result would be: the destruction of the French fleet and loss of French colonies. The editor argued that France would never surrender and that her defeat would be only the first act in a larger, longer conflict. Monson reported this conversation to be merely "an illustration of the state of feeling in France" and dismissed these arguments as the simple speculations of a journalist.[378]

By late January Monson definitively concluded that France had no intention of going to war and that its preparations were strictly defensive. He praised Delcassé's recent speech in the Chamber and the moderation of the ensuing debate as proof that the French government realized how delicate relations had become. Powerful influences existed, he argued, which compelled France to keep the peace: Russian indifference to French colonial ventures; the acknowledgement of French naval inferiority; the continuing discord over the Dreyfus case; and the prospects of prestige from the coming International Exhibition of 1900. The French now understood that Anglo-French relations were passing through "a phase of such extreme delicacy as to render it essential . . . to do nothing which may embarrass the

---

[378]FO 27/3455, D.6, 6 January 1899, Monson to Salisbury; FO 27/3455, D.12, 9 January 1899, Monson to Salisbury; FO 27/3455, D.21, 13 January 1899, Monson to Salisbury; BD 241: 199.

Government." He hastened to add that British representations might still be met with obstinance. The frequency with which French cabinets rose and fell tended to place "excessive power in the hands of irresponsible officials" whose relations with London had always been combative.[379] In addition, the Parisian press resumed its normal tone of abuse: "the mischievous elements which are always at work to irritate . . . the population against England are as busy as ever." Although the French government might have temporarily altered its tone, he concluded, London would continue to see the "obstinate attitude of the past" with respect to future colonial and commercial questions."[380]

Monson's assessment of the French intention to fight ultimately proved to be correct when by late January British naval intelligence concluded that French military preparations were primarily defensive and that France had no intention of going to war. As a result, a gradual demobilization began towards the end of January as discussions between Salisbury and Paul Cambon began in earnest. By the end of February 1899 the war scare had largely passed away.[381]

---

[379]FO 27/3455, D.48, 27 January 1899, Monson to Salisbury. See also: FO 27/3461, Tel.11, 23 January 1899, Monson to Salisbury; FO 27/3455, D.43, 24 January 1899, Monson to Salisbury; FO 27/3455, D.44, 25 January 1899, Monson to Salisbury.

[380]FO 27/3455, D.67, 3 February 1899, Monson to Salisbury; BD 243: 200-201; FO 27/3456, D.119, 27 February 1899, Monson to Salisbury; Marder, 328-329; Rolo, 100.

[381]Marder, 334-335; Sanderson, 365-366.

Craig E. Saucier

Chapter Fifteen

"THE QUEEN WANTS TO ENJOY CIMIEZ"

In November 1898 French officials had anticipated that negotiations concerning claims in the Upper Nile would be taken up as soon as Marchand evacuated Fashoda and that they could therefore consider their withdrawal to be a legitimate step that exposed French honor to "no suspicion of injury."[382] For several weeks, however, both Delcassé and Monson waited for the other to make some proposal that would serve as a basis for opening negotiations. Although Delcassé stated very plainly that he was prepared to begin talks and to cede what he could, Monson's transmissions to London produced no result. When the British did not issue the expected invitation to begin negotiations, Delcassé once again decided to bypass Monson entirely and instructed his new ambassador Paul Cambon to initiate talks directly with the prime minister.[383]

Cambon, recently the French ambassador to Constantinople, arrived in mid-December with explicit instructions to lessen the various sources of friction

---

[382]FO 78/5052, D.566, 30 October 1898, Monson to Salisbury.

[383]FO 27/3400, Tel.273, 10 November 1898, Monson to Salisbury; Wood, 210-212, 219-220.

between Paris and London. He already had a reputation as an Anglophile and was according to Monson the best man that could have been chosen. Although Delcassé intended to keep the Egyptian question on ice until he was ready to reopen it, Cambon wished to begin immediately.[384] He proposed a line of demarcation for the western borders of the Bahr al-Ghazal, which would separate the Upper Nile region from French territory immediately to the west but provide France with a commercial outlet to the tributaries of the Nile. Salisbury agreed to discuss differences but reiterated that British policy and opinion were fixed, and that France would not be allowed any political rights in any part of the Nile valley; he did, however, feel that a commercial outlet should be readily accorded. He agreed to refer the proposal to the cabinet. Within two weeks both the British cabinet and Delcassé accepted the line.

The first serious step to the final agreement was the conclusion on 19 January 1899 of the Anglo-Egyptian Condominium, which gave Britain a predominant voice in all matters connected to the Sudan. Moreover, the British government expected that any advice "they may think fit to tender to the Egyptian Government" with respect to the affairs of the Sudan "will be followed." Salisbury consulted no other Powers, even those that had rights and interests that were violated by the Condominium. Nevertheless, and in spite of certain legal weaknesses, it was never publicly challenged. The British naval mobilization indeed represented a warning, not just to the French to accept the Condominium without fuss but to the Powers in general, that any attempted intervention would invite serious risks. The French accepted the reality of British control over the Sudan with little complaint. In one respect, they believed that they might reasonably be able

---

[384]Andrew, 112-113; Bates, 177-181; Eubanks, *Paul Cambon*, 39-60; Giffen, 88-89; Grenville, 232; Rolo, 92-95.

to extract territorial concessions. Immediate domestic turmoil, however, necessitated an expeditious resolution as the Dreyfus affair reached a critical point in early 1899. Rumors of a military *coup d'état*, which ended following the failed attempt on 25 October, began anew in late November 1898 and intensified in January and February. The Dupuy ministry faced a renewal of disorder, popular demonstrations, political rallies, and the expectation of more labor trouble. Most significant, the unexpected death of President Faure on 16 February inspired an attempt by Paul Déroulède to overthrow the government on 23 February. The attempted coup, however, did not have the support of the French army and Déroulède's bold but ridiculous efforts ended in a comic failure. In addition, Marchand was en route back to France. He was bitter, dispirited, and remained an implacable foe of the British. He was regarded by the anti-Dreyfusards as a national hero, perhaps a new savior of France, perhaps a new Boulanger. Delcassé reasoned that if Marchand returned to Paris amidst internal crisis and another prolonged dispute with London, the consequences might be disastrous to the Republic.[385] The French thus agreed to the Condominium with a minimum of complaint and accepted the reality of British control of the Sudan. British naval preparations were subsequently relaxed.

Thereafter, the negotiations between Salisbury and Cambon proved to be a mere drawing of agreed-upon lines on a map. From late January to March they engaged in detailed discussions over boundaries, frontiers, lines of demarcation, trade routes, and claims to commercial outlets. Negotiations were relatively tame, conducted with exemplary caution, and -- contrary to the earlier apocalyptic predictions of Monson -- Delcassé offered no

---

[385]Bredin, 372-376; Chapman, 253-257; Larkin, 85-86, 92-93, 96-104; Rutkoff, 97-100, 120-133.

serious resistance to the British determination not to share with France any portion of the Nile valley. He also abandoned the French claim to a commercial outlet on the Nile. Salisbury even apologized for the uneasiness caused by the latest inflammatory speech by Joseph Chamberlain on 18 January. The agreement, signed on 21 March and officially designated as an "Additional Declaration" to the West African Convention of 14 June 1898, established the watershed of the Nile and Congo rivers as the dividing line between British and French spheres of influence.[386] Upon hearing the news, the German Kaiser was furious. He tastelessly commented that Salisbury had kept the peace because "the Queen wants to enjoy Cimiez."[387]

Monson took no part in the Salisbury-Cambon discussions that resolved the Upper Nile question and was generally uninformed of their progress. In mid-January, when he expressed his hope to Delcassé that France expedite the treatment of the several outstanding questions between the two governments, the foreign minister confined his response to generalities, noting that all overtures were to be made by the British government and that "he would leave all initiative" to London.[388] At a dinner for the diplomatic body on 19 January, President Félix Faure expressed to Monson how pleased he was at the results of the previous day's Salisbury-Cambon discussion. He asked the ambassador whether he could tell him what had occurred; Monson, however, had to reply that he had heard nothing from Salisbury.[389]

Much of the ambassador's correspondence after mid-

[386]BD: 238, 196; BD: 240, 197-198; BD: 244, 201-202; BD: 245, 202; Bates, 177-181; Eubanks, *Paul Cambon*, 65-67; Grenville, 232-234; Sanderson, 365-373. See Foreign Office reports in FO 27/3454.

[387]Cockfield, 274.

[388]FO 27/3455, D.25, 16 January 1899, Monson to Salisbury.

[389]FO 27/3455, D.33, 20 January 1899, Monson to Salisbury.

February reflected his absence from the negotiations. While Monson spent considerable time away from the British embassy during much of February, the majority of those dispatches he did indeed file involved French domestic politics and colonial issues.[390] Monson's few reports concerning the Salisbury-Cambon negotiations[391] suggested that he was convinced of Delcassé's sincerity, although he believed the French would argue that their evacuation of Fashoda entitled them to reciprocal "generosity" when it came to the actual delimitation of territory. What they had failed to obtain by a direct challenge they would now seek to acquire by placing themselves in a position of exaggerated humility.[392]

From the Fashoda crisis until Monson's retirement in 1905, all important discussions between Britain and France would be conducted in London. Although he had acted as Britain's principal negotiator in the delimitation of the Niger territory and had served as the leading British representative during the Fashoda crisis, Monson never again assumed a leading role in any significant Anglo-French issues or negotiations. He subsequently devoted himself to a role as reporter and analyst, probing the state of French feeling, observing trends in their diplomacy, and keeping his government supplied with intelligence. He was created GCVO[393] when King Edward VII visited Paris in 1903. He remained in Paris until December 1904 and, although his efforts to improve relations with France remained hostage to the frequent unwillingness of his government to respond to French overtures, Monson had

---

[390]See Monson's reports to Salisbury from February to March 1899 in FO 27/3456.

[391]Ibid.

[392]Wood, 220-221.

[393]Knight Grand Cross, the highest grade of the Royal Victorian Order, a dynastic order of knighthood recognizing distinguished personal service to the order's Sovereign.

the satisfaction of seeing a general settlement of the principal issues between the two countries in the Entente Cordiale of April 1904. He retired from the diplomatic service in February 1905, whereupon King Edward VII created him a Baronet. He received from the French government the Grand Cross of the Legion of Honour. After much ill health, Monson died in London on 28 October 1909 and was buried in the family mausoleum adjoining the South Carlton church, near Lincoln. Monson's former colleagues in Paris subscribed for a portrait of Monson by the Hungarian artist, Róbert Berény. The painter, however, became bankrupt and the picture disappeared.[394]

---

[394]*Dictionary of National Biography*, 687-688; *Foreign Office List*, 417-418; Wood, 12, 208, 211-216, 300-301.

Chapter Sixteen

CONCLUSION

The Fashoda crisis represented an overwhelming British diplomatic victory. Lord Salisbury remained skeptical about the extent of this "victory": "[W]e have been so anxious to establish our position against the French, that we have half pledged ourselves to liabilities which will furnish subjects of penitent reflection to the Treasuries both of England and Egypt."[395] Nevertheless, the crisis had two significant and overriding implications for the diplomatic relations between Britain and France. First, it resolved both the Egyptian and Upper Nile questions. It afforded the French a clear demonstration that Britain, its diplomatic and military interests guided by the principles of "Splendid Isolation" and therefore unencumbered by treaty obligations, would indeed fight for its position in the Upper Nile. Many observers in France began to acknowledge that the Upper Nile was not as important as French interests elsewhere and that their policy of opposing the British in Egypt had largely been motivated by national pride rather than by any rational assessment either of its interests or of its diplomatic and military resources. The colonialists and other traditional

---

[395]Peterson, 129.

Anglophobe groups such as the officer corps, the nobility, and anti-Dreyfusards, began to lose ground to the commercial and industrial classes, who regarded their economic interests as adequately safeguarded under the existing situation.[396]

Second, the Fashoda crisis ultimately paved the way for the rapprochement between Britain and France. While Russia, the Ottoman Empire, Austria, Germany, and Italy all at one time or another had encouraged France to confront Britain in the Upper Nile and in Egypt, not one of them had offered any effective help. In particular, the crisis convinced the French that the value of their alliance with Russia had genuine and practical limitations. Certainly from the Russian point of view, the question of support for France during the Fashoda crisis came down to simple balance of interests. First, the Franco-Russian alliance had never been directed against anything but the Triple Alliance; and in recent months, relations between St. Petersburg and Berlin had been growing warmer. Moreover, Russia had been quite open about its reluctance to support France in a war against Britain. Second, Russia was perpetually short of money and as always unprepared for war, as its army was undergoing reform. Third, Russia had been quite open about their utter indifference to imperial quarrels in Africa. Outside of its mild concern to internationalize the Suez Canal, Russia had no interests in Africa. Fourth, there was growing skepticism in St. Petersburg about the stability of their ally. On one hand, they saw little value in an ally paralyzed by the Dreyfus affair. On the other hand, the ministry was under a radical, Henri Brisson, and was supported by other radicals who opposed the Franco-Russian alliance.[397] In Paris, many came to the conclusion

---

[396]Langer, *Diplomacy of Imperialism*, 565-566; Sanderson, 374-376.

[397]Andrew, 121-122; Langer, *The Diplomacy of Imperialism*, 562-563;

that the fruits of the alliance were gathered and reaped principally by St. Petersburg. The Tsar and the Russian aristocratic ruling classes regularly made contemptuous sneers about French statesmen, French institutions, and the French president, but tolerated their ally to ensure a steady source of gold and to guarantee the good behavior of Germany. As the Russians made clear that they had no stomach for African adventures, the alliance therefore proved almost worthless in the recent crisis. At the same time, the French also came to understand that they would never completely resolve their differences with Germany, which would never go beyond mere words and sabre-rattling. Any hope for an arrangement with Berlin remained illusory unless they willingly and completely renounced their claims to Alsace and Lorraine.

It was clear France must come to an accommodation with some other power -- which could only be Britain. Many in France began to work toward a reconciliation with London on the basis of an equitable colonial settlement. They recognized that the Nile valley simply had to be written off but wanted to reach some accommodation of other French colonial aspirations, especially in Morocco. Morocco represented the territory most indispensable for the rounding off of the French North African Empire, built around the shores of the Mediterranean. In the meantime, the British leadership was reaching the same conclusions. As Britain encountered growing industrial competition from Germany and the United States and progressively increasing costs of imperial defense, the British government began moving toward rapprochement with France. London sought to protect its interests from Russian expansion by efforts to reach settlements with Germany (although unsuccessful) and Japan. Because

---

Sanderson, 327, 384.

they remained pessimistic about confronting Russia without resorting to war and because the Boer War revealed British diplomatic isolation to be less than splendid, many in London began to look favorably upon any means to lessen Anglo-French tensions. The result was the initiation of negotiations, which took two years, during which Britain and France finally resolved the primary issue of colonial spheres of influence particularly in Africa. The culmination of this Anglo-French accommodation was the Entente Cordiale in April 1904. This rapprochement proved to be the instrument that effectively ended centuries of mutual Anglo-French antagonism and at the same time effectively established the foundation for the Triple Entente.[398]

The overall assessment of Monson's role and performance as the principal intermediary between London and Paris during the Fashoda crisis, while not necessarily uncomplimentary, proves bland. Several historians consider Monson a diplomat whose skills and ability as an ambassador and negotiator, after forty years service in the diplomatic corps, remained at best mediocre. Raymond Jones, who chronicled the development of the British diplomatic service in the nineteenth century, described Monson's career as among the more exceptional of British diplomats appointed after the civil service reforms in the 1850s and 1860s but primarily in terms of his rapid advancement from attaché to ambassador. By the time of his appointment to Paris, Monson was an old man at the end of his career and did not play any significant role after the turn of the century. Jones suggested that Monson's career reflected those of other nineteenth-century diplomats. Due to the increasing

---

[398]Andrew, 103-110; Grenville, 427-432; Langer, *Diplomacy of Imperialism*, 575-577; Sanderson, 376-380.

professionalization of the diplomatic service and the technological revolution in communications, the great independent British ambassadors of the eighteenth century had given way to bureaucrats such as Monson, "self-effacing, subordinate, and anonymous -- fit persons to execute the policy of the foreign secretary at the behest of the electric telegraph."[399] Zara Steiner wrote that a close examination of some of Salisbury's ambassadors revealed numerous men of mediocre ability and that Monson was a "prime example." J.A.S. Grenville lamented that "it was something of a misfortune that the most senior post in the British diplomatic service was filled by a man of such mediocre abilities as Monson." G.N. Sanderson, who described the ambassador as generally hostile and suspicious, characterized Monson's diplomatic posture during the crisis as the maintenance of a "blank wall of negation."[400]

Monson's bearing on the resolution of the Fashoda crisis followed two general phases. From September to October 1898, he provided Salisbury with a mountain of information and interpretations. He repeatedly engaged Delcassé in formal discussions, sometimes cordial and sometimes combative. With the explosive reemergence of the Dreyfus affair in August, Monson attempted to forecast how the instability in Paris would affect French attitudes and actions during the imminent confrontation on the Upper Nile. Previously in January 1898, following the publication of "*J'Accuse*," he doubted that the issue would have any impact on French diplomacy. Following the August suicide of Colonel Hubert Henry, however, Monson became gradually more concerned with the louder cries for revision and the increasing rumors of a military *coup d'etat*. At that moment, he initially argued

---

[399]Jones, 116; 161-162; 191.

[400]Grenville, 429; Sanderson, 342; Steiner, 176.

that so long as domestic pressures did not force Delcassé's hand, the French would resolve the Fashoda dispute with "calmness." Within this environment, three difficulties frustrated his efforts to negotiate with Delcassé: the possibility that the Dreyfus affair would tempt some in the French government and certainly in the French army to divert public attention away from the domestic chaos with a timely African war against Britain; the nearly desperate efforts by Delcassé to avoid that scenario by obtaining some clear concession in the Upper Nile to soothe French tempers; and the ironclad unwillingness of the British government to negotiate until Marchand had withdrawn unconditionally.

By early October Delcassé grew frustrated with his inability to persuade the ambassador to compromise London's hard-line position, while Salisbury became concerned about the soundness and reliability of Monson's reporting. In one respect, he believed that Monson proved too eager to placate French concerns. Moreover, some of the ambassador's dispatches betrayed excessive excitement and nervousness. Consequently, the discussions that resolved the Fashoda crisis shifted to London and Monson, his role dramatically reduced, was thereafter virtually ignored.

Through the remainder of October, Monson endeavored to supply London with intelligence regarding French policy and to assess possible courses of action in the face of unfolding drama in Paris. The domestic situation in France remained dangerously volatile. The clamor caused by the Dreyfus affair and the labor unrest intensified to the point that the government brought army troops into the city to maintain order, prompting rumors that a *coup d'état* was imminent. Public opinion continued to smolder and grow more bellicose due to heightened political posturing and inflammatory newspaper commentary on both sides of the English Channel, while both governments began to make serious preparations for war. In Britain where it was confidently assumed that the time was right for settling accounts with the French, the cabinet pushed forward naval preparations. In France the government initiated furious defensive preparations and made desperate overtures to secure the active support of their Russian ally. Finally, the Brisson ministry collapsed in late October, prompting renewed fears of a military *coup d'état* and an outbreak of revolution.

In spite of his efforts to remain relevant, to evaluate the French crisis despite his reduced responsibility and influence, four factors generally ensured his relegation to the periphery of the efforts to resolve the Fashoda crisis. The first involved the nature of diplomatic practice in the late nineteenth century. Two separate but interdependent developments, the growth of the professionalism and bureaucracy within the diplomatic service and the development of the electric telegraph, diminished the independence and initiative of ambassadors. Many became mere bureaucrats who simply collected information and executed the policy of the Foreign Office.

The second factor involved the nature of the British embassy in Paris. The international prestige of the British empire in the late nineteenth century meant that foreign governments preferred to conduct their diplomatic relations with Britain in London. The exceptions included those nations that were most remote and those that posed more of a challenge to British interests. The most skilled and most trusted British diplomats were generally those posted in St. Petersburg, Cairo, and Constantinople. By contrast, although the embassy at Paris remained a brilliant and prestigious position in the foreign service, the significance of the post became largely regarded in social rather than diplomatic terms. Moreover, by the 1890s, London no longer perceived its interests to be seriously threatened by French designs. The proximity of Paris to

London meant that it would be easier and more convenient to keep British policy toward France in the hands of the Foreign Office.

Third, both Salisbury and Delcassé preferred to work through the French ambassador in London. Salisbury preferred to conduct his diplomacy in London with resident foreign ambassadors as a matter of course while Delcassé tended to avoid extensive conversations with ambassadors, preferring instead to conduct diplomatic business through his own representatives. In September 1898 Delcassé quickly became weary of dealing with the ambassador. Monson, usually without specific instructions, tended to answer evasively, elaborate on Salisbury's comments to Courcel, or defer the issues to London. By early October the foreign minister, immensely frustrated by his failure to engage Monson in anything more than arguments over established positions, concluded that his efforts to obtain concessions in the Upper Nile would produce more immediate if not positive results by ignoring the ambassador altogether and approaching Salisbury directly.

Salisbury, whose confidence in the ambassador's talents were suspect in any event, generally thought Monson too eager to placate French concerns. This was in fact one of the prime minister's major complaints. Throughout his career, Monson consistently sought to conduct diplomatic business on a personal level and to establish working relations based on friendship and mutual confidence. His tactics paid dividends on occasion. For example, he correctly warned London at least a year before the fact of the Franco-Congolese Agreement of 1894 and of French intentions to drive into the Nile valley. Nevertheless, the practice had its drawbacks. Whenever Monson could not establish strong and confidential working relationships with the resident foreign minister his efforts frequently failed. This was particularly true in Vienna, where Rosebery kept him completely uninformed about British policy with Austria-Hungary, and in Paris, where he did not get along personally with either Hanotaux or Delcassé. In addition, Monson often became too sympathetic to the governments to which he was accredited and tended to project their perspective with too much energy. During the West African negotiations, Monson stressed the importance of a quick response to Hanotaux's requests and argued that the responsibility for the initiative belonged to London. He complained that the claims of the Royal Niger Company were baseless and that no progress would be made at the possible risk of war unless London made concessions. Similarly, during the Fashoda negotiations, he appeared to endorse a modification of the British position a little too enthusiastically. Consequently, when Monson completely succumbed on 30 September to Delcassé's emotional pledge that France would go to war over Fashoda, he sent a strongly worded dispatch to Salisbury that summarized the French position. In mid-October, Monson complained that the rhetorical excesses of British politicians and the London newspapers were having an adverse reaction upon public opinion in France and warned that the chauvinism of the British press might easily provoke a dangerous reaction in France.

Finally, Monson's performance itself proved rather banal and uninspiring. He was ineffective and appeared confused. At the outset of the diplomatic dialogue he did not extend Salisbury's intended carrot, the offer of territorial concessions, due to his misinterpretation of the prime minister's instructions. Furthermore, Monson failed to clarify certain questions that would have a significant bearing on London's policy during the crisis. First, he could not interpret the impact of public opinion on the course of French policy as both sides initiated and intensified military preparations. At times, he argued that because public opinion remained permanently divided over Dreyfus and Fashoda, France could not go to war. At other times, he acknowledged the possibility of war. Second, as the French government continued its extensive use of troops to suppress labor unrest in Paris and began to implement defensive preparations along the coast, Monson grew anxious over rumors of a military coup, followed by war -- rumors he previously discounted. During the final weeks of October, he limited his assessment of the military situation to the transmission of Dawson's numerous reports of French defensive preparations. Monson did not attempt, however, to interpret what these preparations suggested about French intentions; possibly he could not. Third, Monson could never state conclusively whether Russia would actively assist France. At times, Monson reminded London of Delcassé's promises of Russian support and the foreign minister's frequent declarations that France would accept war rather than submit to a national humiliation. At other times, he reminded London of Russian disinterest in virtually all questions related to the Upper Nile. Yet in late October, Monson believed that Delcassé possessed four telegrams that confirmed Russia's promise to support France in the Upper Nile. In London, however, Salisbury and Sir Thomas Sanderson immediately concluded that Delcassé had deceived the ambassador. His dispatches therefore revealed a confused appraisal of the situation and were often contradicted by the reports of other British diplomats. Fourth, his constitution proved weak and uncertain. During critical moments of crisis and confrontation, Monson -- although a generally cautious and conservative diplomat -- tended to become extremely anxious and warned his superiors in London to brace for the worst. After particularly contentious interviews with Delcassé on 28 September, in which the foreign minister threatened the assistance of Russia for the first time, and

30 September, in which the foreign minister emotionally declared that France would go to war rather than endure yet another affront to its honor, Monson abandoned his initial optimism that the French would be prepared to resolve the Fashoda question with calmness and began to warn that the French government would not back down from a confrontation. As a result of the events of 25 October, Monson completely abandoned his previous caution and panicked. As soon as news reached him of the dramatic collapse of the ministry and of the massive demonstrations, he immediately telegraphed London that France stood on the brink of a revolution. Monson feared that this new threat of revolution in Paris made war between Britain and France inevitable. He believed that the establishment of a military government or of a nominally civilian government in the hands of the military party would render the settlement of the dispute almost impossible. A government dominated by generals, he argued, would welcome war with Britain if it could in that way stave off revision of the Dreyfus case.

Without question, Monson played a minimal role in the ultimate resolution of the Fashoda crisis. After actively participating in the initial negotiations, he found himself virtually ignored after early October. Although an extended examination of his function might therefore seem somewhat curious, the consideration of Monson's role helps to provide a more thorough appreciation of the changing nature of diplomatic representation in the late nineteenth century. Given his abilities, personality, and temperament, and given the institutional limitations placed upon him -- notably, the preference of Salisbury to conduct diplomatic business in London with the French ambassador, the practice of several nations to conduct their relations with Britain in London, and the prevalence of the electric telegraph, which further limited the scope of Monson's activities to providing information, answering questions, and responding to orders -- Monson could not have played anything but a peripheral function.

BIBLIOGRAPHY

I. Primary Sources - Unpublished Documentary Sources

Monson, Sir Edmund John. Personal Papers. The Modern Papers Reading Room, New Bodleian Library, Oxford University, United Kingdom.

United Kingdom. Public Record Office. Foreign Office Papers.
   FO 27 (France)
   FO 78 (Turkey)

II. Primary Sources - Published Documentary Sources

Buckle, George Earle, ed. *The Letters of Queen Victoria*. 3rd series. *A Selection From Her Majesty's Correspondence and Journals Between the Years 1886 and 1901*. Vol. 3, *1896-1901*. London: John Murray, 1932.

Bülow, Bernhard Heinrich Martin Karl, Furst von. *Memoirs of Prince von Bülow*. Vol. 1, *From Secretary of State to Imperial Chancellor, 1897-1903*. Translated by F.A. Voigt. Boston: Little, Brown and Company, 1931.

Gooch, G.P., and Harold Temperley, ed. *British Documents on the Origins of the War, 1898-1914*. Vol. 1, *The End of British Isolation*. London: His Majesty's Stationery Office, 1927.

Hertslet, Godfrey E.P., ed. *The Foreign Office List and Diplomatic and Consular Yearbook For 1910*. 83rd publication. London: Harrison and Sons, 1910.

III. Secondary Sources

Andrew, Christopher. *Théophile Delcassé and the Making of the Entente Cordiale: A Reappraisal of French Foreign Policy, 1898-1905*. London: Macmillan and Company, Ltd., 1968.

Balfour, Michael. *The Kaiser and His Times*. Boston: Houghton

Mifflin Company, 1964.

Barclay, Sir Thomas. *Thirty Years: Anglo-French Reminiscences, 1876-1906*. London: Constable and Company, Ltd., 1914.

Barthorp, Michael. *War on the Nile: Britain, Egypt, and the Sudan, 1882-1898*. Poole, New York, and Sydney: Blandford Press, 1984.

Bates, Darrell. *The Fashoda Incident of 1898: Encounter on the Nile*. Oxford: Oxford University Press, 1984.

Benson, E.F. *The Kaiser and English Relations*. London: Longmans, Green and Company, 1936.

Blunt, Wilfrid Scawen. *My Diaries*. 2 vols. New York: Alfred A. Knopf, 1921.

Bredin, Jean-Denis. *The Affair: The Case of Alfred Dreyfus*. Translated by Jeffrey Mehlman. New York: George Braziller, Inc., 1983.

Brown, Roger Glenn. *Fashoda Reconsidered: The Impact of Domestic Politics on French Policy in Africa, 1893-1898*. Baltimore and London: The Johns Hopkins Press, 1970.

Carroll, E. Malcolm. *French Public Opinion and Foreign Affairs, 1870-1914*. New York and London: The Century Company, 1931.

Chapman, Guy. *The Dreyfus Case: A Reassessment*. New York: Reynal and Company, 1955.

Cockfield, Jamie. "Germany and the Fashoda Crisis, 1898-99." *Central European History* 16 (September 1983): 256-275.

Eubank, Keith. "The Fashoda Crisis Re-Examined." *The Historian* 22 (February 1960): 145-162.

_____. *Paul Cambon: Master Diplomatist*. Norman: University of Oklahoma Press, 1960.

Garvin, James L. *The Life of Joseph Chamberlain. Vol. 3, 1895-1900: Empire and World Policy*. London: Macmillan and Company, Ltd., 1934.

Giffen, Morrison Beall. *Fashoda: The Incident and Its Diplomatic Setting*. Chicago: University of Chicago Press, 1930.

Gooch, G.P. *History of Modern Europe, 1878-1919*. New York: Henry Holt and Company, 1922.

Grenville, J.A.S. *Lord Salisbury and Foreign Policy: The Close of the Nineteenth Century*. London: University of London and the Athlone Press, 1964.

Headrick, Daniel R. *The Invisible Weapon. Telecommunications and International Politics, 1851-1945*. New York and Oxford: Oxford University Press, 1991.

_____. *The Tentacles of Progress. Technology Transfer in the Age of Imperialism, 1850-1940*. New York and Oxford: Oxford University Press, 1988.

Hoffman, Robert L. *More Than A Trial: The Struggle Over Captain Dreyfus*. New York: The Free Press, 1980.

Jones, Raymond A. *The British Diplomatic Service, 1815-1914*. Waterloo, Ontario: Wilfrid Laurier University Press, 1983.

Kennedy, Paul. *The Rise of the Anglo-German Antagonism, 1860-1914*. London: George Allen and Unwin, 1980.

_____. *Strategy and Diplomacy, 1870-1945*. London: George Allen and Unwin, 1983.

Langer, William L. *The Diplomacy of Imperialism, 1890-1902*. 2nd. ed. New York: Alfred A. Knopf, 1965.

_____. *European Alliances and Alignments, 1871-1890*. 2nd. ed. New York: Alfred A. Knopf, 1950.

Larkin, Maurice. "'La République en Danger?' The Pretenders, the Army, and Déroulède, 1898-1899." *The English Historical Review* C, 394 (January 1985): 85-105.

Lebow, Richard Ned. *Between Peace and War: The Nature of International Crisis*. Baltimore and London: The Johns Hopkins Press, 1981.

Lee, Sir Sydney, ed. *The Dictionary of National Biography*. Supplement, January 1901-December 1911. Oxford: Oxford University Press, 1912. S.v. "Sir Edmund John Monson" by Thomas Henry Sanderson.

Lewis, David L. *Prisoners of Honor: The Dreyfus Affair*. New York: William Morrow and Company, Inc., 1973.

_____. *The Race to Fashoda: European Colonialism and African Resistance in the Scramble For Africa*. New York: Weidenfeld and Nicolson, 1987.

Marder, Arthur J. *British Naval Policy, 1880-1905: The*

Anatomy of British Sea Power. London: Putnam and Company, 1940.

Massie, Robert K. *Dreadnought: Britain, Germany, and the Coming of the Great War*. New York: Random House, 1991.

Newton, Lord. *Lord Lyons: A Record of British Diplomacy*. 2 vols. London: Edward Arnold, 1913.

Pakenham, Thomas. *The Scramble for Africa, 1876-1912*. New York: Random House, 1991.

Penson, Dame Lillian M. *Foreign Affairs Under the Third Marquis of Salisbury*. London: University of London and Athlone Press, 1962.

_____. "The New Course in British Foreign Policy, 1892-1902." *Transactions of the Royal Historical Society*. 4th series, vol. 25. London: Offices of the Royal Historical Society, 1943, 121-138.

Peterson, Susan. *Crisis Bargaining and the State: The Domestic Politics of International Conflict*. Ann Arbor: The University of Michigan Press, 1996.

Porter, A.N. "Lord Salisbury, Foreign Policy and Domestic Finance, 1860-1900." In *Salisbury: The Man and His Policies*, ed. Lord Blake and Hugh Cecil, 148-184. New York: St. Martin's Press, 1987.

Porter, Charles W. *The Career of Théophile Delcassé*. Philadelphia: University of Pennsylvania Press, 1936.

Ramm, Agatha. "Lord Salisbury and the Foreign Office." In *The Foreign Office, 1782-1982*, ed. Roger Bullen, 46-65. Frederick, Md.: University Publications of America, Inc., 1984.

Riker, T.W. "A Survey of British Policy in the Fashoda Crisis." *Political Science Quarterly* 44 (March 1929): 54-78.

Roberts, Andrew. *Salisbury:Victorian Titan*. London: Weidenfeld & Nicolson, 1999.

Robinson, Ronald, John Gallagher, and Alice Denny. *Africa and the Victorians: The Climax of Imperialism in the Dark Continent*. New York: St. Martin's Press, 1961.

Rolo, P.J.V. *Entente Cordiale: The Origins and Negotiation of the Anglo-French Agreements of 8 April 1904*. London:

Macmillan and Company, Ltd., 1969.

Rutkoff, Peter M. *Revanche and Revision: The Ligue Des Patriotes and the Origin of the Radical Right in France, 1882-1900.* Athens and London: Ohio University Press, 1981.

Sanderson, G.N. *England, Europe, and the Upper Nile, 1882-1899.* Edinburgh: Edinburgh University Press, 1965.

Schroeder, Paul W. "Munich and the British Tradition." *Historical Journal* 19 (March 1976): 223-243.

Schumann, Frederick L. *War and Diplomacy in the French Republic: An Inquiry into Political Motivations and the Control of Foreign Policy.* With an introduction by Quincy Wright. New York: Whittlesey House, McGraw-Hill Book Company, Inc., 1931.

Snyder, Louis L. *The Dreyfus Case: A Documentary History.* New Brunswick, New Jersey: Rutgers University Press, 1973.

Steiner, Zara S. *The Foreign Office and Foreign Policy, 1898-1914.* Cambridge: Cambridge at the University Press, 1969.

Steinheil, Marguerite. *My Memoirs.* New York: Sturgis and Walton Company, 1912.

Stuart, Graham H. *French Foreign Policy: From Fashoda to Serajevo (1898-1914).* New York: The Century Company, 1921.

Taylor, A.J.P. *The Struggle For Mastery in Europe, 1848-1918.* Oxford: The Clarendon Press, 1954.

Taylor, Robert. *Lord Salisbury.* Edited by Chris Cook. New York: St. Martin's Press, 1975.

Tombs, Robert and Isabelle Tombs. *That Sweet Enemy. Britain and France: The History of a Love-Hate Relationship.* New York: Random House, 2006.

Tuchman, Barbara W. *The Proud Tower: A Portrait of the World Before the War, 1890-1914.* New York: The Macmillan Company, 1966.

Uzoigwe, G.N *Britain and the Conquest of Africa: The Age of Salisbury.* Ann Arbor: University of Michigan Press, 1974.

Wood, Leonard Clair. "Sir Edmund Monson, Ambassador to France." Ph.D. diss., University of Pennsylvania, 1960. Unpublished.

Wright, Patricia. *Conflict on the Nile: The Fashoda Incident of 1898*. London: William Heinemann, Ltd., 1972.

ABOUT THE AUTHOR

Craig E. Saucier received his Ph.D. in modern British and modern European history from Louisiana State University. He currently teaches history at Southeastern Louisiana University. He lives in South Louisiana with his wife, a bestselling author, and their two dogs. They are loyal Saints fans. So are Dr. and Mrs. Saucier.

Printed in Great Britain
by Amazon